Objects as Insights: R.H. Codrington's Ethnographic Collections from Melanesia

Nick Stanley

The British Museum

This publication has been supported by Julia and Hans Rausing

Publishers
The British Museum
Great Russell Street
London WC1B 3DG

Series editor
Sarah Faulks

Objects as Insights: R.H. Codrington's Ethnographic Collections from Melanesia
Nick Stanley

ISBN 9780861592357
ISSN 1747 3640

© 2021 The Trustees of the British Museum

Text © 2021 Nick Stanley

Front cover: Dress used in dances (*malo saru*), in four scarf-like divisions united at top into a band with an opening for the neck, woven from narrow strips of buff-coloured vegetable fibre, Banks Islands, l. 148cm (with fringes), w. 156cm (with fringes). British Museum, 1873, Oc.7929

Printed and bound in the UK by 4edge Ltd, Hockley

Papers used by the British Museum are recyclable products made from wood grown in well-managed forests and other controlled sources. The manufacturing processes conform to the environmental regulations of the country of origin.

All British Museum images illustrated in this book are © 2021 The Trustees of the British Museum

Further information about the Museum and its collection can be found at britishmuseum.org

Contents

Acknowledgements	iv
Introduction: A Most Unusual Missionary Anthropologist	1
1. 'I have little doubt but that I can get some good things sooner or later': Codrington as a Collector	14
2. 'Matters that lie upon the surface of native life and are open to the observation of the visitor and traveller': Codrington's Collections Explored	18
3. 'There was a spirit in my pen': Codrington's Visual Documentation	48
4. 'It has rained shell adzes today, large and small': Gifts and Exchange	59
5. On Mana and Poisoned Arrows	65
6. Codrington Today	71
Appendix 1: Codrington's Collection in the British Museum	81
Appendix 2: Codrington's Collection in the Pitt Rivers Museum, Oxford	84
Appendix 3: Codrington's Collection in the Museum of Archaeology and Anthropology, Cambridge	95
Bibliography	96
Index	101

Acknowledgements

I am most grateful to the British Museum for agreeing to publish this text and to Sarah Faulks, Senior Editorial Manager: Research Publications, for all the work involved in its production, and to Sean Kingston for his contribution. I am likewise greatly appreciative of the financial support for this publication from Julia and Hans Rausing. I am indebted to the British Museum, the Pitt-Rivers Museum, Oxford University, and the Museum of Archaeology and Anthropology, Cambridge University, for their support and permission to use material relating to R.H. Codrington and his collections in addition to the photographs provided by them.

At the British Museum my first debt of gratitude goes to Lissant Bolton for her hospitality and support throughout my time in the Department of Africa, Oceania and the Americas, and in particular for her encouragement of this publication. I thank her and Ben Burt most sincerely for reading and commenting on the work. I am also grateful to Jim Hamill and Jill Hasell for their frequent assistance, and to Gaye Sculthorpe and Julie Adams for their support. Thanks are also due to the British Museum photographers for the new photography they took of Codrington's collection at the Museum.

At the Pitt Rivers Museum, Oxford University, I am grateful to Marina de Alarcón, Philip Grover, Nicholas Crowe, Mark Dickerson, Meghan O'Brien Backhouse and Jeremy Coote for making their Codrington collection details so readily available, and for taking photographs of objects reproduced in the book.

At the Museum of Archaeology and Anthropology, University of Cambridge, I am grateful to Nicholas Thomas, Anita Herle, Rachel Hand, Jocelyne Dudding and Lucie Carreau for their assistance, advice and support. I am greatly appreciative of their making available photographs of objects reproduced in this publication. I am also very grateful to Nicholas Thomas for his comments on the manuscript.

I have enjoyed the privilege of reading Codrington's writings at the University of London, School of Oriental and African Studies Library Special Collections. I thank the staff for making photographs of objects reproduced in this book and to the Melanesian Mission UK, the owners of the collection, for permission to use these photographs. I have had similar good fortune to consult the Codrington papers at the University of Oxford Bodleian Library Special Collections. I would like to thank them for making images available from the collections. Likewise, I am grateful for permission to publish an image from the Prints and Drawing Department at the National Art Library at the Victoria and Albert Museum, and to the Warden and Fellows of Wadham College, Oxford University, for the image of the portrait of R.H. Codrington in their collection.

I am particularly grateful to John and Jenny Pinder for their long-term help with matters relating to the Melanesian Mission and for their comments on this work. I likewise thank Brian MacDonald-Milne, archivist at the Melanesian Mission UK, for his assistance and comments on this work. I am also grateful to Terry Brown for sharing documents relating to Codrington. I thank David Vunagi for agreeing to read a draft of this work.

I thank Helen Gardner and Thorgeir Kolshus, both specialists on the work of R.H. Codrington, for their careful reading and numerous incisive comments on this text.

I should also like to thank Andrei Nacu for his work on the museum databases at the Royal Anthropological Institute; and Jill Hasell at the British Museum, Nicholas Crowe at the Pitt Rivers Museum, and Lucie Carreau and Rachel Hand at the Museum of Archaeology and Anthropology for helping to bring the collections' spreadsheets published here as Appendices 1–3 into order.

Needless to say, after receiving such help from so many individuals, the mistakes that remain in this work are my responsibility alone.

Note on geography and place names

Island Melanesia is normally taken to include Solomon Islands, Vanuatu and New Caledonia, often also including the islands of Papua New Guinea (the Bismarck Archipelago, Buka, Bougainville, and the islands of Milne Bay Province, Papua New Guinea). The Melanesian Mission focused particularly on the northernmost province of Vanuatu, Torba, comprising the Banks Islands and Torres Islands, the eastern part of Solomon Islands including Guadalcanal, Malaita, Savo, Rennell and Bellona, Makira and Ulawa as well as the southerly region of Temotu. The western Solomon Islands were missionised by the Methodists. For a brief period, the Melanesian Mission also had stations in the Loyalty Islands, the easternmost part of New Caledonia.

In northern Vanuatu Codrington frequently mentions islands that are now known by different names: These include Whitsuntide Island (Pentecost also sometimes known as Raga), Lepers' Island (Aoba/Ambae) and Aurora (Maewo). In Solomon Islands San Cristoval is now known as Makira, Ysabel is now spelt Isabel.

Abbreviations

The following abbreviations have been used throughout the book to identify sources:

- AIML: Auckland Institute Museum Library, New Zealand.
- BOD: Oxford University, Bodleian Libraries Special Collections R.H. Codrington MSS.
- EP&H: Edge-Partington, J. and Heape, C. 1890. *An Album of the Weapons, Tools, Ornaments, Articles of Dress, etc, of the Natives of the Pacific Islands*, 3 vols, Manchester.
- LT: Letters to Tom [Codrington], 1867–82 (SOAS, MM box 9, folders 2/1–2/6), 116 numbered letters, dated on sending and on receipt.
- PRM: Pitt Rivers Museum, Oxford University, Collections IV: 'Chamberlain Codrington Czaplicka Dunn'.
- SOAS, MM: School of Oriental and African Studies Library, University of London, special collections, Melanesian Mission.
- *TM*: Codrington, R.H. 1891. *The Melanesians: Studies in their Anthropology and Folklore*, Oxford.

Figure 1 Photograph of R.H. Codrington by Charles Dodgson (Lewis Carroll), Oxford, c. 1855. Victoria and Albert Museum, 1686E-1956. © Victoria and Albert Museum

Introduction: A Most Unusual Missionary Anthropologist

This publication examines the writings and collections made by R.H. (Robert Henry) Codrington – a prominent Anglican missionary and a founding figure in the anthropology of Oceania – and their continuing significance today (**Fig. 1**). He was born in Wroughton, near Swindon, Wiltshire, on 15 September 1830 and died at the age of 91 on 11 September 1922. After graduating from Wadham College, Oxford, he spent 20 years, continuously, from 1867 to 1887, in Melanesia as one of the first generation of Europeans to work in Oceania as a missionary. He had a keen interest in language and became one of the most proficient speakers and writers in the *lingua franca* of the Melanesian Mission, Mota, the language of Mota Island in northern Vanuatu. His collecting of local cultural knowledge was made possible through his command of the languages of the region; his fluency in Mota enabled him to understand some related languages. But, most importantly for this work, Codrington was a regular and knowledgeable collector of what were known at the time as 'curios' (objects of material culture from the region), as he sought to preserve a record of the cultures he saw as under threat from the process of colonisation. His documentation of objects, from large buildings to the smallest item, was of an exceptional quality, combining acute and forensic analysis of the objects with detailed information on aspects of their provenance. This documentation is now recorded both in the accession registers of the major museums that acquired his collections, and in his magisterial work *The Melanesians: Studies in their Anthropology and Folklore* (1891). Unlike most other collectors he lived in the region from which the objects came, and he had both the time and interest to discuss their significance with members of the source communities.

Codrington's opportunity to work with Melanesians and to study their customs came through membership of the Melanesian Mission. He joined this in 1865, when the mission was still based in Auckland, New Zealand. The Melanesian Mission had been founded by Bishop George Augustus Selwyn in 1849, to help introduce Christianity to the western Pacific. The strategy that Selwyn and his successor, Bishop John Coleridge Patteson, employed was of inviting local young men, a few young women and some older men and women to attend the 'Central Boarding School' on an annual basis, first in New Zealand, but after 1867 on Norfolk Island (where it was known as St Barnabas College), situated between New Zealand and Melanesia. Numbers were not large. From 1849 to 1860, 152 Melanesians attended the school in Auckland (Hilliard 1978: 17). These students provided Codrington with basic information about the societies from which they came.

As headmaster of St Barnabas College from 1867, when it moved to Norfolk Island, Codrington was in a position both to converse with his pupils and to start his collection of artefacts from the islands from which they came. The collection (of which 606 artefacts survive) became one of the most comprehensive from the Melanesian Mission (for a list of mission collectors, see Stanley 1994a: 38, table 1). Of these, 215 items came from northern Vanuatu (the Banks and Torres Islands groups in what was formerly the New Hebrides), and 380 from the central and eastern Solomon Islands (**Fig. 2**). There are a handful of items from elsewhere, such as Fiji, and some items have no definitive provenance.

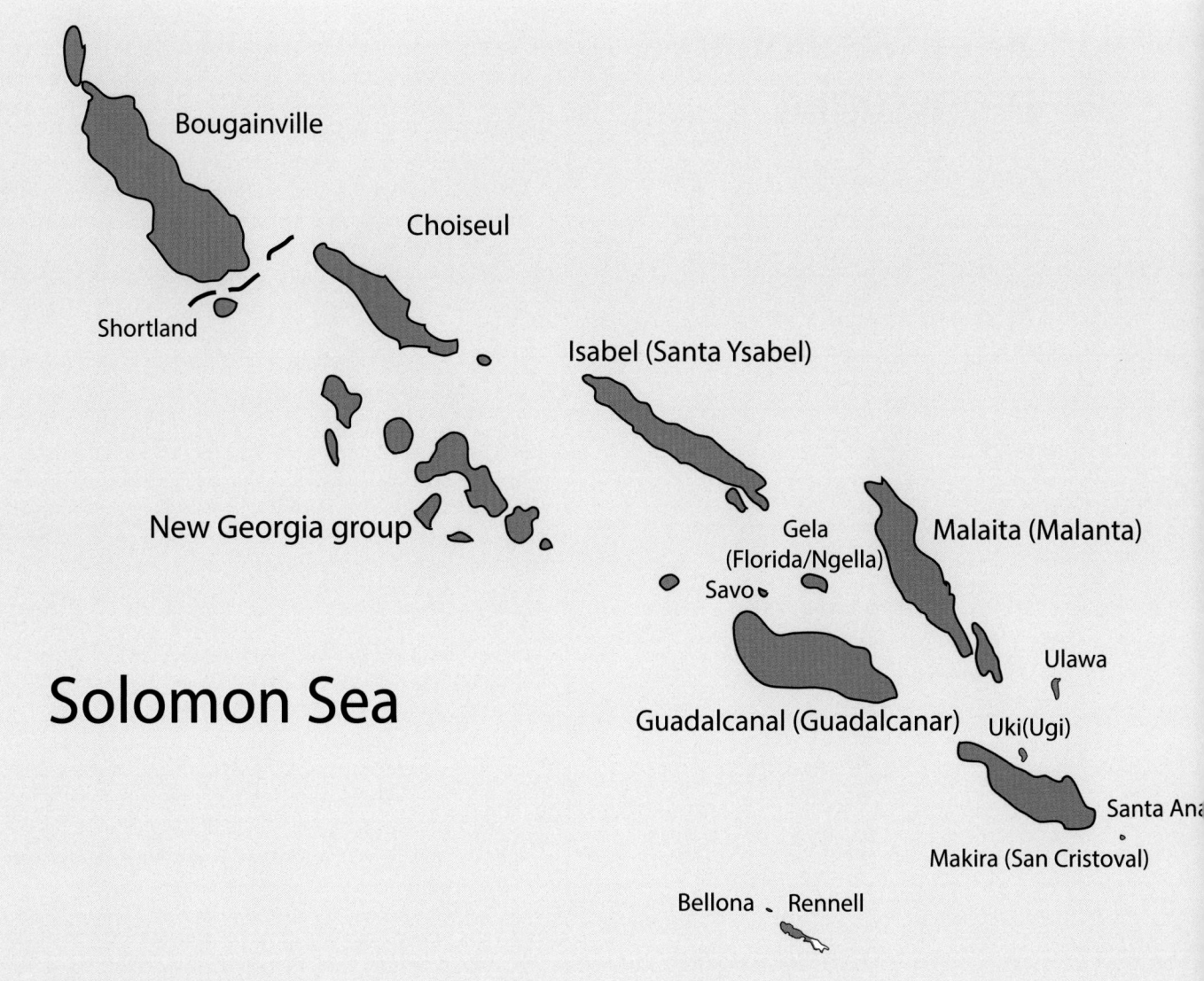

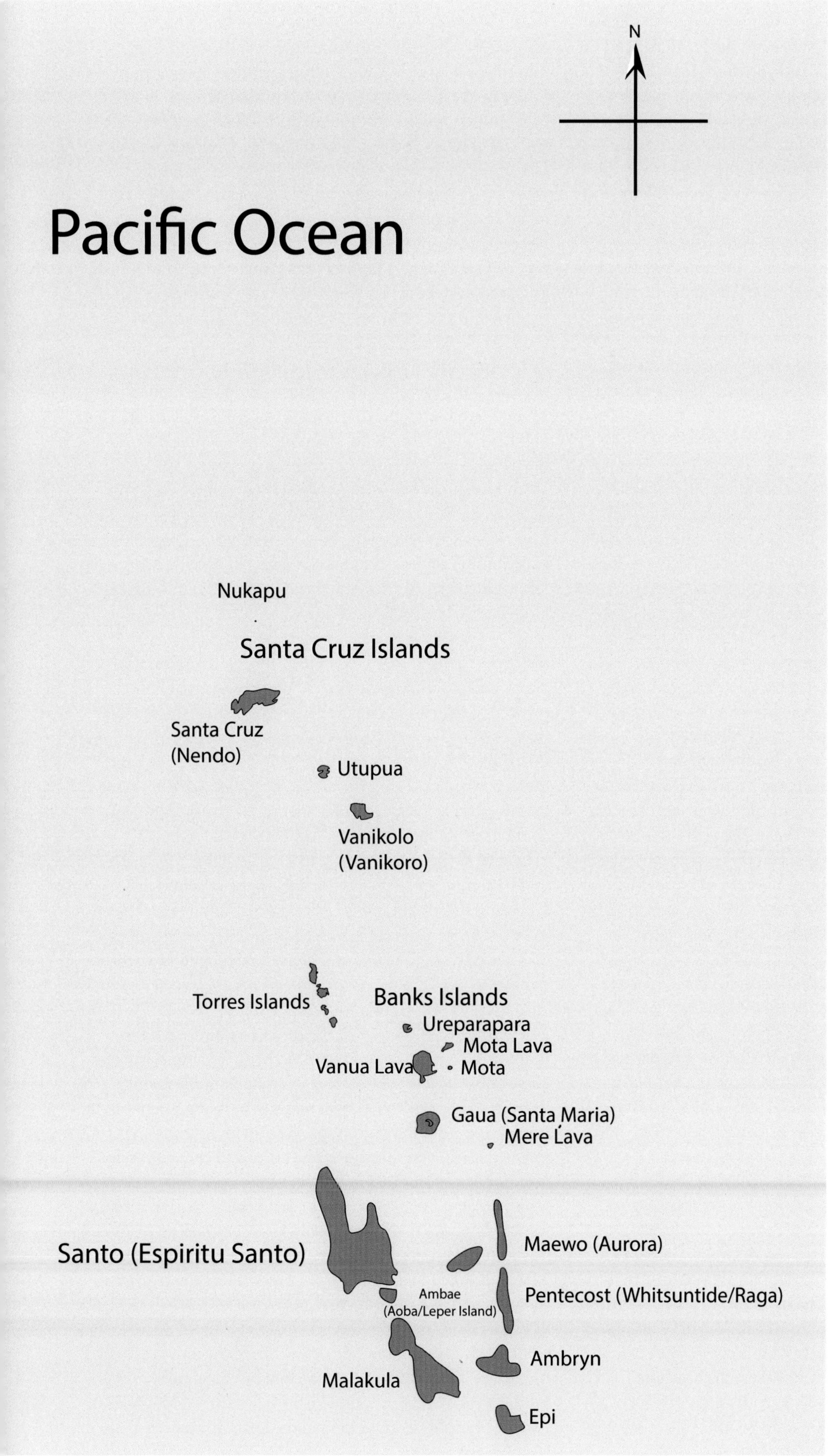

Pacific Ocean

Nukapu

Santa Cruz Islands

Santa Cruz (Nendo)

Utupua

Vanikolo (Vanikoro)

Torres Islands

Banks Islands

Ureparapara
Mota Lava
Vanua Lava • Mota

Gaua (Santa Maria)
Mere Lava

Santo (Espiritu Santo)

Maewo (Aurora)

Ambae (Aoba/Leper Island)

Pentecost (Whitsuntide/Raga)

Ambryn

Malakula

Epi

Figure 2 Map of the western Pacific (drawn by Louis Kingston)

The destinations for his collections were, firstly, the Blackmore Museum in Salisbury, Wiltshire; then the British Museum, London; the Pitt Rivers Museum, Oxford; and the Museum of Archaeology and Anthropology, Cambridge. The Blackmore Museum's collection was later dispersed, and several of the objects it formerly housed found their way into the other three museums. The collections currently consist of 122 objects in the British Museum; 463 at the Pitt Rivers Museum; and 21 at the Museum of Archaeology and Anthropology.

This book argues that the focus of Codrington's collecting changed over time, and that this is reflected in the differences between the types of objects in each museum. Codrington's underlying relationship to the various local constituencies is here critical. Exchanging gifts with students and their relatives was a very different context to trading on the island foreshore through barter. His collection strategies are explored here in some detail.

The argument

This work consists of seven chapters dealing with different aspects of Codrington's collecting, his philosophy and his life in Melanesia. The current chapter provides an introduction to his philosophy, emphasising his humanist perspective, which contrasts sharply with the prevalent evolutionary orthodoxy in both anthropology and missionary theology at that time. It also gives details of Codrington's range of practical aptitudes, which were to be of critical importance in his comprehensive study of Melanesian culture. Chapter 1 traces the process of the formation of the museum collections and the role played by museum personnel in the collections reaching their destinations. The second chapter discusses the three collections at the British Museum, the Pitt Rivers Museum and the Museum of Archaeology and Anthropology, and their special features, and speculates on Codrington's own collection before its incorporation into these three museums. Chapter 3 explores how Codrington went about providing visual documentation, in particular through photography, but also and more extensively through drawing and sketching. This chapter considers how his use of verbal description was combined with the visual record in order to provide a more complex understanding. Chapter 4 considers the circumstances through which Codrington acquired his artefacts, including the processes of exchange. The discussion contrasts the gifts given by Codrington, and the objects that he sought in return. Usually, however, this involved purchase which raised questions about how to conduct equitable exchanges with Melanesians. Chapter 5 discusses Codrington's most significant theoretical ideas. Mana, as a Melanesian concept of 'efficacious force, sometimes sacred, sometimes profane that infused all things' (Mazzarella 2017: 38), was explored and discussed by Codrington. Subsequent anthropologists have argued over the appropriateness of the concept and whether the term has a useful purpose. There has been a very active discussion about the impact of Codrington's publications on some Melanesian communities, at the time and subsequently. These topics are taken up in the final chapter. Finally, the book concludes with an assessment of R.H. Codrington's achievements and how his collections are important today.

Biographical background

R.H. Codrington was a quiet but talented polymath, not only a gifted linguist and translator but also one of the founding scholars of Pacific ethnography. He became a major figure in the Anglican Melanesian Mission in what are now the nations of Vanuatu and Solomon Islands. He was the first headmaster of St Barnabas College, Norfolk Island, which trained Melanesian catechists from 1867, when he was 37 years old, until his departure in 1887. He acted as head of the mission from 1871–7. At the same time, he was translating the majority of the New Testament into the Mota language, and was responsible for the building of St Barnabas Chapel on Norfolk Island. Codrington was also a pioneer in the anthropology of Island Melanesia, writing the standard text, *The Melanesians: Studies in their Anthropology and Folklore* (1891), recognised as authoritative for many decades, and a linguist who wrote a comparative study of Melanesian languages (Codrington 1885). And yet, although authors have acknowledged his importance in the development of the Anglican church in Melanesia (Armstrong 1900; Gardner 2006; Hilliard 1978; Kolshus 1999; Samson 2010; Whiteman 1983; Yonge 1875) and historians of anthropology have similarly recognised his contribution to their discipline (Gaillard 1997; Kolshus 2013; Lonergan 1991; Stocking 1987), no full biography of R.H. Codrington has yet been written.

This monograph does not fill this gap, but instead has a narrower focus. It seeks to explore how Codrington went about understanding the way the people he taught and served led their lives. In particular, this study concentrates on his reliance upon the observation of, and careful listening to, local inhabitants. A key issue that he explored was the material culture through which people expressed themselves and lived their lives. One of Codrington's most significant actions in this respect was his systematic collection of artefacts, to preserve them from disappearing, physically and mentally, and to act as anchors to the past and pre-Christian life and practices – 'it is more difficult every year to find things which rapidly disappear as trade advances' (Codrington: Letters to Tom, henceforth LT, 19 July 1875). This study uses Codrington's collections of objects, together with his published and unpublished articles, books, journals and letters about them, to gain an understanding of his motives, collection criteria and aesthetic preferences in his choice of artefacts. The comments that he made about individual objects in his collection throw further light on the underlying principles he adopted. Codrington was always suspicious of armchair theorists and casual collectors who expressed opinions on Pacific island societies. His disdain for writers on the Pacific was total. 'The more I read of books the less I believe their writers, but by a comparison of mistakes and ignorance, one can get knowledge' (LT, 25 March 1881). He seldom ventured into the realm of grand theory and had a healthy disregard for evolutionary theories of staged human development. He was far more interested in what people said about themselves, and how they conducted their lives. For Codrington, material artefacts were fundamental to the grounded understanding of Melanesian life. The humble stone provided the basis for his best-known concept, mana.

While this study does not offer a complete biography of the man, it does require some brief contextual information to situate his achievements in the field of cultural anthropology. R.H. Codrington came from a well-connected Anglican family with a lively interest in culture and literature. Both his father and his grandfather before him were clergymen. His father was the vicar of Wroughton, Wiltshire, where he raised his family. Robert was the second of six boys. Although Robert never married, he remained close to his siblings, in particular his elder brother Tom; he also took a keen interest in Tom's son, Oliver, with whom he corresponded and to whose school fees he contributed. Tom became a civil engineer and an inspector of roads, first in Ireland and then in South Wales. Like Robert, he was a keen antiquarian and wrote *Roman Roads in Britain* in 1905. This book has two similarities with Robert's writings, firstly in its display of a deep suspicion of received wisdom not based on verifiable evidence, in this case the spurious history of Roman names, stations and roads that had been accepted unquestionably for over a century (T. Codrington 1918: 25); secondly, it was also disparaging of new types of roads (turnpikes) that destroyed the remains of their Roman predecessors, in a way that paralleled Robert's desire to document Melanesian society before it was overtaken by modernity. For both brothers, maintaining continuity with the past was an enduring ambition. Robert entrusted Tom with many Melanesian curios over the years, and these formed Tom's personal collection. Throughout their lives, he and Robert remained close correspondents.

During his years as a missionary, Tom acted as his uncomplaining agent supplying him with whatever needs Robert expressed, such as boots, trade goods, lamps and clothes for his personal use. Robert's instructions were often very specific: 'Most of all I want some flannel shirts. Those one buys in Auckland shrink so in washing as soon to be useless and some I have had made here are already as bad besides not fitting. I got very good ones made when I came out at Whiles in Shoreditch' (LT, 9 October 1871). Many of the goods supplied by Tom were often disparaged by Robert when they arrived. So, although the lamp supplied on one occasion was satisfactory it would not last. 'The lamp and its box are just what I want, but since the glass shade is but one I feel that it will soon be broken' (LT, 10 June 1874). Similarly, the next consignment brought defective boots: 'The boots I see are in the box but once again are enormous. Whether made on the last [sic] or not I don't know, but they are as wide as a boat and much heavier than is bearable in a hot country' (LT, 25 Nov 1874). Although we have no copies of Tom's correspondence with his brother, he seems never to have ceased to attempt to meet the demands made of him.

A third brother William served in the navy, rising from captain of HMS *Narcissus*, to Private Secretary to the First Lord of Admiralty, Director of Naval Ordnance and Aide de Camp to Queen Victoria, before retiring as a Rear Admiral. A fourth brother, John, became a priest, but died at the age of 35. The fifth, Oliver, was an army doctor, reaching the rank of Deputy Surgeon-General. He was also, in the family tradition of antiquarianism, a numismatist, linguist and writer on Muslim culture (Blain 2019). He published *A Manual of Musalman Numismatics* in 1904. No details are known concerning his sixth brother, James.

After two years at Charterhouse School with his elder brother (1845–8), Robert attended Wadham College, Oxford (1851–6). Whilst there he became acquainted with Lewis Carroll (Charles Dodgson), who took a photograph of him (**Fig. 1**). He was made a Fellow of the College in 1855 and gained his MA in Theology the following year. He was ordained a priest in 1857. Wadham College was a constant source of support. There was a stipend attached to the fellowship, and when R.H. Codrington retired from his life in the mission field, he went to a parish, Wadhurst in Sussex, for which Wadham College was the patron (Blain 2019). The fellowship stipend meant that he retained financial independence throughout his life, and he was able to use his income to support his interest in creating material collections wherever he ventured.

R.H. Codrington spent a short time after his ordination as a curate to Edmund Hobhouse at St Peter-in-the-East in Oxford. Both shared an interest in antiquarianism, and in early church history. These were topics that Codrington was to turn to at the end of his life, when he composed his Wittering lectures (see Chapter Six). Evidently the men got on well together, and when Hobhouse was made the first Bishop of Nelson in New Zealand, he persuaded Codrington to join him in 1860. At the invitation of the Bishop of New Zealand Codrington visited the Melanesian Mission field in 1863, before joining the mission in Auckland in 1865. He moved with the mission to Norfolk Island in 1867, and remained there until his retirement in 1887, when he took up the post of vicar of Wadhurst, where he remained until 1893. He remained a Canon Prebend of Sidlesham at Chichester Cathedral until 1895. He continued to correspond with Melanesian friends until his death in 1922.

The band of missionary anthropologists

On his move to the Pacific, Codrington became a member of a small band of four missionaries working independently in the region, all of whom were to become informants for British academics as well as be anthropological investigators in their own right. They shared distinctive characteristics that set them apart from their fellow missionaries. Each of them respected local religious belief systems; were committed to learning the vernacular, preaching and translating the Bible into local languages; and were prolific writers on anthropology and folklore. Significantly, they were all serious collectors of ethnographica.

The four were all of a similar age. The eldest was William Wyatt Gill (1828–96) of the London Missionary Society, and he was based in Mangaia, Cook Islands from 1877 to 1883. He published two works, *Historical Sketches of Savage Life in Polynesia* (1880) and a compilation of folklore and song, *Myths and Songs from the South Pacific* (1876). Professor Max Müller, Chair of Comparative Philosophy at Oxford University, provided an enthusiastic preface for this work:

> Now what are these Myths and Songs which Mr WW Gill has brought home from Mangaia, but antiquities, preserved for hundreds, it may be for thousands of years, showing us, far better than any stone weapons or stone idols, the growth of the human mind during a period which, as yet, is full of the most

perplexing problems for the psychologist, the historian and the theologian. (Gill 1876: vi)

Müller was the focus of this group of missionary scholars, corresponding with each of them. The second and third members of the group, Lorimer Fison (1832–1907) and George Brown (1835–1917) were both Methodists, working in Fiji and New Britain, respectively, the latter also making museum collections (Eves 2000). Fison produced a compendium, *Tales from Old Fiji*, in 1904, and Brown a study entitled *Melanesians and Polynesians: Their Life-Histories Described and Compared* in 1910. In this book Brown recorded, 'On my return from New Britain to Sydney I had the privilege of corresponding with Dr. Codrington, both directly and also through a mutual friend, Rev. Dr. Fison' (Brown 1910: 369). As Gunson has noted, 'Brown's scientific correspondence included Müller, Lorimer Fison, E.B. Tylor, Sir James Frazer, J.J. Lister and R.H. Codrington' (Gunson 1969). The fourth member of the group was, of course, R.H. Codrington, who was particularly pleased when Müller highlighted his work in his highly influential Gibbert Lectures in 1876. There was a widespread discussion of anthropological and folklore among the group, and in the cases of Fison and Codrington, this grew into a lifelong academic friendship and constant correspondence (Gardner 2006).

Codrington's reflections on missionaries and others

Codrington's relationship with other missionaries was far less cordial. From the beginning, he held a low opinion of many, whom he felt were morally unfit, ignorant or intellectually lazy. Perhaps the most serious of these charges was that of moral unsuitability. Towards the end of his life he reflected on what he saw as the unwillingness of missionaries to share in the lives of their converts:

> It conduces to the health of missionaries that they should be affectionately attached to their native people. It is obvious, when one thinks of it, that loneliness tends towards ill health, and that friendly intercourse prevents loneliness. Therefore men ought to be reproved when they complain often in a self-satisfied way, that they are so lonely; and if a man says that of course he can't associate with the natives he should be told by the bishop that if he can't he would be better away. (Letters 1891–1922, to C.H. Brooke, 22 November 1912)

But the most frequent of Codrington's complaints about missionaries was their wilful ignorance. He wrote in his major study, *The Melanesians: Studies in their Anthropology and Folklore*:

> Few missionaries have time to make systematic enquiries; if they do, they are likely to make them too soon, and for the whole of their after-career make whatever they observe fit into their early scheme of the native religion … Besides, every one, missionary and visitor, carries with him some preconceived ideas; he expects to see idols and he sees them; images are labelled idols in museums whose makers carved them for amusement; a Solomon Islander fashions the head of his lime-box stick into a grotesque figure, and it becomes the subject of a woodcut as a 'Solomon Islands god'. (*TM*: 117, 118)

Furthermore, Codrington maintained that missionaries commonly made major mistakes in their choice of local informants:

> A missionary has his own difficulty in the fact that very much of his communication is with the young, who do not themselves know and understand very much of what their elders believe and practice. Converts are disposed to blacken generally and indiscriminately their own former state, and with the greatest zeal the present practices of others. (*TM*: 116)

The result was that missionaries were ill-informed. Again, he laid the charge directly at their lack of understanding:

> I have a very poor opinion of the knowledge of missionaries. They are concerned with other matters, and I think know very little generally of what natives really believe. I think their answers in these days are less trustworthy than they would have been in the days before Anthropology became a popular science: i.e. I think that they now find in their own people whatever they have heard about or read about. (Letter to Cambridge correspondent, 27 September 1888, G.W. Stocking papers)

What Codrington had in mind here were the papers written by scholars like Tylor and Müller that had entered into widespread circulation, and which Codrington supposed had led less-enquiring missionaries to lend credence to these authorities without matching them with their own experience in the field.

There were, perhaps, other reasons for Codrington's distain for his fellow missionaries. In an unguarded moment he wrote to his brother, no doubt mourning the death of his mentor, Patteson (for more details, see p. 75):

> It is a hard thing to keep up the tone of the mission. They are very good fellows, all but one, who are here, but the tone is not what it was, and will sink if we don't have more gentlemen who have had an English education. (LT, 30 September 1872)

But in Codrington's view missionaries were not the only culprits. His complaint extended to popular writers, such as John Lubbock, an author on archaeology and etymology, 'notorious for his somewhat indiscriminate use of observations made by transient visitors' (Samson 2017a: 28), who came in for particular criticism from Codrington:

> To my mind it seems after reading Lubbock that the savages of the scientific men recede farther and farther from my experiences and my belief is that if you could get the evidence of the people who really know and live with these savages who are considered the lowest you would find that the savages of the very low type do not exist in the world. Scientific men fit their evidence to their preconceived ideas of how things ought to be! (LT, 8 November 1871)

As Sohmer has noted, there was a fundamental disagreement between Codrington and Lubbock, 'For Lubbock, the evolutionary, ultimately progressive process of human development had passed the "savage" by' (Sohmer 1988: 232).

From 1871 Lorimer Fison was a regular correspondent with Codrington, who warned Fison about the limitations of popular writers on Melanesia. Codrington 'was especially scathing of Lubbock's populist analyses that were based almost entirely on published travellers' tales and lacked any systematic evidence' (Gardner 2006: 127). What disturbed Codrington about Lubbock was his promotion of an evolutionary theory of cultural development. This classical evolutionism enjoyed widespread popularity and it held that:

human beings progress through a universal sequence of stages from primitive to civilized. To comprehend the origins of modern civilized society, one had to look to the 'primitive' societies of the contemporary present … the non-European world provided theorists with a living museum of the history of present-day Western society. (Weir 2008: 282)

As Stocking observed, 'He [Codrington] never really became a convert to evolutionism' (Stocking 1995: 39). In fact, as Gardner has persuasively argued:

> The first principle was human similitude and the capacity to come to the full potential of human ability within the single life span. Thus there was no contradiction for most missionaries of that generation in the islander who was born a cannibal and died a clergyman. Yet missionaries rarely persuaded their anthropological interlocutors that their new converts were their equals in intellectual ability and potential. (Gardner 2006: 131)

Codrington's distrust extended to most authors, and certainly to Solomon Islands Government Resident Commissioner, Charles Woodford, whose account of life in Solomon Islands was at best colourful and more often fanciful (Woodford 1890). Codrington affected to be much more impressed by a fictitious account written supposedly by a Melanesian about his conversion to Christianity. The narrative by Percy Pomo (1884) bears striking resemblance to accounts from Melanesian members of the Melanesian Mission. This is hardly surprising, as it was written anonymously by Charles Brooke, Codrington's colleague (Whiteman 1983: 164n. 151). Codrington wrote approvingly, 'there is no picture of native life as good as that given in Percy Pomo' (*TM*: 9). This judgement was in sharp contrast to his views on colonial writing about Melanesia. As Codrington wrote to Fison:

> It is as you remark a great calamity that in Australia and N. Zealand alike the people who write and read papers are not really competent. They get the reputation, and are puffed up by their fellow colonists, being themselves quite unconscious of their ignorance. They want someone among their own set who will learn – outsiders they despise. (Codrington to Fison, 22 November 1893, Pacific Manuscript Bureau MS 1042)

Codringon's vigorous dismissal of such views was based on his desire to strip away prejudice and to discover the common humanity that all people shared. He emphasised the importance of local knowledge using the example of growing crops:

> I think that it is probable that most people are little aware with how much skill and care those whom we call savages carry on their cultivation … in the island of Mota there are 80 varieties of cultivated yams recognised and named. How many well-known varieties of bananas have their own names I cannot tell; but a native knows them by the look of their stems and leaves. (Codrington 1889: 13)

He wrote emphatically: 'The point with Melanesians was not to turn them into Englishmen but to make them Christians, and, as a first step, to convince them that, in the sight of God who made them, and redeemed them, Englishmen and Melanesians were alike equal' (Campbell 1873: 5). In a rather florid note to his aunt he explained:

> The most wonderful thing about heathen savages is that they are so extremely like other people. When one gets used to the colour, which is certainly the best wear for the climate, it is absurd to see the exact likeness of people you see in everyday England. My particular old friend, if white, would keep a general shop in the village and be Church warden. (Letters 1891–1922, to aunt, 27 October 1870)

His 'particular old friend' was Vetpepewu, who he first met on his preliminary visit to Mota in 1863, and whom Codrington mentions in his diaries of 1869 and again in 1875.

Another important figure who features early in Codrington's *The Melanesians* was George Sarawia (**Fig. 3**), with whom he worked and who become the first Pacific Islands-ordained priest in the mission. Sarawia was not only an informant but a major source of knowledge about the people and their customs, and, most important of all, a tutor in local languages. He is discussed in greater detail in Chapter 5. In his introduction to *The Melanesians* Codrington emphasised Sarawia's significance:

> I had, as regards the Banks Islands, the very valuable assistance of a native who was a grown youth before his people had been at all affected by intercourse with Europeans or heard any Christian teaching – the Rev George Sarawia, the first, and now for many years the leader of the native clergy of this group. (*TM*: v–vi)

Sarawia's value to Codrington lay in the fact that he had grown up in a pre-missionary era and so could understand and explain previous cultural practices. Other specialists assisted Codrington in checking the accuracy of his accounts:

> I was able to go through the subjects which are treated in this book with native instructors from the Solomon Islands, and the Northern New Hebrides: with Marsden Manekalea from Ysabel, Benjamin Bele from Florida, Joseph Wate from Saa, Walter Woser from Motlav, Arthur Arudulewari from Aurora, Lewis Tariliu from Pentecost, Martin Tangabe from Lepers' Island; every one of them, in my opinion, a competent and trustworthy witness. (*TM*: vi)

Characteristically, Codrington added a qualifying comment, 'though all were not equally intelligent'. This reliance on local personal knowledge was part of a more general principle that Codrington adopted, to pay close attention to what people said:

> I have endeavoured to collect what as well as I can make out the natives themselves think, and I have carefully abstained from writing down what I have heard from white men, missionaries or others. I don't in the least suppose that I understand it all, but I desire to ascertain as far as I can the facts and make them known. (Letter from Wadhurst, 4 December 1888, G.W. Stocking papers)

He restated his principles in *The Melanesians*:

> It has been my purpose to set forth as much as possible what natives say about themselves not what Europeans say about them. For this reason, though the results of my own personal observation are given, I have refrained from asking or recording, except in a few instances where acknowledgment is made, the information which my colleagues in the Mission would have abundantly and willingly imparted. (*TM*: vi)

The sting was in the tail: 'which my colleagues in the mission would have abundantly and willingly imparted'. For Codrington the key to understanding was a proper study of local languages. Relying on previous visitors'

Figure 3 Photograph of George Sarawia and family, c. 1870. SOAS, MM box 40, file 08/46

misunderstanding, he warned, was perilous: 'A correct native name, it may be said, is rarely obtained from a trader; the early sea-going visitors make the form which is to stand for the native name, and hand it on. The only security is the writing of a native who knows' (*TM*: 5).

On language

Codrington was deeply indebted to Bishop John Coleridge Patteson, his mentor, who introduced him to the Melanesian world (**Fig. 4**). Both men immediately took to one another. On Codrington's arrival at the mission in 1867, Patteson said, with evident relief, 'Somehow I think that all is well, and, if so, what a gain, what a blessing to me and to all' (Gutch 1971: 177). Patteson had a gift for languages; Codrington noted with admiration, 'Bishop Patteson was generally conversant with the people and languages of the islands from New Zealand to Ysabel' (*TM*: 10) (**Fig. 5**). As important for Codrington was Patteson's tolerance of local customs, the male secret societies called *tamate* (*TM*: 74; see Chapters 3 and 5 this volume). Had the two men not been so compatible, Codrington's career might have taken quite a different direction. The next bishop, John Richard Selwyn, who took up post in 1877, was not as congenial and Codrington exercised some reserve in his relationship with him.

Patteson had insisted that the missionary endeavour should be conducted in local languages. Codrington was firm in his conviction that compromises like Pidgin English were to be repudiated as 'wretched childish stuff, and degrading to people who have a real language' (LT, 4 December 1884; Nash 2012: 478). Codrington reflected:

> Bp Patteson said that it was most important to prepare besides the native Teachers, native laymen, Churchwardens. What is the good of simplified English to the working layman? He must be preached to in his own language, and in his own language he ought to pray. (Letters 1891–1922, to C.H. Brooke, 12 October 1917)

But what was the native language? This was not an easy question to answer. Patteson abandoned English as the language of instruction in favour of Mota, selected as a language from the Banks Islands group, the heart of the early mission. Codrington reflected: 'He [Patteson] saw so clearly the great advantage … of throwing together in every possible way the boys from all the islands, which was much helped by the use of one language' (Yonge 1875, vol. II: 178). The choice of Mota was explained by Awdry: 'It so happened that several of the most intelligent of Bishop Patteson's early converts came from the little island of Mota, so that it was possible to get translation into that earlier than any other, so it came to be adopted as the training language' (Awdry 1902: 11). Whiteman came up with a more prosaic reason: 'There was an increasing percentage of scholars from the Banks Islands who spoke Mota, and, with Pritt's linguistic limitations, this was the only language that he learnt to speak' (Whiteman 1983: 125). Pritt was Codrington's immediate predecessor as headmaster of St Barnabas College.

Roger Tempest, a member of the Melanesian Mission, offered another generic reason for the choice:

For Mota, this or any other Melanesian language is the idiom in which people think, any native or any white man who tries, can learn Mota quickly and easily and by this means you can teach religious texts or anything else you like without having to spend all your time explaining the meaning of the language. (R.E. Tempest. 'Memories' ms, 1959: 6)

Kolshus provides another more specific explanation:

The Melanesian Mission soon chose the language of Mota as its language for hymns, liturgy and teaching. The reasons behind this were its phonetic simplicity compared to many other Melanesian tongues; its rich vocabulary on cosmological and ethereal phenomena; and the mission's first impressions of Mota climate as less humid than other surrounding islands and therefore more suitable for Europeans. (Kolshus 2011a: 10)

Mota acted as a consolidating language, facilitating the generation of a specific Melanesian Anglicanism. This was important for Codrington, as he felt that Melanesia was widely seen as inferior to Polynesia. He was aware that Melanesians suffered in their dealings with others, especially Polynesians, but was insistent that this should not be taken to mean that they were in any fundamental sense inferior: 'the Melanesians are the poor relations at the best, of their more civilised and stronger neighbours; but a question of language must be discussed in its own merits' (Codrington 1885: 13). Indeed, as Gardner has noted, Codrington 'strenuously argued, based on the incontrovertible evidence of island languages, that his flock were members of the "common brotherhood"' (Gardner 2006: 131).

Codrington was always alert to the difficulties that operating in a local language presented:

It is probable that some corruption of a native language is inevitable in mission work, in which the language must be used before it is known; and no great harm is done. But great mischief is done when a native language is impoverished for teaching and translating by the use of an incorrect and narrow vocabulary. It is not only that the usefully effective richness of the native vocabulary is lost, but with it is lost, to probably, some of the activity of the native mind, for natives will follow their teacher. (Codrington and Palmer 1896: viii)

Nevertheless, Codrington insisted, local language was always to be used: 'The white missionary's chief work is to teach teachers first, and then to supervise them. To teach them their language and native views of things must be learnt by the teachers and that can only really be done in the islands' (Journal 1881: 100). Codrington's approach to teaching was generally appreciated, as one of his successors noted:

He was not a great disciplinarian, like Pritt, yet he was so great a teacher, so wise and patient, so loved by the boys, that he held them in the hollow of his hand. His lessons on the parables and miracles, written in the Mota language, are magnificent teaching. They show deep understanding of the Melanesian mind and the power of a born teacher. (Fox 1958: 220)

If the study of language was to be the key to understanding, other more sensorial approaches were not to be neglected. Codrington tried chewing betel nut: 'Since we were leaving the region of betel nut, I carried out a second determination I had made, which was to chew some of it, in native fashion. I thought it so good, that I'm sorry I didn't begin before. Of course I was very moderate for a good

Figure 4 Photograph of George Sarawia, his son and Bishop Patteson, c. 1870. SOAS, MM box 40, file 08/46

mouthful would have made one giddy' (Journal 1881: 87). He also took the opportunity to experiment with kava, despite the disapproval of his fellow missionary, Charles Bice:

I was guilty of corrupting the whole thing by drinking kava. I was not aware that Bice had considered it criminal to drink kava on Sunday. It was another of those things I had determined to do and that now we were not to go to Araga or Lepers' Island, it was my last chance. (Journal 1881: 95)

Codrington's practical skills

Practical activities took up much of Codrington's time working for the Melanesian Mission. He complained to his brother Tom:

I had no idea before we settled down again how few boys had gone and how few teachers remained. Besides school I have to become cook again, which is a nuisance, and have the care of the sick, and of the printing press. Moreover I have undertaken to teach the two little Bices for an hour a day ... I have got off the arithmetic lesson three times a week, and have done my translations in that time, but now I am obliged also to do that out of school, and I can hardly get any time for getting language matters written down. In fact I begin to believe that I must not only get away if I am to print anything, but also get away if I am to write anything. (LT, 21 April 1881)

Allan K. Davidson lists other accomplishments that Codrington acquired. 'On top of his teaching responsibilities Codrington designed the dining hall, which seated 140, acquainted himself with printing, taught some students to play the harmonium and made wedding rings for the Melanesian brides and plum puddings for the

Figure 5 Group portrait of scholars with Codrington, Bishop John Selwyn and Mrs Selwyn, Norfolk Island, date unknown. SOAS, MM box 40, file 08/46

community breakfasts' (Davidson 2003: 172). Codrington also proudly reported, 'I have learnt how to make guava jelly, and people who have been in the West Indies say it is the correct thing' (Letters 1867–87, to aunt, 27 May 1869). Gutch characterises Codrington at this time thus: 'He was lively and sociable and had many accomplishments – a keen botanist and naturalist, interested too in art and architecture: he was decorating the little wooden chapel with his own carving' (Gutch 1971: 181). Early on in his time in Norfolk Island, Codrington reported to his aunt, 'I have spent much of my time in carving some ornaments of the chapel which is part of the buildings being put up but the buildings like all these colonial wooden buildings with planks with thin and mean features there is nothing to carve that makes any shew' (Letters 1867–83, to aunt, August 1867: 2).

Nelson Drummond, a later head of St Barnabas College, also reported that Codrington made the lectern for the chapel, 'with revolving top and provision for the Old and New Testaments on either side'. Drummond also added somewhat less charitably, 'If anything, it is rather too large, obstructing, as it does, the view of the Altar' (Drummond 1930).

Codrington not only carved in wood, but also in stone. Gutch and Pinder reported:

> The caps and bases for the marble shafts [of the pillars in the chapel] were missing and must have gone astray in transit. Codrington says that he is trying to screw up the courage to try and carve replacements. He had never tried to carve stone before but the local stone was so soft that he thought he might manage it. Lack of time would be the difficulty. In the event he managed to complete the carving. (Gutch and Pinder 1980: 7)

At the same time, he was engaged in sewing. 'I kept at home all morning beginning a kind of altar cloth for the little chapel out of some red stuff got for trade' (Blue Journal, 22 August). Two days later he recorded: 'I finished roughly the altar cloth', suggesting that perhaps his needlework skills were somewhat rudimentary. Carreau also suggests that Islander students at St Barnabas College may well have been involved in the construction of the chapel (Carreau 2018: 243). If this were the case then Codrington would inevitably have had a significant role in their supervision.

On self-reliance

It might appear that Codrington lived a quiet life among his students, leading by example. But he was keen to see his converts establish their own polity and governance. Towards this goal his first principle was non-interference in local custom. As he recorded in *The Melanesians*:

> It was a matter of principle with Bishop Patteson not to interfere in an arbitrary manner with the institutions of the people, but to leave it to their own sense of right and wrong, and their own knowledge of the character of what they did, to condemn or tolerate what their growing enlightenment would call into question… The bishop would therefore not condemn the societies, and in the Banks Islands they continue to exist, and indeed to flourish more than it is at all desirable that that they should. (*TM*: 74)

That last phrase betrays Codrington's ambivalence as to how far practices like *suqe* (a graded secret society; see also Chapter 5 this volume) should be respected and permitted. But he was convinced that the future lay in political self-governance. He advised George Sarawia:

> … the grown-up fathers of families must look after things themselves and not rely upon their teacher but above all things to keep their own houses in order, since family life is the basis of everything. These people, having no political organization whatever, are in hard case [sic] when the law of the bow and arrow are put down. I told them they must try and get a village council of elders into play. We have been accustomed to abhor the common assumption of political power by Missionaries, but we must keep in view their political as well as spiritual advancement. (Journal 1872, 1 September)

For Codrington, to engender a sense of self-reliance required a radical critique of colonial policy. Naval patrols were at fault for their punishment raids on coastal villages, in which 'these little men-of-war go about to protect the traders and not the natives' (Journal 1875, 7 May). Traders in turn were responsible for despicable practices in labour recruitment:

> Europeans have from the beginning of intercourse with Melanesian natives kidnapped them, and have persuaded themselves that they were doing them a service by bringing them into what is called contact with civilization; the natives have from the first resented the kidnapping of their sons, and their sons, however much they have wished to go away and have rejoiced in what they have learnt and acquired, will hardly be said by any impartial observer to have done any good when they have returned. (*TM*: 12)

Ultimately these recruitment practices were a threat to the very viability of the island communities. Codrington wrote passionately:

> It [the labour trade] is a most serious obstacle in the way of evangelization of the natives… It is not a question of more or less difficulty in carrying on the mission; it is a question in some islands already whether the population is to be utterly destroyed instead of being evangelized. (Melanesian Mission Annual Report 1873: 23–4)

Like many other commentators, Codrington feared the total destruction of Melanesian island societies through labour recruitment, which with the voluntary departure of able-bodied males had rendered populations unstable. In the 1860s kidnapping was certainly employed by labour recruiters, and this enraged the anti-slavery societies in Australia, New Zealand and Britain. Codrington worked against the practice: 'We have met with a good many slavers but it seems to me that that they are not so successful in our islands as they were. It is a good sign that they hate us and abuse us, which looks as if they found we hindered them' (LT, 21 October 1874). Even when the trade became loosely regulated the problems did not cease. As Shineberg (1999: 6–7) has noted, 'The Reverend R.H. Codrington even considered that the situation deteriorated after kidnapping largely gave way to trading for workers, since it was then possible to enlist more recruits when youths, as he believed, were traded by their seniors for their own gain.'

The situation was made even worse by the devastating imported illnesses that returning labourers brought back. These factors, exacerbated by the importation of guns, led to the collapse of traditional authority structures. Codrington not only condemned the recruiting practices, but went to Queensland himself, the destination of most of the indentured islander recruits, to argue against the practice.

In the face of the potential catastrophe that labour recruitment represented, Codrington was determined to depict a disappearing world before it was too late, and to do this he made skilful and reputable records permanently available, both for scientific study and, more importantly, for future Melanesian people, thus providing an enduring link to their cultural heritage.

Codrington's writing

To record this changing world Codrington kept regular journals, and these also give a good indication of the interplay that occurred on a daily basis between himself and those he taught. His first journal, composed on Mota Island in 1870, exemplifies this well:

> September 2nd. Could not sleep for rats, and the strangeness of the place, got up early but things were late. Clock an hour behind till yesterday. School for an hour. I took down 33 names of boarders yesterday, 2 were in school. After school took George's report for rewards etc and gave a fishing line apiece to all. They range from men of 25 to boys of only 9, mixed up in the classes. Unpacked and stuck up Scripture prints, and Ellen's clock. An old man brought an old native stone adze damaged, which I bought. (1870 Journal, 2 September)

It was in these journals that Codrington was able to depict the wide variety of everyday activities. Koshus (2011: 7) insists that Codrington's various writings represent a composite artefact in their own right. The corpus includes the most valuable set of 116 letters written to his brother Tom, from May 1867 to February 1882, each numbered and dated on their receipt. Thankfully these letters to Tom were bequeathed to the Melanesian Mission by the family and were later recovered from the floor of the Melanesian Mission headquarters in London in the 1970s (pers. corr. Jenny Pinder 2019). They were written on two-sided semi-transparent blue onion-skin octavo notepaper and require patience of the modern reader to decipher: the writing is often cramped, with old-fashioned handwriting getting smaller as the page is covered, often resulting in curious palimpsests (**Fig. 6**).

They do, however, provide Codrington's reflections on life in the mission field, thoughts on indigenous beliefs and practices, and the role of the missionary, as well as his response to the harshness of the climate and its effects on his health. They likewise give us a good insight into his collecting practices, as well as how he undertook these activities.

Codrington wrote for a larger audience than his immediate family. He completed four substantial journals, each composed on his visits to the islands. The first in 1870 was 74 pages long and copied into a quarto blank-page book. He explained his purpose in writing in a letter to his brother:

> I have kept a journal at Mota which I send to you and which will give you all the news and more than ever I should have written in letters. I thought that being then alone and my own master it was a good chance to write what once written would save me a world of letter writing and give a certain amount of pleasure to my friends. (LT, 12 October 1870)

The following journal in 1872 was in the same format and had 143 pages. The third, composed in 1875, was 80 pages long, and the final 1881 journal had 101 pages. These were all

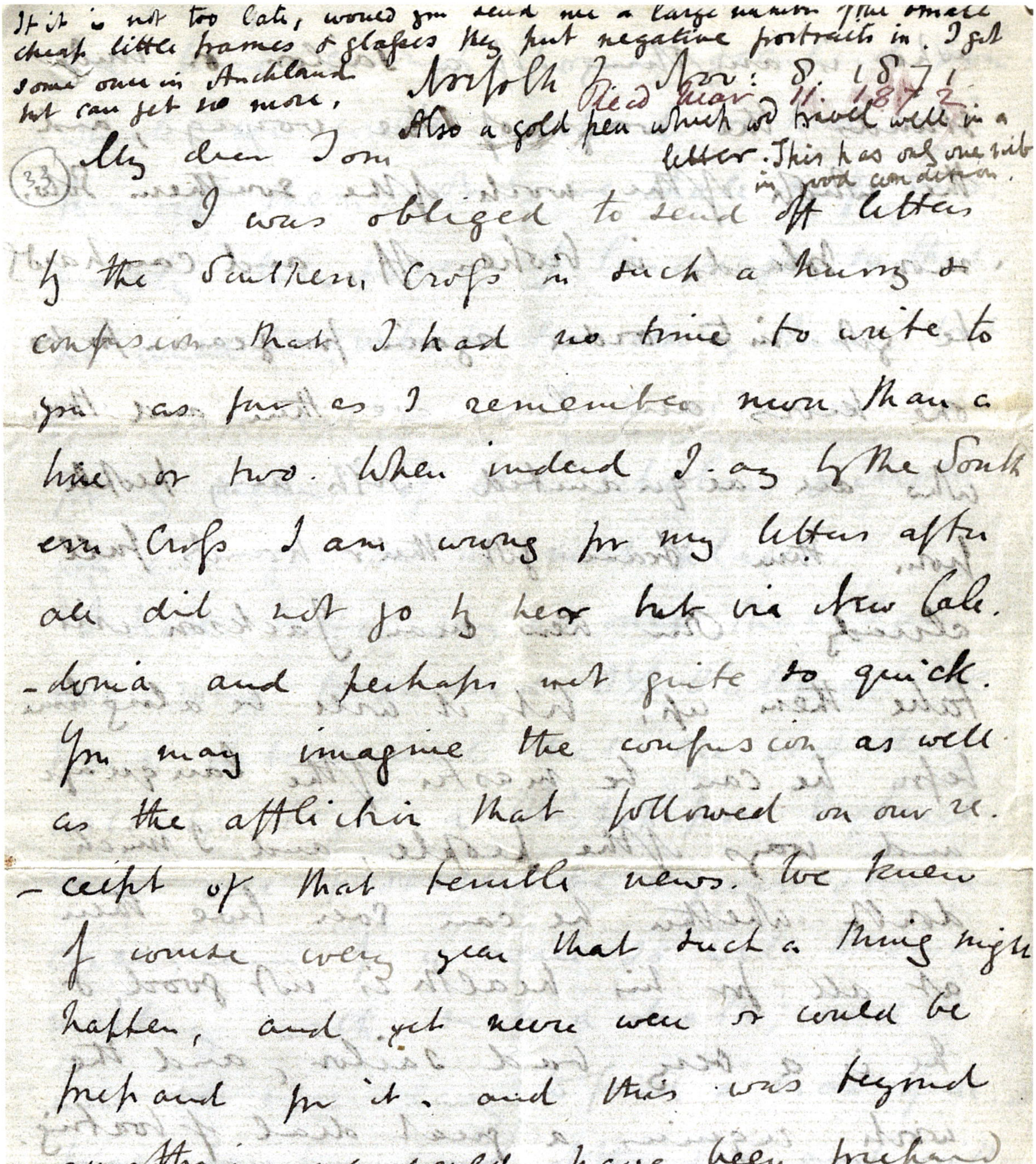

If it is not too late, would you send me a large number of the small cheap little frames & glasses they put negative portraits in. I got some once in Auckland but can get no more.

Norfolk I[sland] Nov: 8. 1871
Rec'd Mar: 11. 1872

Also a gold pen which wd travel well in a letter. This has only one nib in good condition.

My dear Tom

I was obliged to send off letters by the Southern Cross in such a hurry & confusion that I had no time to write to you as [far] as I remember more than a line or two. When indeed I say by the Southern Cross I am wrong for my letters after all did not go by her but via New Caledonia and perhaps not quite so quick. You may imagine the confusion as well as the affliction that followed on our receipt of that terrible news. We knew of course every year that such a thing might happen, and yet never were or could be prepared for it. and this was beyond anything we could have been prepared for, as it was not only the Bishop, but Joe Atkin also that we had lost, not only the head but the right hand of the mission also, and in the good old Taroniara the most influential and steadiest of all our native helpers out of Mota. For example there is no one left more

Figure 6 Copy of a page from a letter from R.H. Codrington to his brother Tom, 8 November 1871. SOAS, MM box 9, folder 2/1

written to be circulated among the mission supporters in Britain. They thus act as a series of examples of missionary activity, but more importantly, they give us an insight into Codrington's personal relationships with Melanesian people. What is remarkable about the journals and also the letters is how little space is given to daily interaction with other missionaries. The focus remains consistently on efforts to understand the context in which he found himself both at school as well as in the islands during his visits. A note written on Pek, Vanua Lava, gives a hint of Codrington's intimacy with his students and their networks:

> Two boys have lived in my house for four years and have now been baptized, the first from this neighbourhood, who are particular favourites of mine, and two others who have been 2 years with me, are just as good. They are all returning, and an excellent Mota young man with another to assist him goes to begin school. The two boys, whose Godfather he is, invite him to live with them and they are all to stay together with the father of one of them, have prayers and school and make a beginning. It is such things as these that give a promise of something being done, hopes and prospects to be thankful for. (1875 Journal, 12 May)

Codrington's most serious literary and intellectual preoccupation was translation. Mota was the destination language for his texts. Beside the dictionary of the Mota language that he co-authored with John Palmer, he steadily worked his way through key biblical texts throughout his time in the mission. To make effective translations he needed to gain an understanding of the mental construction of the Melanesian world, so language acquisition was the most vital element in creating workable texts. It remained a constant preoccupation throughout his stay in Melanesia. He was fortunate in that he had a constant source of information from scholars from across the region at St Barnabas College, and when accompanying them home, with members of their families and villages. He employed a scientific mode of experimentation with all these scholars, so as to obtain not only a real correspondence with the English, but also to the earlier Greek and Vulgate biblical texts.

Codrington also wrote for the general public and specifically for anthropologists. This monograph attempts to bring together and provide something of a synthesis of his writings. The only corpus that is not readily accessible is that of Codrington's correspondence with his ex-pupils, written in Mota. Fortunately, Kolshus has provided some translations of letters to and from Codrington that help make up this deficiency. He remarks that Codrington's writings in Mota are quite different to his other correspondence with the outside world. He notes, 'The Mota letters are infinitely more personal and emotional… the tone of his letters in the Mota language sent to his Melanesian friends is much more expressive and unconditionally affectionate' (Kolshus 2011a: 12, 14).

Kolshus exemplified this with a quotation from Codrington's letter to the students on Norfolk Island written in the Mota language during his tour of the United States:

> Today I will again embark on the steamer and six days after I will see my island again. But how do I feel? It is not with happy feelings, it is not possible because my thoughts stay with you, and the way I left you behind… I keep thinking about you, and I feel sad. Because I was always happy when I stayed with you, and I really long to assist you, and now we are separated. Only this, I always implore you not to forget me but to think about me and write me letters, so that we can always remain friends. (Codrington 1887b)

The contrast is significant. On reading Codrington's English-language writings, both published and, especially, those written privately, there is an otherness and emotional distance from the scenes that he depicts. They provide a tale told without over-embellishment, pride or self-justification. Indeed, his concern to gain interpersonal understanding with Melanesians excluded speculative theorising in favour of an experimental approach, trying out a variety of possible synonyms with local speakers to obtain a 'best fit'. This makes them valuable resources in considering his work on Melanesian material culture. It is a pity that more of these letters did not survive. As Codrington confessed late in life, 'I have a lot of letters from Melanesians which I must burn, for no one would ever read them if they could. I cannot hope to read them again myself' (Letters 1891–1922, to C.H. Brooke, 13 September 1917).

Chapter 1
'I have little doubt but that I can get some good things sooner or later': Codrington as a Collector

It is often assumed that collections arrive ready-made at the destination museum and are then assimilated by the curator in the most practicable way. This chapter shows how false this picture is in the case of R.H. Codrington. His dealing with museums were long-term, fitful and sometimes tortuous. As will become apparent, each of Codrington's donations took a different route and involved different forms of negotiation.

There is no indication that Codrington knew much about museums in his youth. Neither is there evidence that he spent any time at university museums, and the Pitt Rivers Museum was not opened until 1884, long after he left Oxford. It seems that Codrington learnt as he progressed in his missionary career. It is also quite likely that his interest in material culture was stimulated by the antiquarianism he shared with his brothers Tom and Oliver.

The Blackmore Museum
Prior to his appointment as headmaster at the new mission school on Norfolk Island, Codrington was in contact with the Blackmore Museum in Salisbury, which held a collection consisting mainly of stone hatchets and other '"minor monuments" of that early period known as the Stone Age' (Haddow 2020: 119–20; Wiltshire Archaeological and Natural History Society 1864: 105). This was near his family home at Wroughton, Wiltshire, and had been set up in 1864 by William Henry Blackmore with assistance from his brother, Dr Humphrey Purnell Blackmore, and his brother-in-law, Edward Thomas Stevens. This was a very modern museum created as a result of the archaeological revolution of 1859 devoted to flints (Gamble 2021). These had, as a result of new theory, become seen as proxies for human activities, their presence in soil strata enabling archaeologists to date the prehistoric past and so revise our understanding of human antiquity. Flints thus took on a fundamental significance in this new archaeology. The Blackmore Museum held an extensive collection of flints, but also incorporated a section devoted to 'Implements, weapons and ornaments of modern savages, which serve to throw light upon the use of similar objects belonging to prehistoric times' (Wiltshire Archaeological Society 1864: 109). Edward Stevens in his guide to the museum (*Flint Chips: A Guide to Pre-Historic Archaeology as Illustrated in the Blackmore Museum, Salisbury*) wrote, 'a collection such as that at the Blackmore Museum, is calculated to throw much light upon the *progress* of civilization in various countries'. 'Furthermore,' he argued, 'it is our desire to *improve* the "general collection" rather than to extend it; we seek to render it more illustrative, and more generally representative of the industry of the Stone Age of various countries' (Stevens 1870: xv, xvi). This focus on the stone age gave Codrington an early impetus for collecting, but, as will become clear in his later writing, this did not mean that he became a cultural evolutionist.

Soon after his arrival at Norfolk Island, Codrington sought to establish a policy and strategy for collecting for the Blackmore Museum. He wrote to his brother Tom:

> About the things for the museum I will very gladly do what I can and I have little doubt but that I can get some good things sooner or later. The great difficulty would be to send them

Figure 7 Adze with tridacna shell blade, wooden haft and rattan binding, given by R.H. Codrington to his brother Tom Codrington, who used it as a walking stick, before 1894, Bellona Island. British Museum, Oc1907,-.37. The inscription reads 'Adze of clam shell, Bellona. Donated by T Codrington'

home. The best thing, I think, would be for the Blackmore Trustees to appoint an agent and receive and ship things and pay me for such things through him. Mr Shirley Hill our agent of Fort Street, Auckland would do very well I have no doubt. It would be a long time before £50 would be spent in the islands but when you come to shipping and packing expenses would begin. From here it would be impossible to ship and I would have to supply Mr Hill. When and if he were their agent it would much simplify money transactions. I don't mean that they should appoint him to buy for them though he could do in Auckland and probably would buy rubbish. Mr Hill is a very respectable man I am told. (LT, 22 September 1868)

So an agreement was reached whereby Codrington would collect specimen items for the trustees of the museum, and receive an advance of £50 to defray his expenses. This arrangement was to prove uncomfortable for Codrington, as he later complained. In September 1869 Codrington did receive lists from Stevens of objects that the museum would like to receive and, he shared these with his missionary colleagues. But he asked querulously, 'Why should he [Stevens] not send me his Handbook to the Museum which would be very useful?' (LT, 22 September 1869). Codrington did receive a copy of Stevens' *Flint Chips* from the author soon after its publication in 1870. He wrote to his brother Tom that he was immersed 'for light reading a letter of P. Grantry, for severe Liddon's Bampton Lectures. These with "Flint Chips" are all I have brought with the notion that I should have no time for reading, and now I am afraid to read them too fast for fear that I should be left with nothing' (LT, 6 September 1870). A month later he wrote, 'I shall write to Mr Stevens to thank him for Flint Chips and also I shall send him some notes on the subject he deals with according to the light my experience and enquiry throws upon them' (LT, 12 October 1970). Six months later he admitted that he had not got round to responding to Stevens with his reflections from the field.

In the absence of direct instruction from Stevens, Codrington formed his own strategy. 'For the voyage now in progress I furnished some trade [goods] from my own resources and if anything comes out of it I shall present them to the Museum as a beginning, that they may not spend money without seeing a sample.' He continued:

The main expense in point of fact will consist of getting the things to England – in fact unless I get poorer than I am, or prices rise in the Islands I should be ashamed to ask for payment for most things. But if Mr Shirley Hill has authority from the Blackmore Trustees to supply me – or failing me (Atkin, e.g.) somebody of our party – with the necessary axes, beads tobacco for trade; and makes his charge for that and other expenses to them, I shall be more than well pleased – and the business I should suppose sufficiently simple. (LT, 22 September 1869)

Codrington augmented his collection with a set of drawings by one of his pupils, as he reported to his brother:

I am having much for Mr Stevens, a series of tamates drawn by my son Robert [one of his pupils whom he affectionately called his 'son'], who does them very well. I buy them at sixpence apiece at the Blackmore expense. I had begun to get them done before I heard from you if my former drawings had been worth copying. They are certainly enormous things, and are the only examples of art in these parts. (LT, 7 August 1871)

Thus began an annual shipment from Norfolk Island to Salisbury via Auckland. He wrote to his brother:

I am getting ready things in expectation of the *Southern Cross* which may be in now any day. There is no news at all since I last wrote so I had better begin business at once. I am going to enclose a box to you in the annual contribution to the Blackmore which I consider I may do if I pay the proportion of the freight. You must get your box from Mr Stevens. It will contain curiosities and photographic negatives. As for the curiosities Miss Mackenzie (Woodfield, Havant) is to have some, and she must fetch them when she hears from you that they are arrived. In fact I imagine that a good many will be given for her by the bishop when he come back. But all that come are to be subject to selection by yourself, of anything scientifically valuable, or otherwise to your mind for yourself or others. (LT, 9 October 1871)

This latter recommendation meant that Tom was to create his own collection, and some of these items found their way eventually into the British Museum collection (**Fig. 7**). The following January he wrote a similar note: 'I am going to send off to you a box for the Blackmore and yourself and I think I shall send it to you because I want you to have the pick' (LT, 23 January 1872). Four months later the shipment had still not left Auckland, but Codrington assured Tom that they soon would. Again, he enjoined, 'divide at your discretion' (LT, 10 April 1872).

In the next year Codrington again wrote to his brother:

Shirley Hill complains that the Blackmore things are never acknowledged. There is heaps of the money still left and what is to be done? All the stone and shell things in the islands will soon be bought up. If I can get better opportunities these next two years I may spend more but in fact I have never charged anything for the purchase of the specimens. (LT, 23 June 1873)

His frustration mounted and in September he came to a decision, as he reported to Tom:

By the way it would be very desirable of Mr Stevens or somebody would let me know about the things which I have sent, whether they have arrived, whether they are satisfactory, and whether I should get more of the same kind or look out for something else. It is not encouraging to hear nothing, nor comfortable to have received so much money, for the use of which I am responsible without any knowledge of satisfaction or dissatisfaction given. This year I will send as usual, but I think that unless I hear more before next year it would be better to send the considerable balance of their money back and only look hereafter for really remarkable things which I would get at my own expense. (LT, 17 September 1873)

Codrington's dissatisfaction grew. Next year he confided to Tom:

As to Mr Stevens I certainly think he has been negligent. He knew on the one hand of money sent out here to be conserved and he has not looked after it, and he has on the other hand received advice of one case at least and has not enquired after it. It is also very disheartening to me never to know whether I get the right things or not. I shall certainly, if you wish it, send for the future to you. It will have the great advantage that I can put in a few things for you that I should like to send. (LT, 10 June 1874)

The decisive moment came a few months later. He noted, 'We have got very little for the museum this year. It is difficult to get things and it is unsatisfactory not to know what to get. I can get stone adzes and that is about all, unless I am told what to get' (LT, 21 October 1874). He was worried that the opportunity to acquire objects was slipping away, as other were collecting the remaining available stone and shell axes and adzes. Traders and naval patrol ships were collecting haphazardly but regularly, and also contributing to Labour Trade collections in Australia (Quanchi and Cochrane 2007: 4).

The British Museum

By this point Codrington had decided that the time for change had arrived and on 21 October 1874 he wrote to his brother, 'I shall send these to the British Museum, for I am tired of Mr Stevens.' But this did not resolve his collecting dilemma. He raised the same issue with Augustus Wollaston Franks at the British Museum that he had not resolved with Edward Stevens. He wrote again to Tom: 'I wish Mr Franks would write and tell me if there is anything I can do before it is too late. Other people buy curiosities while I am concerned about other things, but if I knew of the things wanted I would get agents to work to buy them' (LT, 21 October 1874). The urgency of his request was reinforced by a follow-up letter: 'I wish also that Mr Franks would write. If he does not before we make the next voyage it may be too late. as I don't think I shall make many more' (LT, 14 November 1874). In the same letter Codrington confided that he was not impressed by one of the few authoritative accounts on collecting the Pacific, Julius Brenchley's *Jottings during the Cruise of HMS Curacao among the Pacific Islands in 1865* (1873):

I have had Brenchley's book on board and have been amused at it, and more than that I think his general views are good. It is one other example however of what I find everywhere, that a traveller puts his own notion into the actions or words of savages then the philosophers at home quote him as an authority. (ibid.)

So, no easy answers would do for Codrington.

The following year Codrington was excusing his lack of collecting success:

I ought to mention that I have got very little indeed for the Christie [*sic*] collection [at the British Museum] this year. It is partly because it is more difficult every year to find things which rapidly disappear as trade advances and partly because I have to be occupied about other things than trading when trading is going on onboard or we are visiting people on shore. (LT, 19 July 1875)

Codrington had evidently entered into a formal relationship with the British Museum by this point, as the Christy funds were devoted to making acquisitions for the Museum. Nevertheless, his request for direction does not seem to have been answered to his satisfaction. He grumbled, 'I don't find that the little book you sent out, from Mr Franks I suppose, tells me what sort of things he wants' (ibid.).

The last links with the Blackmore Museum were severed in 1879. Codrington wrote to his brother, 'Shirley Hill has ceased to be my agent. In fact, poor man, he went bankrupt or something' (LT, 17 March 1879). What Codrington may not yet have known was that both Edward Stevens and William Blackmore had died in 1878, the latter in April, as a result of financial ruin that led him to commit suicide. Consequently, the contents of the Blackmore Museum were progressively dispersed by the Salisbury and South Wiltshire Museum. The precise details of this transfer have been lost; no records survive at Salisbury and the only clues remaining at the British Museum are laconic comments in the accession register, 'ex Blackmore'. The Codrington collection in the British Museum ceases abruptly in 1876. The link through the Blackmore Museum became broken and annual donations stopped appearing. This does not mean that Codrington ceased to collect, but evidence for such collecting becomes fugitive.

James Edge-Partington and the Pitt Rivers Museum

The only real evidence that Codrington continued to collect comes from two sources. The first is James Edge-Partington, who created a visual catalogue of Pacific Islands artefacts held in Britain. Edge-Partington was also a voluntary curator at the British Museum. As he wrote in the preface to his two-part album of drawings made in 1890:

> The purpose of this publication is two-fold: the first intention of the authors was to provide fellow collectors a means of classifying their specimens, but a more permanent object is served by this work, in that it places on record the more important objects to be found in collections both public and private in England and the Colonies. In all probability the public museum will have continuous existence, but the private collections are usually destined to dispersal. (Edge Partington and Heape 1890: n.p.)

This was very prescient prediction. Several private collections of Pacific artefacts were to be auctioned off in the following decades as their creators died. Codrington was one of the major collectors that Edge Partington visited. He recorded and drew 82 objects from Codrington's collection, which he noted were still in Codrington's possession when he visited him in 1889. The second source gives a better idea of what use Codrington put his collection to. A few years before his death, Codrington befriended a young correspondent, Geoffrey Haines, who preserved their correspondence. Codrington wrote to him:

> I received a party of Blue Boys from our school here a fortnight ago to shew them what they call my curios, a very well mannered and intelligent set. I expounded flints, neolithic tools and Island weapons to them, and shewed them curiosities such as water from Jordan, things from mummies, weapons and tools from the Islands and, what impressed them a great deal, gave them chocolate. (Letters 1922–6, to G.H. Haines, 1 October 1919)

But by 1916 Codrington was close to completing his negotiations with Henry Balfour at the Pitt Rivers Museum. Balfour visited him in Chichester, as Codrington recorded:

> I am exceedingly sorry to think you had so unfortunate a journey. It is good of you after all to say that you enjoyed your visit. I certainly did enjoy it and thank you very much for coming. It is only very rarely that I see anyone who cares for these things. I will take care to mark particularly the articles you mention as particularly desirable, so that they may be known to be your property. I aspire to the making of a catalogue. According to the will have made everything will come to you – that is not otherwise disposed of, but some of the things are probably not worth taking away. (Letters 1916, to H. Balfour, 13 July 1916)

The significance of this letter was that it underlined his determination that his collection should find its final destination at Oxford University, which had given him his start in life.

Codrington completed his letter with a reference to Charterhouse School, which they had both attended:

> There is one thing more to say. I see that you are a Carthusian [a student at Charterhouse]. So am I, though I have seen nothing of the place for 50 years and know nobody. Have they a school museum? I think a school museum among other things shows usefully how the old boys go all round the world, and the school does its duty. I should like therefore to give a matted club to the museum if there is one. What do you say? (ibid.)

Charterhouse, the school that he and his brother Tom attended between 1845 and 1847, did go on to create a museum with an eclectic range of material, though it did not open until 1872 (pers. corr. Smith 2019). Perhaps there were earlier donations that formed the Charterhouse School Museum, but there is no surviving record to support this suggestion. Sadly, there is no record of Charterhouse receiving Codrington's donation. Apart from his brother Tom, the only beneficiary of Codrington's final bequest was the Pitt Rivers Museum.

In December 1919 Codrington wrote to his former missionary colleague, Charles Brooke, 'I am just occupied in the conveyance of my collection of Melanesian weapons and curios to the Pitt Rivers Museum. Things of this sort have a very poor chance when they fall into the hands of Executors. I have got but few, but I have got some good [ones]' (Letters 1891–1922, to C.H. Brooke, 16 December 1919). Perhaps he had some lingering regrets as he confided to Haines in March 1920: 'My collection of Melanesian things is gone to Oxford and the house looks empty' (G.H. Haines 1922, extract 29). But in May he wrote defiantly to Brooke, 'I have sent all my Island Collection of weapons and such things to the Pitt Rivers at Oxford, and I am very glad to be quit of them' (Letters 1891–1922, to C.H. Brooke, 28 May 1920).

The Cambridge Museum of Archaeology and Anthropology collection came partly through the Blackmore link, but in 1890 the museum director, Anatole von Hügel, solicited both a copy of Codrington's forthcoming *The Melanesians* (1891) and details of his collection. It seems that Codrington became a regular visitor to the museum and contributed further items to the collection, as will be detailed in the next chapter.

Chapter 2
'Matters that lie upon the surface of native life and are open to the observation of the visitor and traveller': Codrington's Collections Explored

Nicholas Thomas has argued that there are two important characteristics that define historic ethnographic-object collections: they are both portable and durable (Thomas 2018: 296). In this chapter I want to consider these aspects in both R.H. Codrington's collecting practices and the objects to which we still have access. As will become clear, the collections under examination consist of items which are nearly all easy to carry, unlike some later collections that contain large objects, such as Julius Brenchley's bonito canoe from Ulawa (BM Oc1870,0209.1; Bolton *et al* 2013: 237) or Edward Davis's crocodile feast bowl from Roviana (BM Oc1903,1007.1; Bolton *et al* 2013: 210). But it is the issue of durability that intrigues me most. Thomas maintains that such objects 'are distinctively immediate, powerfully physical, yet also more or less indeterminate, in the sense that one may examine the physical expression of an artistic motif, but not have straightforward access to its intended effect or meaning' (Thomas 2018: 296). I would like to see whether in the case of Codrington we may narrow this sense of indeterminacy, as we explore his collecting strategies and, in the next chapter, what he brought to the bargain at the sea-shore, in villages and at St Barnabas College on Norfolk Island.

As described in the previous chapter, Codrington collected for two major institutions, the British Museum and the Pitt Rivers Museum, as well as offering items to Cambridge Museum of Archaeology and Anthropology. But he also contributed to private collections, particularly that of his brother Tom, to whom he regularly sent objects for him to select from. Other British collectors of Pacific curios also obtained artefacts collected by Codrington from public sales of Melanesian Mission material, including Harry Beasley and Captain Fuller (Stanley 1994a: 30, fig. 1). The Melanesian Mission depended upon such sales to supplement the salaries and pensions of its poorly paid missionary personnel.

The oldest holding of Codrington's artefacts is the British Museum's. The majority of the items were given by him to the Museum between 1873 and 1876, while he was the acting head of the mission. Some 16 objects of roughly the same provenance came indirectly, through the collector William Blackmore and the Blackmore Museum. Unsurprisingly, all the items originate in the southern and original field of the mission's operation (Banks, Florida, Makira, Malaita and Savo islands). Axes and fishing equipment figure prominently. The Pitt Rivers Museum's holding demonstrates clearly the relationship between Codrington's interest in objects and their context. This large Oxford collection is well balanced in the range of artefacts it contains. The earliest donations (1886, 1888 and 1912) contain a heterogeneous range of largely domestic artefacts. From 1916 onwards, however, there starts to emerge a sense of purpose in the arrangements. Particular objects are selected to illustrate his *The Melanesians* (1891). The largest bequest (1920) is divided into artefact types, reminiscent in style to the standard anthropological fieldwork guide *Notes and Queries on Anthropology* (British Association 1874).

The British Museum Codrington Collection
The British Museum's collection of artefacts from Codrington (see Appendix 1), consisting of 122 items, was

made early in Codrington's time whilst working for the mission. His was amongst the first made by members of the Melanesian Mission to arrive at the Museum. Of the 14 such collections, it is by far the largest, representing nearly 40 per cent of the total of 281 items from members of the Melanesian Mission. The earliest Codrington donations, from 1870 to 1872, came largely via the Blackmore Museum, which suggests that they were sent directly by Codrington to the curator there, Edward Stevens, and were then passed onto the British Museum. Unsurprisingly, they consist mostly of simple objects of stone or shell, in keeping with the Blackmore's primary interest in the 'Stone Age'. Codrington was worried that he had arrived in Melanesia too late to make any useful collection. He wrote to his brother, 'Mota is wonderfully destitute of museum specimens. The progress of European implements in supplanting the old ones is amazing. The aspect of the place is changed since I was here 6 years ago owing to the introduction of iron.' He lamented, 'I could only get two objects, an axe and an adze.' To sharpen the blades of these, local men 'took up any handy stone and threw it down again. In grinding the shells into shape they used convenient surfaces of walls and larger stones' (LT, 30 October 1869). These were the sort of objects that modern iron tool were rendering redundant, and Codrington was keen to obtain as many types and examples as he could before it was too late.

Throughout the period of his collecting Codrington paid close attention to the way in which axes and adzes were manufactured. The earliest pieces were mostly of shell, and some of them were very beautiful in their markings, and this may well have recommended them particularly to him (**Figs 8–9**). Other shell objects also displayed considerable ingenuity and skill in their manufacture. In particular, Codrington selected *dala* forehead ornaments from Malaita made from a disc of tridacna shell with a fretted pattern cut out of a piece of tortoiseshell superimposed (**Figs 10–11**). But

Figure 8 Clam shell axe blade, Gaua, Banks Islands, h. 21cm. British Museum, 1874, Oc,RHC.21

stone became more popular in his collecting over time, so that in the largest donation in 1875, the majority of the axe and adze blades came from Solomon Islands and were made of stone rather than shell. Again, the simplicity and fineness of shape are immediately striking (**Fig. 12**). They could also comprise dramatic composite forms of wood and stone, as an adze from Solomon Islands shows (**Fig. 13**).

Later, Codrington was to offer a systematic analysis of the ways in which adze heads could be classified by material composition:

Figure 9 Four clam shell blades from Ureparapara (from left to right): h. 19.5cm. British Museum, 1875, Oc,RHC.17; h. 14.5cm. British Museum, 1875, Oc,RHC.18; h. 14cm. British Museum, 1875, Oc,RHC.19; h. 11.2cm. British Museum, 1875, Oc,RHC.22

Figure 10 *Dala* head ornament from Malaita, with a disc of tridacna shell overlaid with a fretwork of turtle shell, diam. 8.5cm. British Museum, before 1874, Oc,RHC.32

Figure 11 *Dala* head ornament from Malaita, with a disc of tridacna shell overlaid with a fretwork of turtle shell, diam. 11.5cm. British Museum, before 1874, Oc,RHC.33

Figure 12 Five adze blades (from left to right): of dark grey stone, Florida, h. 16.9cm. British Museum, 1876,Oc,RHC.53; of dark green stone, Savo, h. 16.5cm. British Museum, 1876, Oc,RHC.69; of dark green stone, Savo, h. 16.5cm. British Museum, 1876, Oc,RHC.70; of dark green stone, Savo, h. 16cm. British Museum, 1876, Oc,RHC.71; of dark green stone, Savo, h. 15.7cm. British Museum, 1876, Oc,RHC.72

The islands may be roughly classified according to the use of stone or shell implements in them. In the Banks' Islands, Torres Islands, and Santa Cruz, they had only shell adzes, and used obsidian flakes for cutting and scraping. In the Solomon Islands, except in Rennell and Belona, and the New Hebrides, the implements were of stone, and flakes of chert were used; but in the latter group on Lepers' Island, where the volcanic force is not yet exhausted, shell was the ancient use. Stone adzes in my possession from the Solomon Islands are of Andesite, a basaltic lava, from Florida compact Andesite; from the New Hebrides, one from Ambrym is Gabbro, one from Pentecost is Bastite serpentine. (*TM*: 16)

As an afterthought, he considered: 'In preparation of food they use large wooden platters and sticks for pestles of which I had better get one or two I suppose' (ibid.). This he made good in the consignment of 1873 (**Fig. 14**).

The first recorded items Codrington sent to the Blackmore Museum were 'two or three different bits of rock', although he regretted that he was unable to supply fossils. 'Here I never heard of fossils nor can I find any myself, and I suppose to send a bit of coral rubbish or whatever is hardly worthwhile' (LT, 29 November 1869). There seems little distinction in Codrington's mind between archaeological and anthropological specimens. As Gosden (1999: 2) remarks, at that time 'archaeology and anthropology can be seen as a double helix with their histories linked but distinct' (prior to their 'divorce' – Shankland 2012: 4). For Codrington the distinction appears not to have been important. The next year he was still seeking suitable material. He wrote, 'I enclose in this a bit of flint or something used in the Solomon Islands for various purposes. You will observe that it is a regular flint chip' (LT, 12 October 1870). The 1871 consignment appears to have been much dissipated before it reached the Blackmore Museum, as Codrington sent it directly to his brother, Tom, who was told, 'all that come are to be subject to selection by yourself, of anything scientifically valuable, or otherwise to your mind for yourself or others' (LT, 9 October 1871). He repeated this instruction twice early the next year: 'I am going to send off to you a box for the Blackmore and yourself and I think I shall send it to you because I want you to have the pick' (LT, 23 January 1872) and 'divide at your discretion' (LT, 10 April 1872). Things improved for the museum in 1872. He wrote, 'I have got together this year a good lot of stone and shell adzes which I send down to Shirley Hill for the Blackmore Museum' (LT, 30 September 1872).

In the same consignment he also included a fishing lure. This was one of Codrington's favourite objects, featuring human ingenuity using simple materials, and he collected many specimens throughout his time in the mission. He explained, 'I send also a curious lure for catching fish commonly used in the Solomon Islands of which I sent in a letter. The bait, a piece of spider's web. This is a kite which keeps the bait dragging on the surface of the sea' (LT, 30 September 1872) (seen at the centre of the display in **Fig. 20**). Elsewhere he added, 'A large garfish with a long snout bites and entangles its teeth and is caught' (1876: 11).

No collection made in the Western Pacific at the time, or since, could ignore the beauty and simplicity of fish hooks, and Codrington dutifully supplied three specimens (two of which are shown in **Figs 16–17**), as well as fishing floats (**Figs 18–19**). He also contributed to the British Museum display of 50 Solomon Islands fish hooks captured in an early 20th-century photograph (**Fig. 20**).

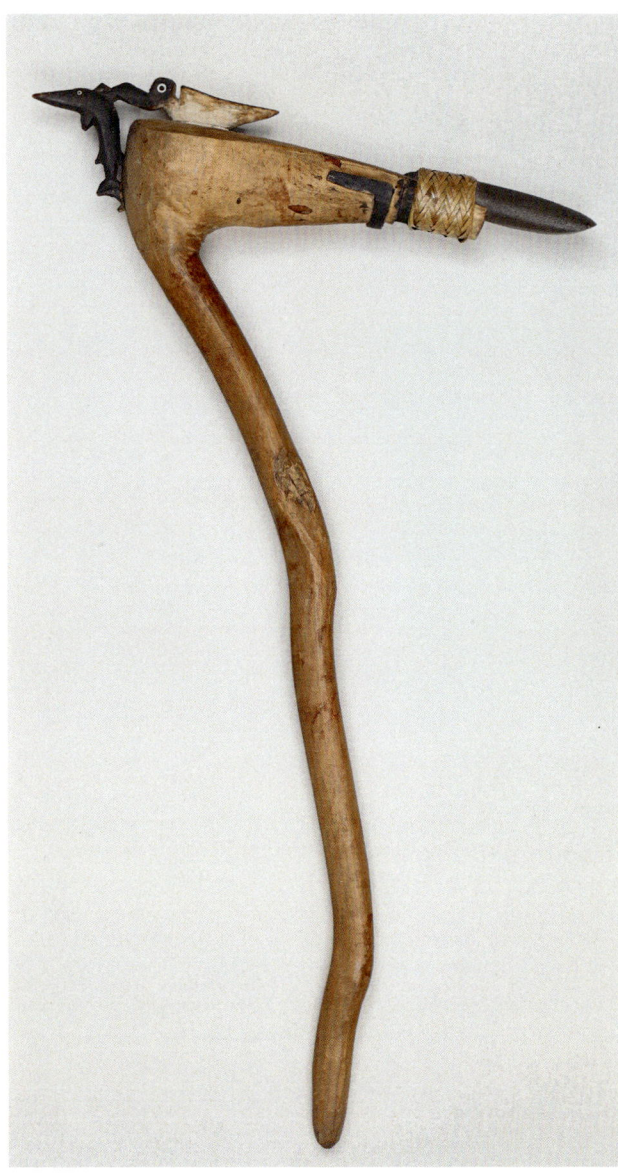

Figure 13 Adze with stone blade bound with vine-strip to wooden haft carved with bird motif, Makira, h. 24cm. British Museum, 1876, Oc,RHC.48

Two items that Codrington included in the 1872 consignment were textiles from Santa Cruz. Although this was not a region that he had visited, he recognised the uniqueness and importance of the cloth that was manufactured there. As he noted: 'The remarkable thing is that in Santa Cruz alone is found a loom with which beautiful mats are woven with the fibre of a banana cultivated for the purpose.' What interested him most was the cross-cultural potential such manufacture represented. He continued: 'These looms are identical with those in use in the Caroline and Philippine islands and in Borneo' (*TM*: 316). So he obtained pieces of cloth still on the loom, which he forwarded with the following commentary and drawing on the accession slip, 'Cloth in process of weaving together with the apparatus employed. The cloth is very closely woven of dark cream coloured vegetable fibre with a double band patterned at one end. The sticks and pieces of wood and bamboo used in the weaving are shewn in the sketch' (**Figs 21–2**). This description in its brevity and detail demonstrates the attention that Codrington paid to the accurate depiction of objects for the new museum context to which they were destined.

The majority of these objects came to the Museum in 1874 (21 items) and 1875 (55 items), after Codrington had made tours of the islands, in 1870 to Mota, and in 1872 to Ambrym, Florida and Mota. Whilst it is by no means certain that Codrington obtained all of these items in person (such as small objects like the currency string in **Fig. 15**) – he commissioned other missionaries to act on his behalf from time to time – his journals and letters do confirm his direct involvement and his personal reasons for selecting specific items.

Pottery has been a subject that has fascinated both archaeologists and anthropologists in the Western Pacific. Whilst shards have been found in a wide variety of locations, modern people living in these places do not in general make it themselves. Early on Codrington had a false start regarding pottery, as he commented:

> I asked a man here the other day about pottery in one island where I had heard of it. He said there was none when he had been on that island but in San Cristoval they had plenty. A little lad of that island, passing by at the moment, explained that these were wood. (LT, 22 September 1869)

Figure 14 Food vessel made of wood and vegetable fibre, Banks Islands, h. 22cm, w. 67cm, d. 21cm. British Museum, 1874, Oc,RHC.28

22 | *Objects as Insights: R.H. Codrington's Ethnographic Collections from Melanesia*

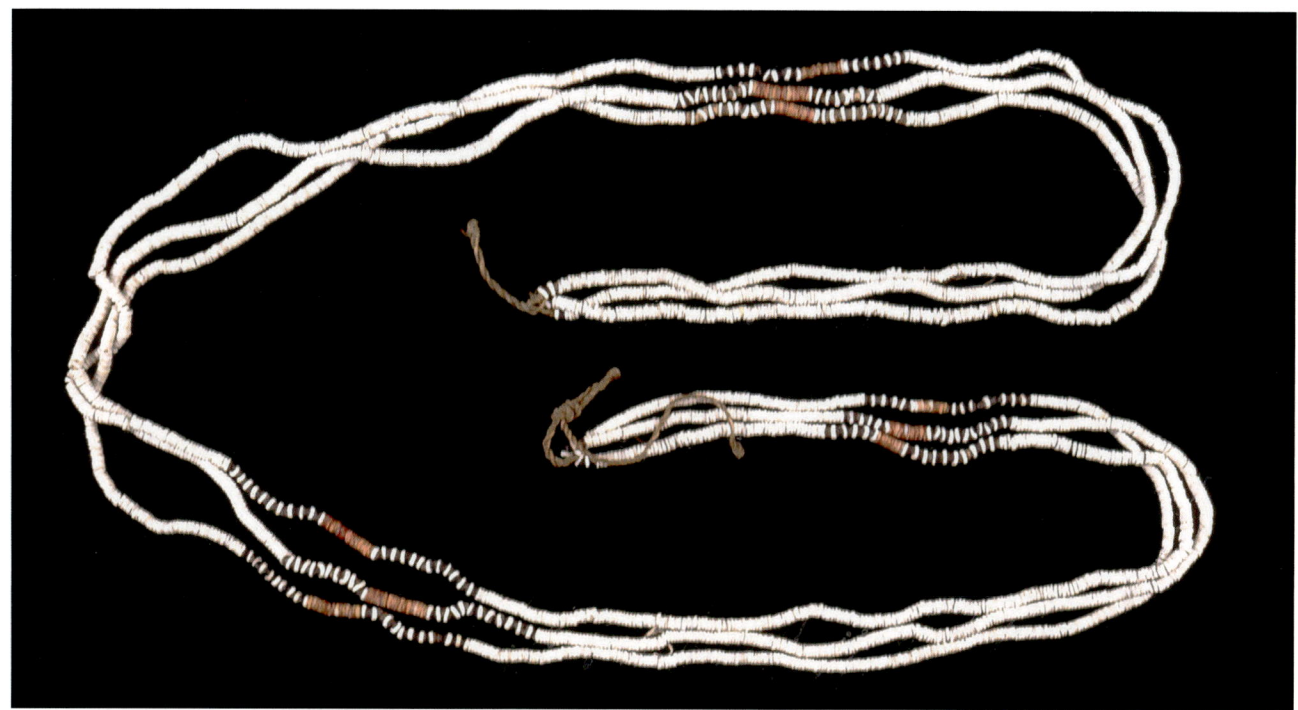

Figure 15 Currency made of seeds and three strings of shell, Solomon Islands, l. 155cm. British Museum, pre-1873, Oc.7903

Figure 16 Pearl shell trolling lure fish hook, Savo, h. 8cm. British Museum, 1875, Oc,RHC.67

Figure 17 Fish hook: back made of mother-of-pearl, with curved barb of amber-coloured turtle shell; fixed at the end is a tuft of red feathers for bait, Solomon Islands, h. 12cm. British Museum, 1875, Oc,RHC.68

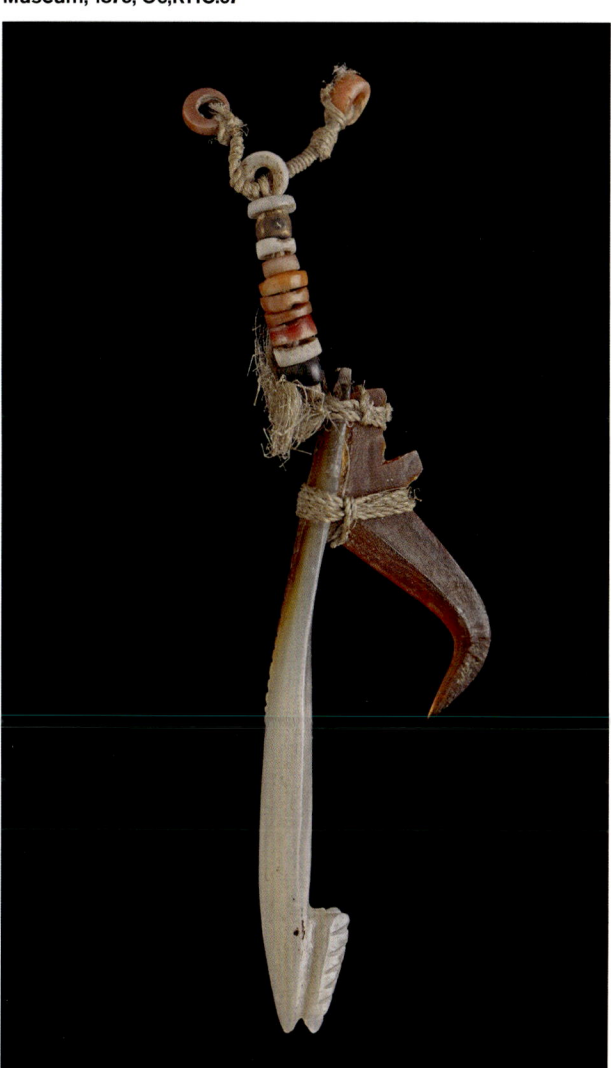

Figure 18 (far left) Fishing apparatus carved out of a lightwood which has been coloured black, with lower end weighted and covered with black gum, Malaita, h. 43cm. British Museum, 1876, Oc,RHC.37

Figure 19 (left) Fishing apparatus made of light wood which has been coloured black, weighted one end, Malaita, h. 40cm. British Museum, 1876, Oc,RHC.38

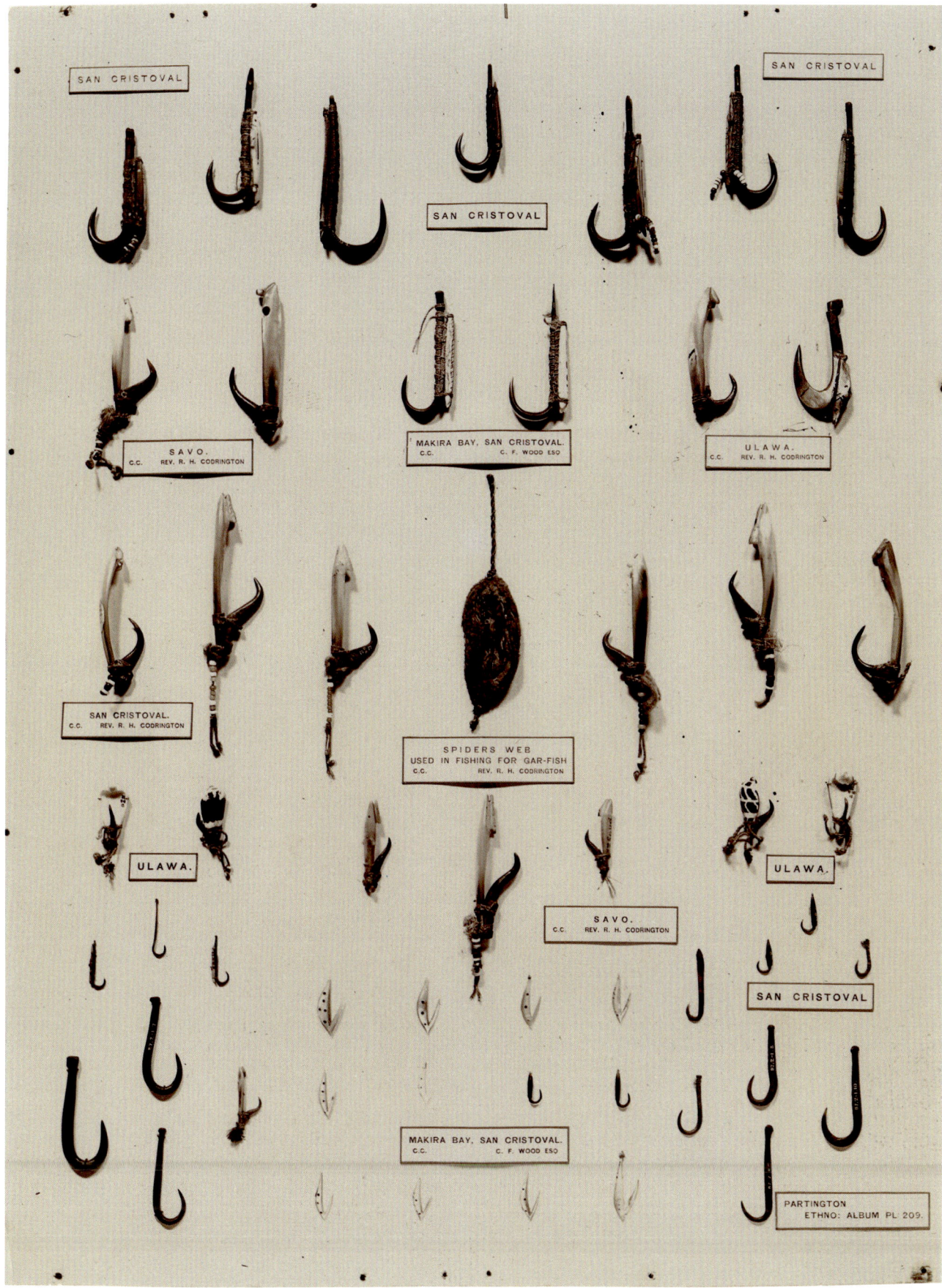

Figure 20 Photograph (gelatin silver print) of board of fish hooks, several with cord and beads attached, hooks made from bone, Makira (San Cristoval), Savo, Ulawa, Solomon Islands, h. 14.4cm, w. 10.9cm. British Museum, early 20th century, Oc,B33.24

Figure 21 Cloth in process of being woven, closely woven of dark-cream coloured vegetable fibre, patterned at one end, l. 85cm. British Museum, Santa Cruz, 1872, Oc.7620

Figure 22 Cloth in process of being woven, similar to Oc.7620 but shorter length, Santa Cruz, l. 165cm, w. 23cm. British Museum, 1872, Oc.7621

Codrington was not put off by this setback, and remained keen to enter the debate about the provenance of pottery in Melanesia. He wrote to his brother Tom:

> I got what I am extremely glad to get for the Blackmore, specimens of pottery from Espiritu Santo. I have always heard of this pottery, but never could verify it, but here it is and very large vessels are made of it. There can be no question that the Espiritu Santo people are all the same as these, and certainly they are in no other respect more advanced. But I imagine that their very large island is not wholly volcanic like all the others in these parts; and my theory is that the original immigrants into these islands knowing the use of pottery found clay there and nowhere else so that the art is elsewhere dead. (LT, 17 September 1873)

He was particularly pleased to be able to offer an example of this ware, describing the specimen he acquired as a 'bowl of red earthenware, hand-made with four ears and a very convex base' (British Museum catalogue entry written or dictated by R.H. Codrington) (**Fig. 23**).

Codrington's donations to the British Museum ended with a small collection of five artefacts, the by now usual assortment of adzes and a fishing float, which were registered in 1876. Significantly, this date immediately follows Codrington's last major tour as head of the Melanesian Mission in 1875, which took in the islands of Pentecost (Whitsuntide), Santa Maria, Mota, Vanua Lava, Malaita, Ugi and Florida. He returned to England in 1877 and made no further donations to the British Museum.

Figure 23 Bowl of red earthenware, handmade with four ears and very convex base, Espiritu Santo, diam. 35.5cm. British Museum, 1875, Oc,RHC.26

One stray item, another shell adze with a wooden handle from Bellona, arrived in the museum in 1907. The handle was inscribed 'Donated by T. Codrington', which suggests that Codrington's brother Tom offered this object from his own collection. A drawing in the British Museum archives illustrates seven objects given by Tom at about this time (**Fig. 24**).

Another dozen objects deriving from Codrington joined the Museum catalogue from Harry Beasley's collection in 1944, and three other early adzes have also recently been located.

Codrington's own collection (Edge-Partington)

What did Codrington's personal collection look like? There are no extant photographs of his display in Chichester but there is one fascinating glimpse into the missionary style of personal display in a photograph of the room of his colleague Richard Comins, who joined the Melanesian Mission in 1877 (**Fig. 25**). The photograph was taken in his study on Norfolk Island in around 1904. With careful scrutiny a wide range of artefacts can be seen adorning his study. Among these are a model canoe strung from the ceiling, paddles, spears, arrays of arrows, pig-tusk and shell armlets, a circular disk of clam shell with a tortoise-shell decoration hanging on the wall to the right, a fishing net, pan pipes, pandanus baskets, coconut water bottles and Malaitan ornamental combs. What is immediately evident is the intimate juxtaposition of Melanesian artefacts surrounding the bed, with folders and books on the chest (a missionary chest?) beside the bed. Both material worlds appear in easy congress. It is, in my opinion, very likely that Codrington's own living spaces would have looked much like that of Comins.

Codrington's correspondence with G.H. Haines alerts us to the personal collection he kept in his house in Chichester, and which James Edge-Partington visited as part of his national survey of ethnographica. Beside documenting items in the British Museum, the Pitt Rivers Museum and Bristol Museum, Edge-Partington explored the collections of Charles Longuet Higgins at Turvey Abbey, The Lady Brassey Collection at Durbar Hall, and the private collections of Walter Coote, Alexander Lister-Kaye and Anatole von Hügel, as well as that of Codrington. Both he and Codrington had similar views about the importance of recording and documenting the material culture of the Western Pacific. Edge-Partington was also equally opposed to the labour recruitment schemes operating out of Australia. As he stated:

> Men of mature age are deported from their own islands, often many hundreds of miles away, and they thus carry with them and introduce what may be described as foreign arts into the culture of their new homes. It becomes, therefore, specially important to render permanent with the least possible delay all the information which can be obtained with regard to this part of the world. (Edge-Partington 1890: n.p.)

This agreement about the changes occurring in the Pacific and their impact on local culture did not, however, preclude Edge-Partington from holding what we would nowadays consider racist views about how to treat island people, which including shooting them into submission (Edge-Partington 1883: 257). He could hardly have been unaware how unacceptable these views would have been to Codrington; nevertheless, he was given full access to Codrington's personal collection and visited him regularly. He made drawings of a selection of the artefacts. These he published in *An Album of the Weapons, Tools, Ornaments, Articles of Dress, etc, of the Natives of the Pacific Islands* (1890) together with Charles Heape. Charles Read of the British Museum, in his introduction to the third volume, gave a further explanation of why Edge-Partington had undertaken the painstaking job of recording private collections like Codrington's:

> In all probability the public museum will have continuous existence, but private collections are usually destined to

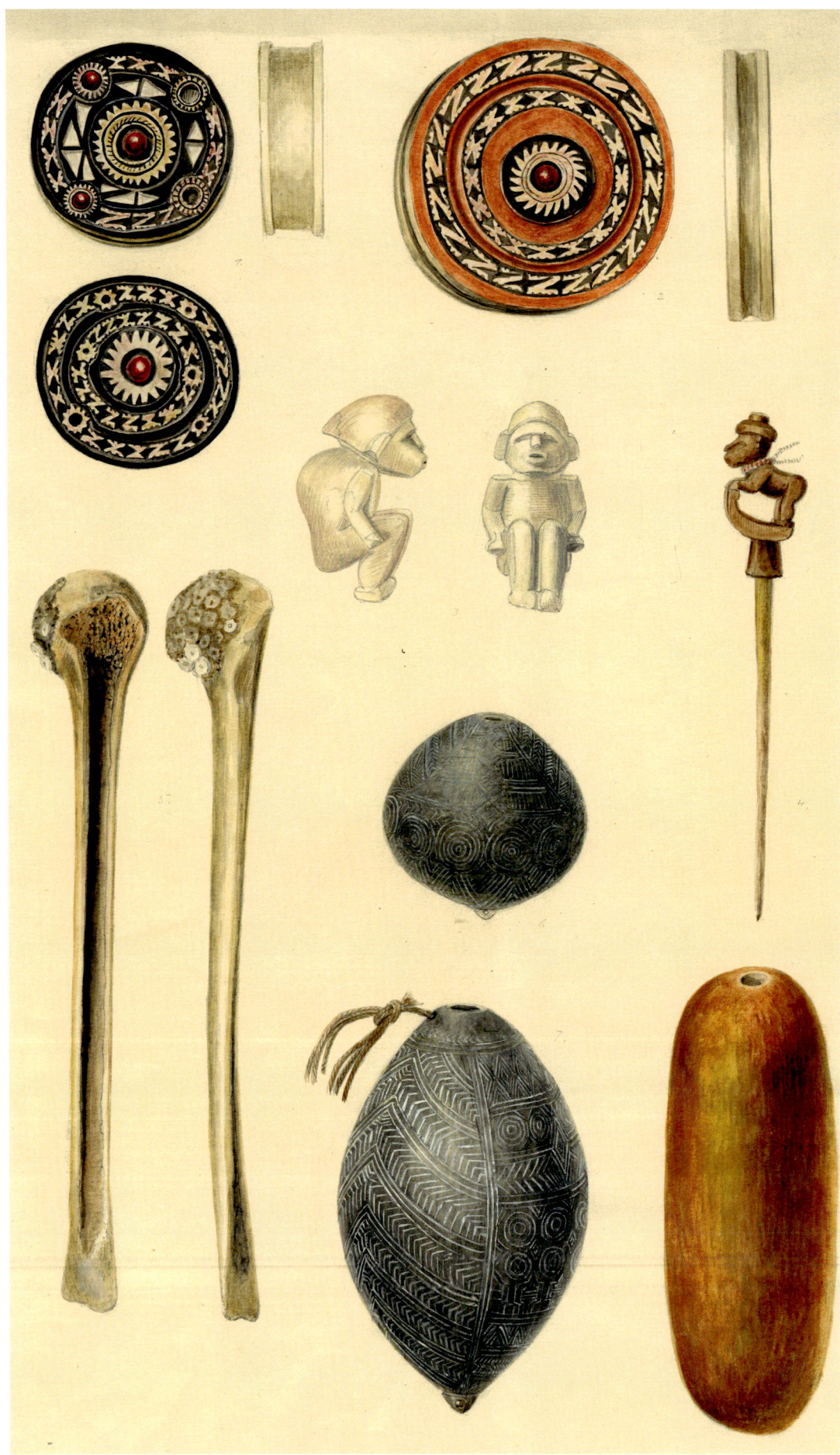

Figure 24 Photograph of a drawing of seven objects sent home by R.H. Codrington, in possession of his brother Tom Codrington. British Museum, no date, Oc2006,Drg.311

Figure 25 Photograph of Revd Richard B. Comins's study, Norfolk Island, *c.* 1904. SOAS, MM box 40, file 08/46

dispersal, and it is not easy to estimate the value that such a record as this will have in a few generations. It is a commonplace that within a limited number of decades the study of ethnography will only be possible within the walls of museums. (Read 1898: n.p.)

This warning about the vulnerability of private collections was born out by events. The Blackmore Museum did not long survive William Blackmore's death in 1878; Harry Beasley's Cranmore Museum closed after his death in 1939 (Carreau 2009: 194); and Captain A.W.F. Fuller's collection was sold in 1958 shortly before his death (Waterfield and King 2005). Read's prediction echoed Edge-Partington's earlier warning in his catalogue, in which he emphasised the danger of the imminent demise of both tangible and intangible culture.

Edge-Partington devoted 11 plates to Codrington's personal collection. In total, he selected 79 of his objects: 31 from the New Hebrides, 11 from the Santa Cruz group and 37 from across the central and eastern Solomon Islands. The drawings he made were presented according to the location the objects derived from. The first plate (**Fig. 26**) displayed six objects from the New Hebrides: two woven girdles from Mai, stone axe blades from Ambrym and Lepers' Island (Ambae) and a bamboo nose flute. The second and third pages (**Figs 27–8**) showed, respectively, 13 and 5 objects from the Banks Islands group. These included bags, baskets, arrows and a pudding knife. Particular mention was made of a *mateout* (choice stone) which is described in the album, probably by Codrington rather than Edge-Partington, as 'threaded with strings of money. It is found on only very rare occasions in a giant clam. The hole is pierced by means of a rat's tooth (Mota).' The fourth page (**Fig. 29**) was devoted to seven objects from the Torres Islands group, mostly made of wood. One object was selected for further comment so as to help in its identification, namely an 'adze head with shell blade fastened to the handle with string, the wood is stained a light yellow with nutmeg, as is the case with nearly all wooden things from this group'. The fifth plate with five objects (**Fig. 30**) and the sixth (not illustrated here) with six, were from further north to the Santa Cruz group. Here Codrington supplied more contextual information to underline the significance of two of the items. A seemingly mundane object is described as a 'carved wooden foreshaft of arrow. On this point "a" is a wrapping which is supposed to contain the charm as during the process of wrapping they sing the incantation song which passes the charm into the arrow.' Another small woven object is similarly identified as a 'finger charm for shooting straight worn on the fingers of the hand holding the bow. It most probably contains the teeth of some well-known man. The covering is of red cloth ornamented with white shell beads.' The remaining five pages covered Solomon Islands (**Figs 31–5**).

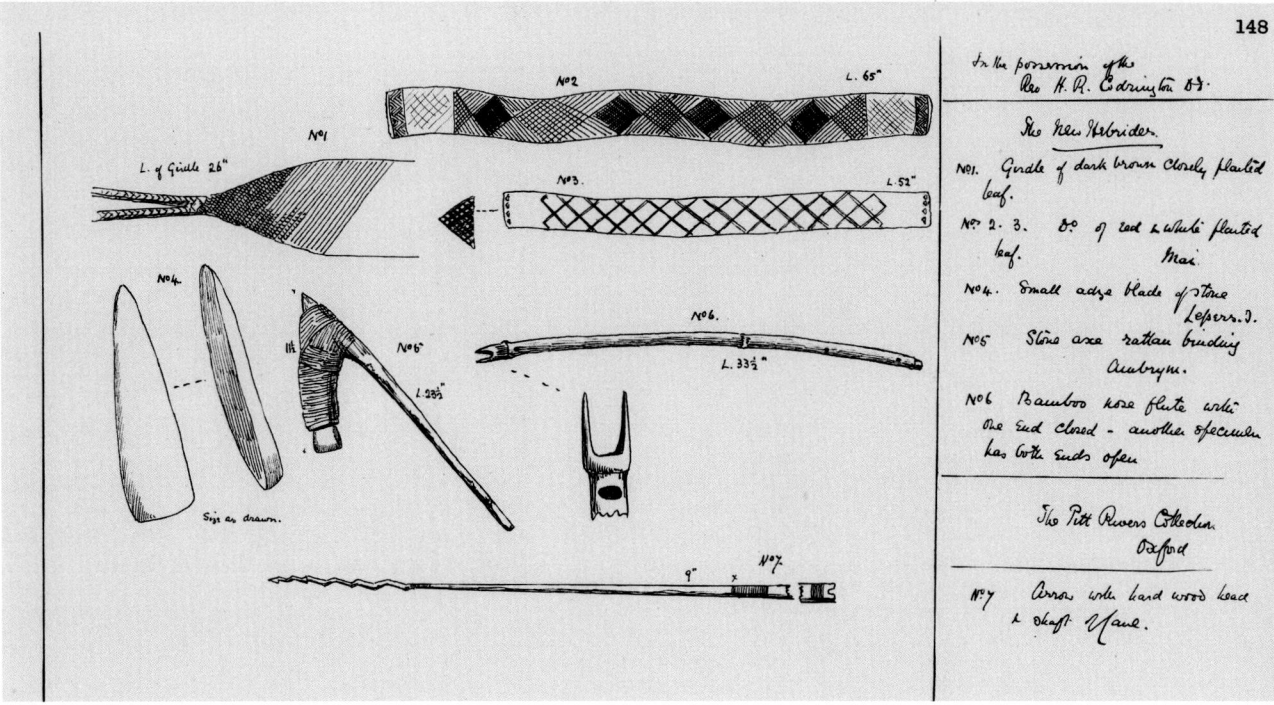

Figure 26 Page from J. Edge-Partington and C. Heape, *An Album of the Weapons, Tools, Ornaments, Articles of Dress, etc, of the Natives of the Pacific Islands*, 1890, pl. 148: New Hebrides

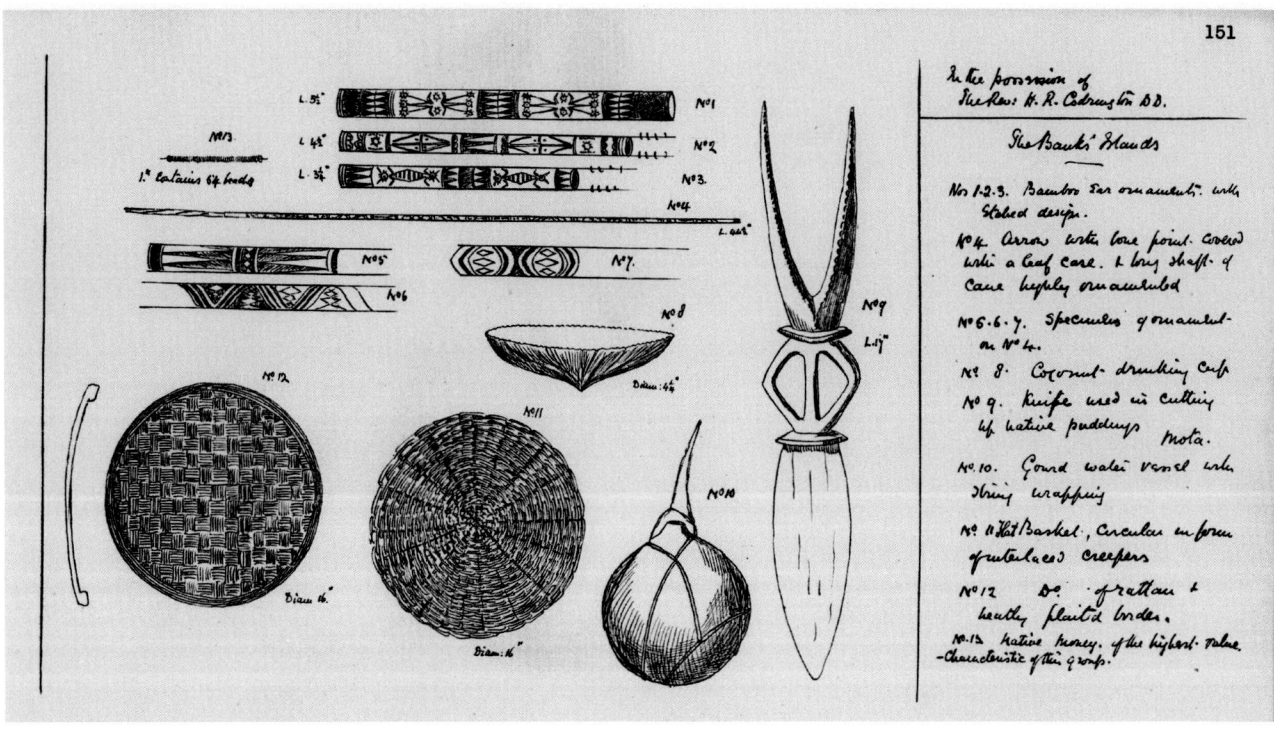

Figure 27 Page from J. Edge-Partington and C. Heape, *An Album of the Weapons, Tools, Ornaments, Articles of Dress, etc, of the Natives of the Pacific Islands*, 1890, pl. 151: Banks Islands

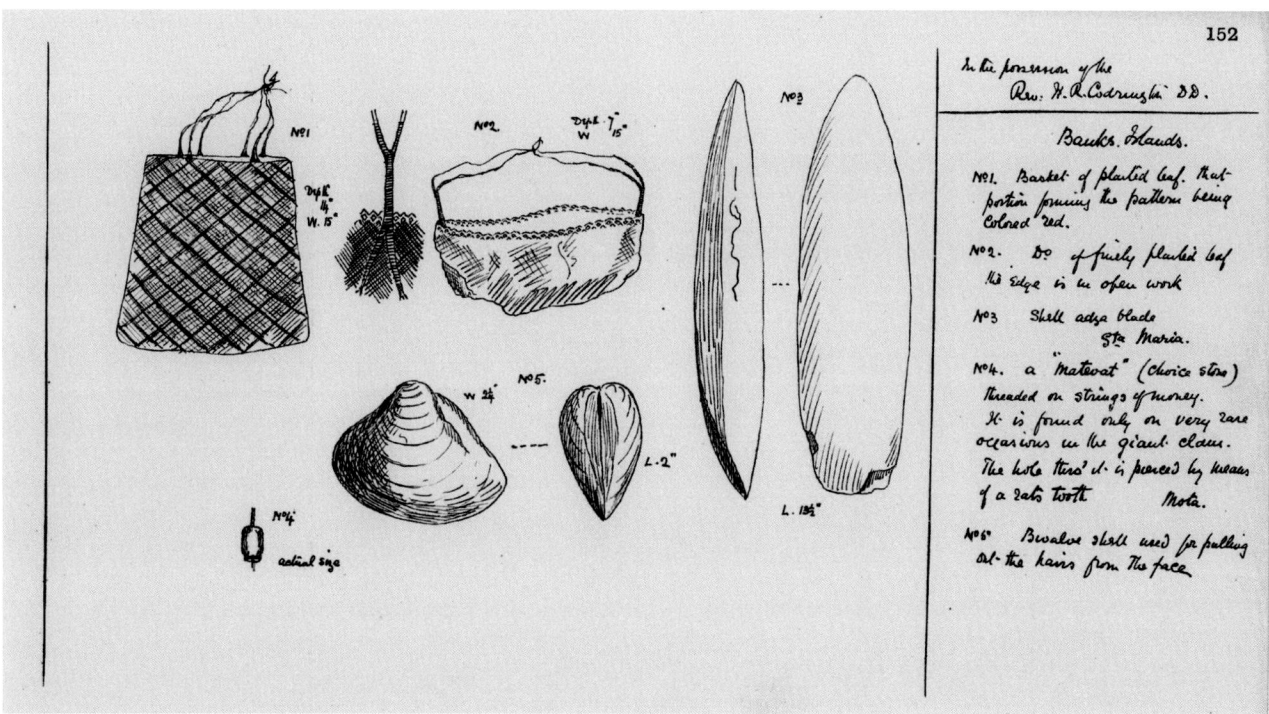

Figure 28 Page from J. Edge-Partington and C. Heape, *An Album of the Weapons, Tools, Ornaments, Articles of Dress, etc, of the Natives of the Pacific Islands,* 1890, pl. 152: Banks Islands

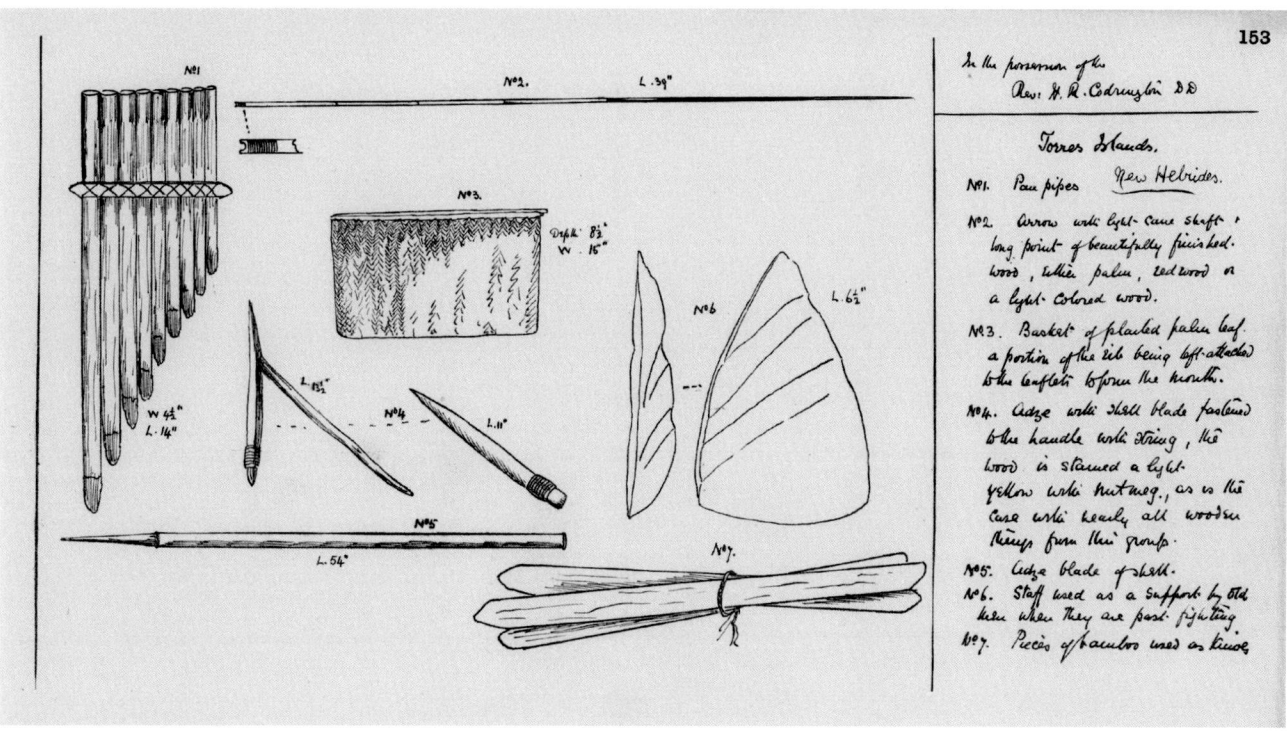

Figure 29 Page from J. Edge-Partington and C. Heape, *An Album of the Weapons, Tools, Ornaments, Articles of Dress, etc, of the Natives of the Pacific Islands*, 1890, pl. 153: Torres Islands

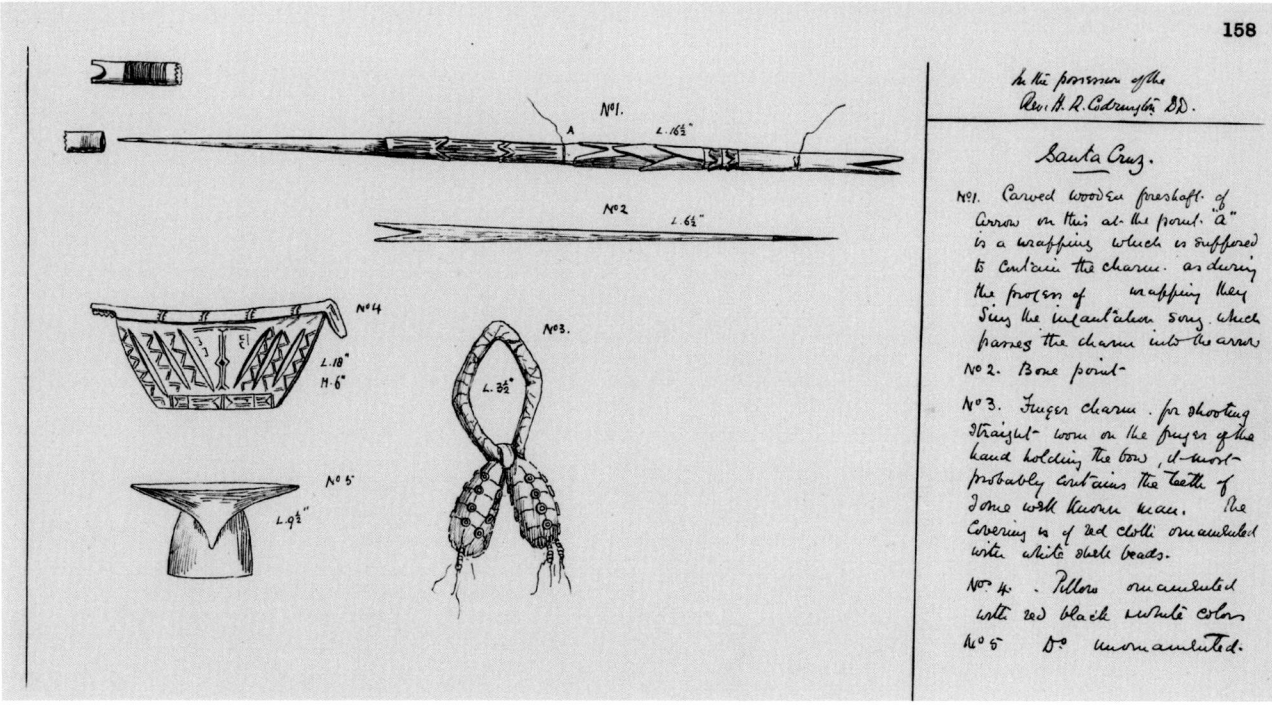

Figure 30 Page from J. Edge-Partington and C. Heape, *An Album of the Weapons, Tools, Ornaments, Articles of Dress, etc, of the Natives of the Pacific Islands,* 1890, pl. 158: Santa Cruz

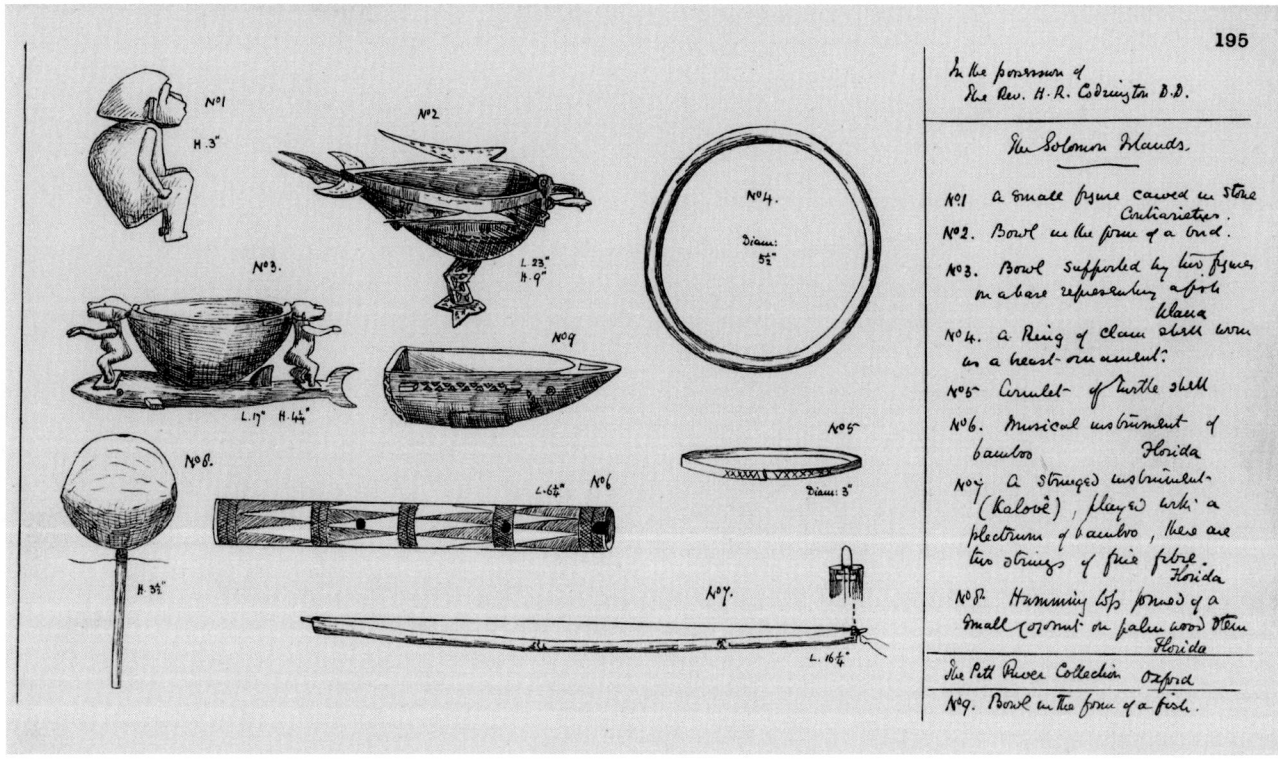

Figure 31 Page from J. Edge-Partington and C. Heape, *An Album of the Weapons, Tools, Ornaments, Articles of Dress, etc, of the Natives of the Pacific Islands,* 1890, pl. 195: Solomon Islands

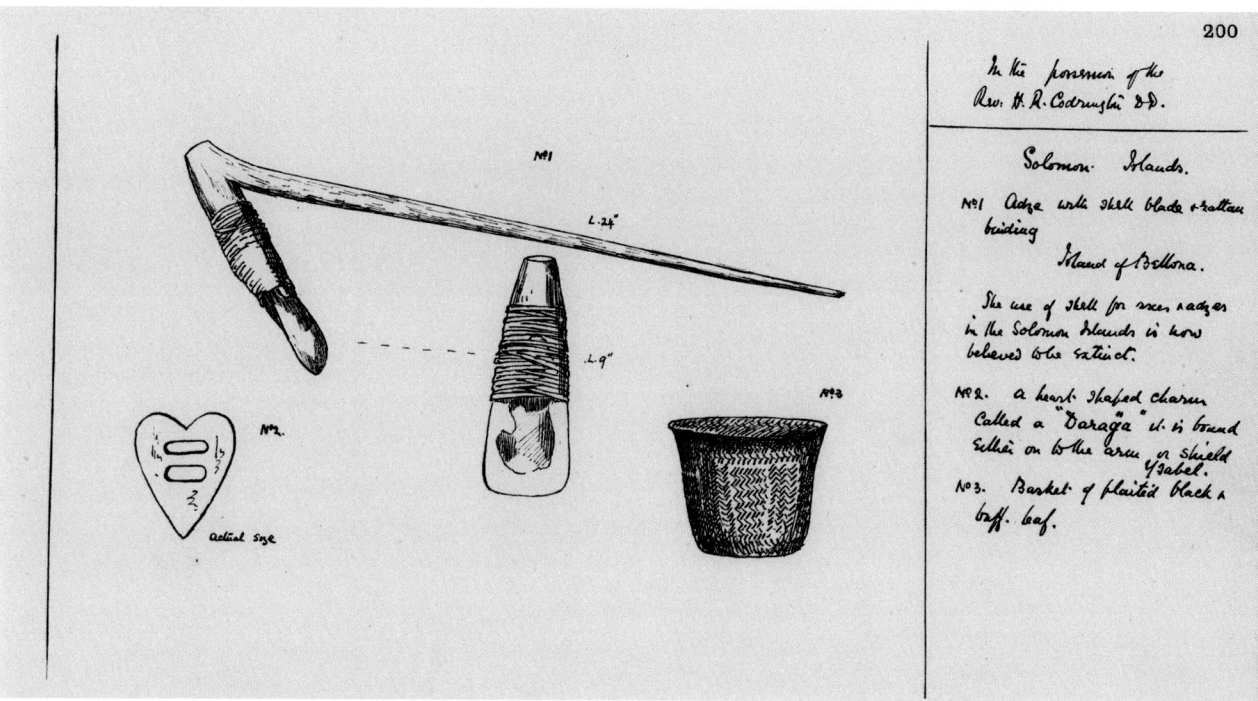

Figure 32 Page from J. Edge-Partington and C. Heape, *An Album of the Weapons, Tools, Ornaments, Articles of Dress, etc, of the Natives of the Pacific Islands*, 1890, pl. 200: Solomon Islands

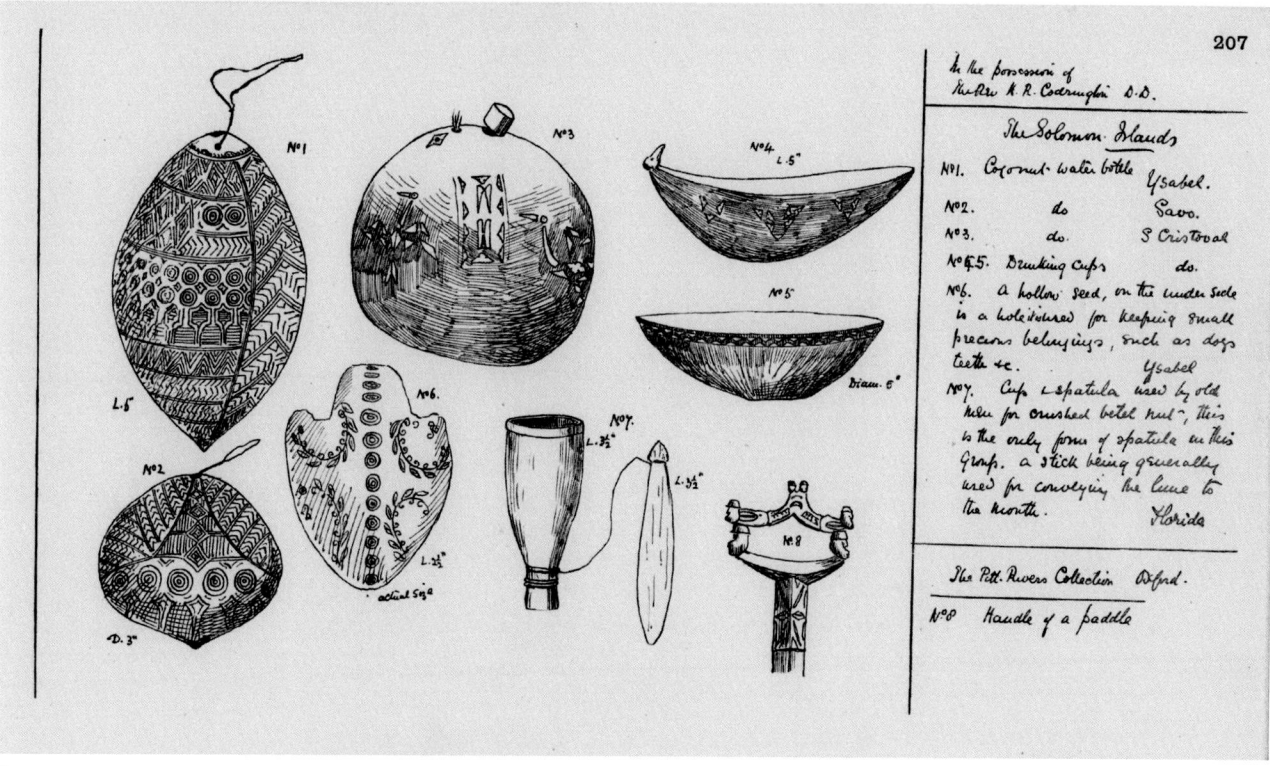

Figure 33 Page from J. Edge-Partington and C. Heape, *An Album of the Weapons, Tools, Ornaments, Articles of Dress, etc, of the Natives of the Pacific Islands*, 1890, pl. 207: Solomon Islands

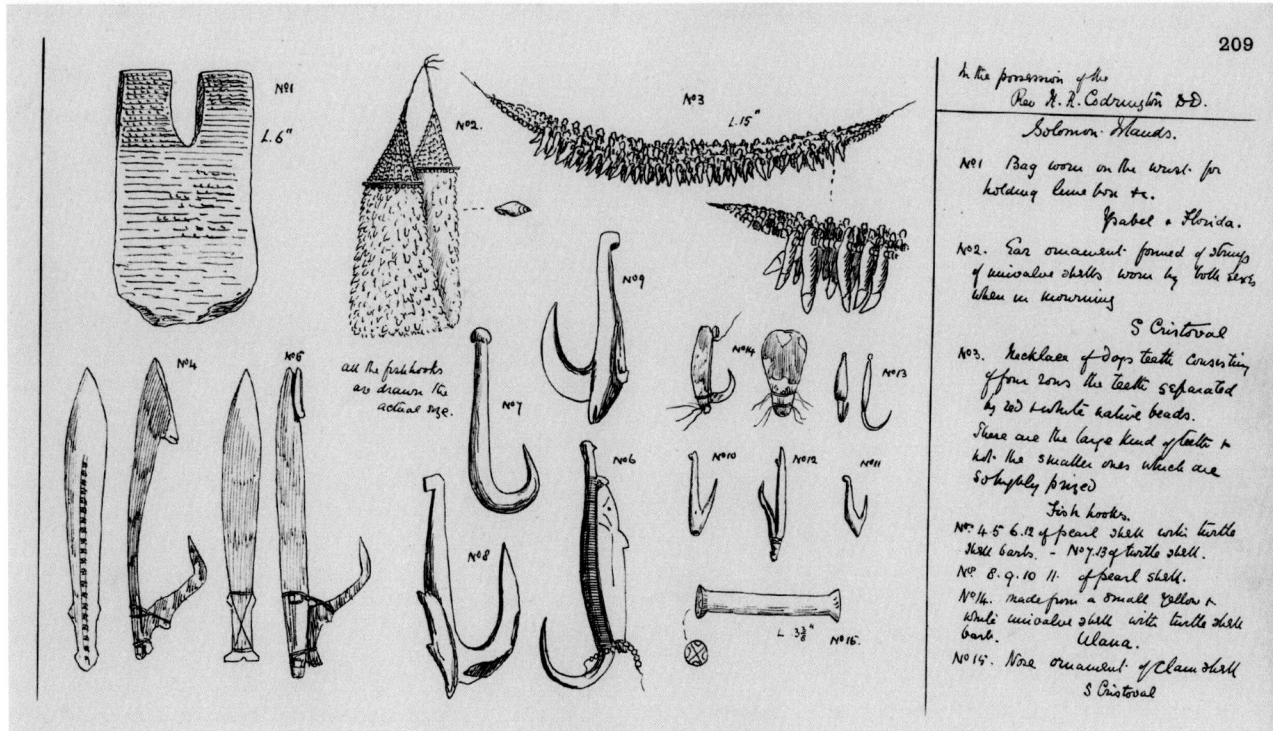

Figure 34 Page from J. Edge-Partington and C. Heape, *An Album of the Weapons, Tools, Ornaments, Articles of Dress, etc, of the Natives of the Pacific Islands,* 1890, pl. 209: Solomon Islands

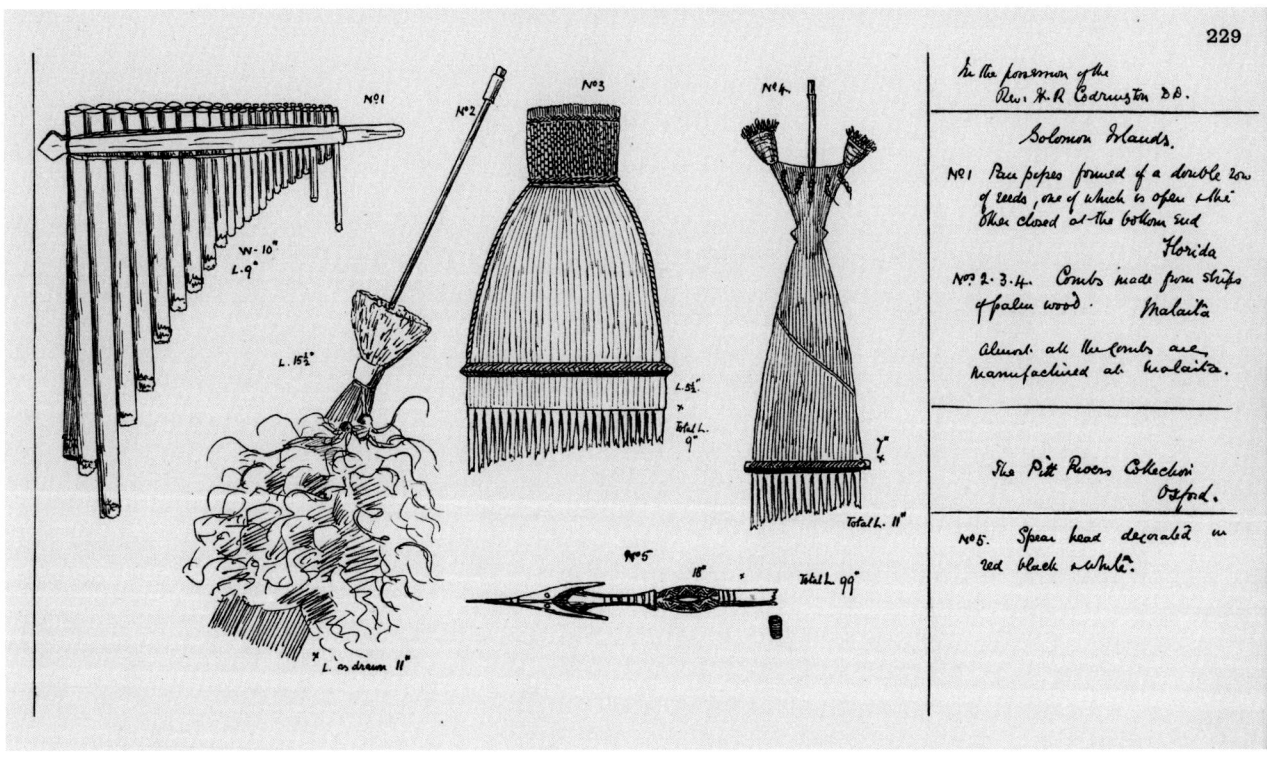

Figure 35 Page from J. Edge-Partington and C. Heape, *An Album of the Weapons, Tools, Ornaments, Articles of Dress, etc, of the Natives of the Pacific Islands,* 1890, pl. 229: Solomon Islands

Figure 36 Notched flute reed, ornamented with incised designs, Pentecost, l. 3.33cm, diam. 1.7cm. Pitt Rivers Museum, 1885, 1920.100.14 (photo: Suzy Prior)

What is immediately clear is how varied the items depicted are. The proportion of shell and stone axe and adze heads is very much lower than in the British Museum collection. Other manufactured items are far more prominent. It would appear that Edge-Partington was particularly interested in pattern and decoration, especially those either woven into cloth or incised on the surface of hard objects. Not only are the drawings remarkably detailed, but they offer a sense of the three-dimensional form, whether in larger bowls and figures (pl. 195) or the minutiae of fish hooks (pl. 209). Edge-Partington's selection celebrates the diversity and ingenuity of Pacific Islanders' visual imagination in a way that mirrors the 'Ornament of savage tribes' by Owen Jones (1856), or Christopher Dresser's (1873) related exploration of decorative design across time and place. Perhaps, he appreciated Jones's argument that in 'savage' designs, 'nothing … can be more primitive and yet the arrangement of the pattern shows the most refined taste and skill' (Jones 1856: 14). He was likely to have endorsed Jones's view that 'The ornament of a savage tribe, being the result of natural instinct, is necessarily always true to its purpose; whilst in much of the ornament of civilized nations, the first impulse which generated received forms [is] enfeebled by constant repetition' (1856: 16).

Edge-Partington, like Jones and Dresser, was seeking underlying principles of design which rely upon artistic prowess demonstrated particularly in ornamentation. As Dresser used Egyptian water-lily drawings to exemplify the virtuoso skills of the carver, so Edge-Partington concentrated upon the designs to be found on textiles, woven baskets and wooden and shell objects from the Pacific. Edge-Partington can hardly have failed to study Jones's examples of designs taken from across the Pacific. Codrington had a similar eye for design as evidenced by the acquisition of a flute reed from Pentecost (**Fig. 36**).

Whilst the quality of the objects that Edge-Partington chose to draw was of a very high standard, it is not immediately apparent whether these choices were his alone or whether he received guidance from Codrington. In all probability there was an agreement between the two based on Codrington's personal preferences but also reflecting Edge-Partington's desire to create an overall balance geographically and by object type across his book. But perhaps the style of display in Edge-Partington's album reflects a prior arrangement already effected by Codrington in his displays throughout his house in Saint Richard's Walk in Chichester Cathedral Close. Was the display geographically based or typological, or perhaps a mixture of both? Evidence is so far lacking, but in Bruce Miller's expanded and revised edition (1996) of *An Album of the Weapons, Tools, Ornaments, Articles of Dress, etc, of the Natives of the Pacific Islands*, Codrington's importance for the book is signalled by reference to his *The Melanesians* (1891) which appeared just one year after Edge-Partington's first edition. Reference to illustrations in *The Melanesians* are frequent and detailed. Both scholars continued to hold each other in some esteem. In a letter composed in 1889, Codrington wrote, 'I went to see Partington, whom you no doubt remember. He has a wonderful collection of Pacific things in his house, and he knows where everything comes from, which is a rare accomplishment' (Letters 1891–1922, to Lorimer Fison, 11 July 1889). Edge-Partington continued to visit Codrington until late in his life. Codrington noted in his diary, 'Edge Partington from Bognor to tea' (1892–1922 Diaries, 8 March 1919).

The Pitt Rivers Museum's Codrington Collection

The same question arises about the organisation of Codrington's collection at the Pitt Rivers Museum (see Appendix 2). Was the prior arrangement at Saint Richard's Walk replicated in the accessions register, on which he offered advice when the material moved to Oxford? The Pitt Rivers accessions register offers some interesting clues though no conclusive evidence. But, before pursuing the question further, some more background information is required and the collection details displayed in Appendix 2 need to be examined.

The Codrington Collection is recorded in a total 463 entries to the Pitt Rivers accessions register, spanning the years 1886 to 1920. As the list below shows, the pattern of donations by Codrington was uneven. Initially, they were sporadic and small, though it should be borne in mind that

Figure 37 Ear plug of wood inlaid with pearl shell and seeds, diam. 7cm, Florida Island. Pitt Rivers Museum, 1916, 1920.100.96 (photo: Suzy Prior)

the dates recorded may reflect their registration at the museum, rather than their donation.
- 1886: 10 items, all from Florida Island and all of currency fathoms, suggesting a prototype collection;
- 1888: 32 items from a wide variety of locations, and of a wide variety types;
- 1890: 2 kites from Santa Maria;
- 1891: 1 flute from Pentecost (Whitsuntide Island) and 1 kite from Torres Islands;
- 1896: a set of fire-making sticks from Mota;
- 1897: 1 drill from Alite, an axe from Santa Cruz and a piece of bark-cloth from Fiji;
- 1902: 1 fishing float from Santa Cruz and 1 comb from Malaita;
- 1903: 1 fishing kite from Santa Ana and 1 piece of bark-cloth from the New Hebrides.

The size of donations then increases substantially:
- 1912: 13 items from across the region, nearly all of which are manufactured objects;
- 1916: 34 items again from across the region, all of which are manufactured;
- 1920: 362 items from across the region, including 58 arrows, each separately listed.

The 1916 donation followed the visit of Henry Balfour, the Pitt Rivers' Director, to Codrington in Chichester (see Chapter 1, p. 17). Codrington subsequently wrote to Balfour:

> I will take care to mark particularly the articles you mention as particularly desirable, so that they may be known to be your property. I aspire to the making of a catalogue. According to the will [I] have made everything will come to you – that is not otherwise disposed of, but some of the things are probably not worth taking away.

He concluded his letter:

> It would be a pleasure to see you again, and my brother wishes for you to see his collection. (Letters 1916, 13 July 1916)

A wood and shell ear disk from Florida Island duly arrived from Tom Codrington that year (**Fig. 37**). Balfour returned to Chichester on 12 December 1918, when a final selection of donations was agreed (1892–1922 Diaries). Codrington spent the following week labelling, packing and dispatching the collection.

This last and largest donation registered in 1920 forms 80 per cent of the Pitt Rivers Codrington Collection. Interestingly, it was also divided into sections. Did it follow the order of the promised catalogue? The first category was weapons (**Fig. 38**), followed by walking sticks (**Fig. 39**), tools, domestic tools (**Fig. 40**), mats, baskets and bags (**Fig. 41**), domestic (**Fig. 42**), money (**Fig. 43**), lime and betel nut,

Figure 38 Arrow with cane shaft and painted and carved fore-shaft with pointed bone coated in resin, Santa Cruz, l. 120cm. Pitt Rivers Museum, 1920, 1920.100.101 (photo: Suzy Prior)

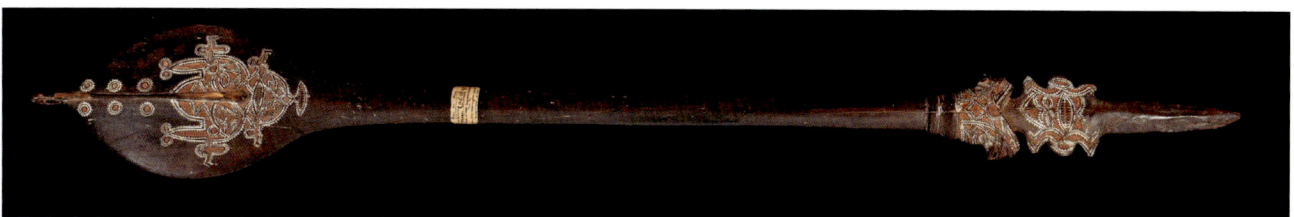
Figure 39 'Walking' club with elaborate carvings of faces and frigate birds, wood, Isabel, l. 118cm. Pitt Rivers Museum, 1920, 1920.100.165 (photo: Suzy Prior)

Figure 40 Carved wooden headrest with six long perforations, white pigment and linear designs, h. 16.8cm, w. 45cm. Pitt Rivers Museum, 1920, 1920.100.238 (photo: Suzy Prior)

Figure 41 A circular dish of shallow wicker basketry, Banks Islands, h. 9cm, diam. 4.65cm. Pitt Rivers Museum, 1920, 1920.100.249 (photo: Suzy Prior)

'Matters that lie upon the surface of native life and are open to the observation of the visitor and traveller': Codrington's Collections Explored | 37

Figure 42 Wooden lenticular food bowl with two protruding handles, Banks Islands, h. 4.3cm, w. 43cm, d. 13.1cm. Pitt Rivers Museum, 1920, 1920.100.283 (photo: Suzy Prior)

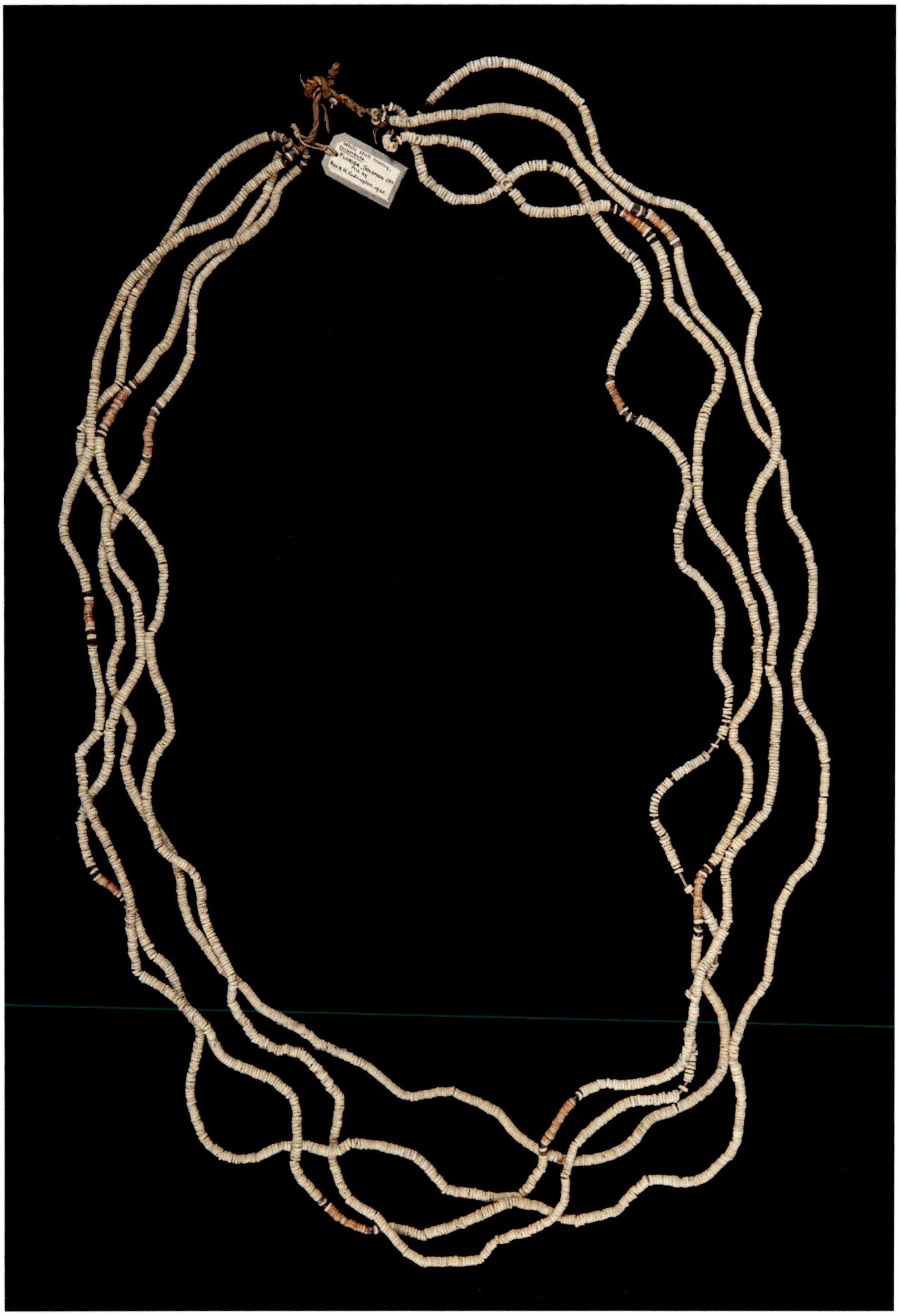

Figure 43 Two strings of white shell beads, tied together, Florida Island, l. 140cm. Pitt Rivers Museum, 1920, 1920.100.285 (photo: Suzy Prior)

Figure 44 Woven mat-work dress, fibre, w. 19.5cm. Pitt Rivers Museum, 1888, 1920.100.328 (photo: Suzy Prior)

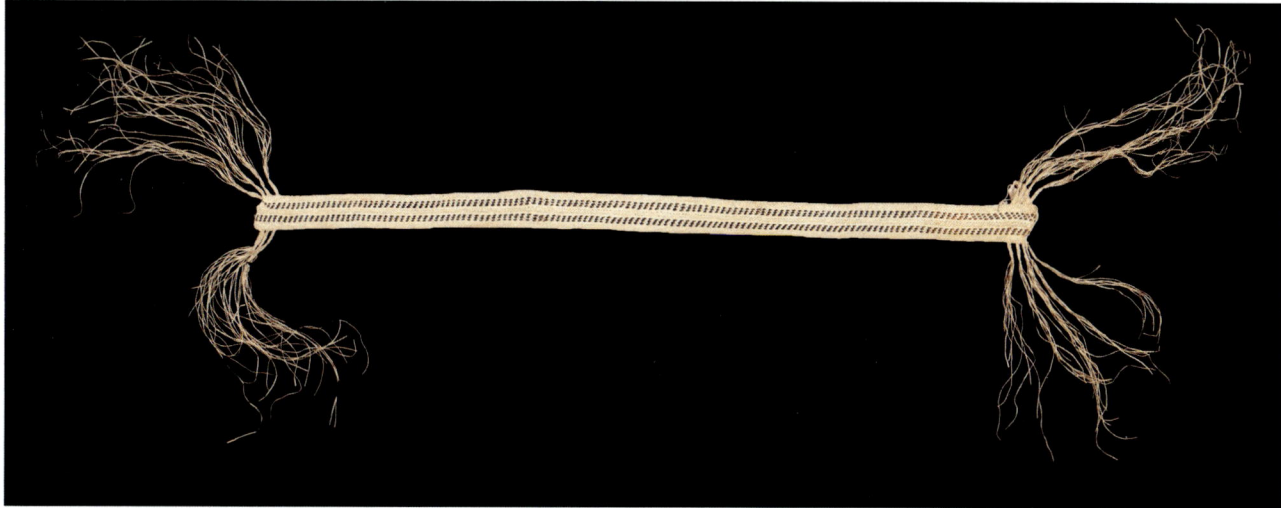

Figure 45 Woman's dress, brown fibre, Torres Islands, max. w. 3cm. Pitt Rivers Museum, 1888, 1920.100.336 (photo: Suzy Prior)

dress and clothing (**Figs 44–5**), combs, armlets, necklets, ornaments (**Fig. 46**), decorative arts (**Figs 47–8**), musical instruments (**Fig. 49**), toys and charms.

This grouping of items by type is very similar to the way in which Codrington treated objects in his book *The Melanesians*. The headings used in chapter xvi, 'Arts of life', have a strong resemblance to the list above (*TM*: xiii). Codrington advised his readers that in this chapter he was cataloguing the material culture of Melanesia:

> The present chapter will contain notices of such matters as lie much more upon the surface of native life, and are open to the observation of the visitor and traveller; the arts, namely, in which the culture of the people expresses itself, by which they build and decorate canoes and houses, plant and cultivate their gardens, furnish themselves with weapons and implements for war and work, catch fish, prepare their food, furnish themselves with clothing and ornaments, make and use money as a medium of exchange. (*TM*: 290)

The objective of this enumeration was, Codrington continued in a somewhat elliptical fashion, to demonstrate the Melanesians' practical accomplishments. 'So long a catalogue of their arts of life shews that Melanesians do not take a very low place among the backward people of the world.' This echoes his attempt to raise the cultural profile of Melanesians in relation to Polynesians in his earlier book, *The Melanesian Languages* (1885: 12).

The Pitt Rivers accessions register for Codrington's collection (PRM Collections IV) offers a concordance between the items and their discussion in *The Melanesians*. Notes in the accessions register against 37 of the objects offer page references to *The Melanesians*. This suggests that

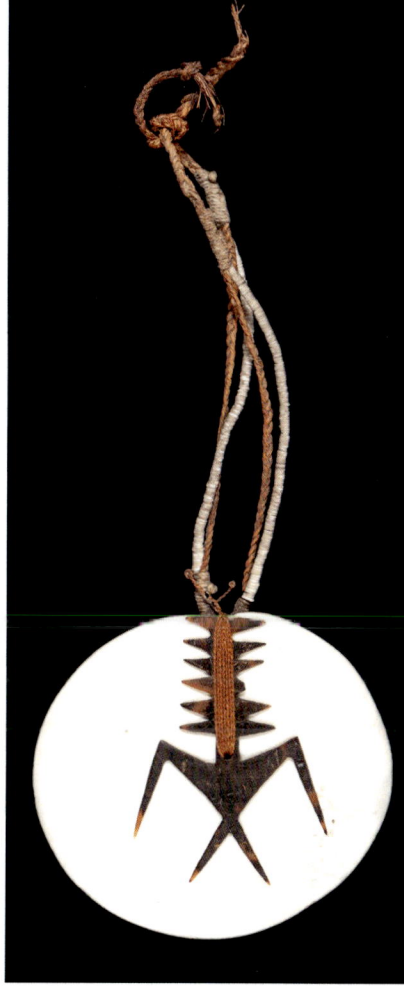

Figure 46 Breast ornament of tridacna shell overlaid with turtle shell bird design with plaited plant-fibre string of shell-disc beads, Santa Cruz, length 12cm. Pitt Rivers Museum, 1888, 1920.100.389 (photo: Suzy Prior)

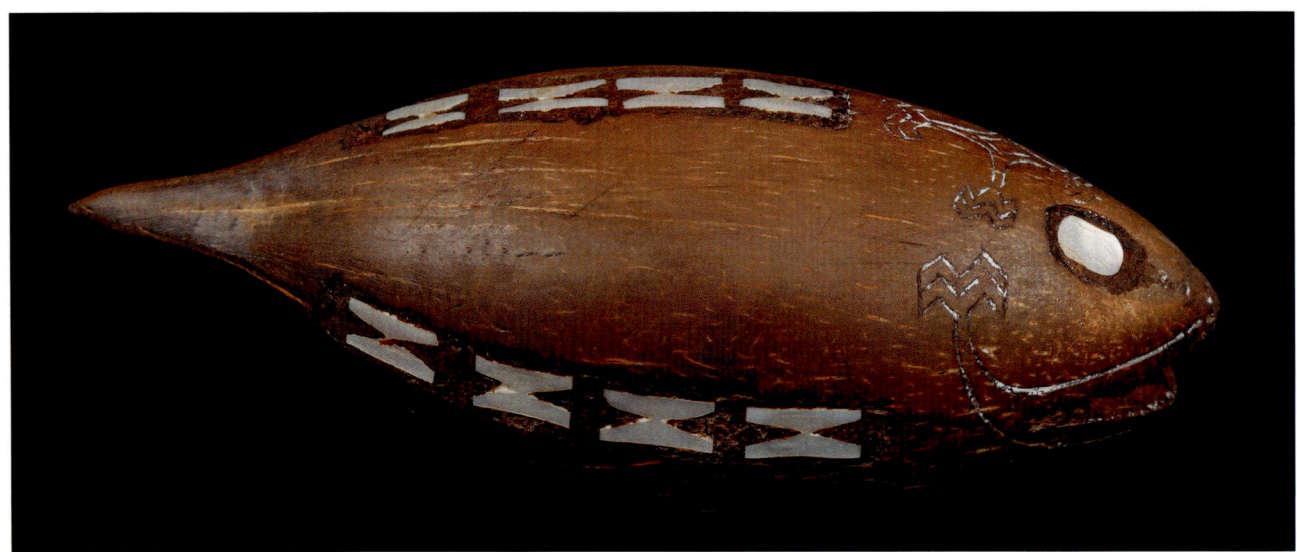

Figure 47 Coconut shell box, inlaid with mother-of-pearl shell in the shape of a fish, coconut husk, pearl shell, lime, Makira (San Cristoval), max. l. 11.5cm, max. h. 4.5cm. Pitt Rivers Museum, 1888, 1920.100.427 (photo: Suzy Prior)

Figure 48 Carved figure of a man and a dog on a canoe, inlaid with shell, wood, Makira (San Cristoval), h. 23.1cm, w. 27.7cm. Pitt Rivers Museum, 1888, 1920.100.437 (photo: Suzy Prior)

Codrington's collection was either physically or conceptually ordered so as to provide the substance for his discussion of Melanesian material culture in his book. This conjecture is further supported by the illustrations in the book, many of which reproduce objects 'in the Author's collection'.

The museum accession register benefits from personal input from Codrington. There is a close correspondence between the first 50 items listed from 1886 to 1897, and their appearance in the text of *The Melanesians*. Second, the voice of Codrington intrudes into the descriptions of the objects. He had two objectives here. The first was to provide cultural context. So, a knotted-string calendar (1920.100.39 from Isabel) had the following commentary:

> Used for marking the days after the death of some person in whose memory feasts were held. The feast days are marked with shell beads. 5 knots are first made as the ghost of the deceased is supposed not finally to depart before five days. Afterwards the knots are in a group of 10 (not quite accurately) every 10th day being a feast day.

A similar entry for a string of money (1920.100.35) emphasised the relationship between the object and the context in which it originated:

> A string of white and red (dyed) feathers taken near the eyes of fowls, worn by males as necklets or anklets as a sign of social status called *wetapup*, Santa Maria, Banks Islands.

A similar description was given for another object (1920.100.376 from Santa Maria). The accession entry texts may well have derived from Codrington's text in *The Melanesians*:

> The little feathers near the eye of fowls are bound on strings, and generally dyed a fine crimson; these are used as necklaces or anklets, by way of ornament and distinction. (*TM*: 324)

The other purpose behind Codrington's comments was to emphasise the technical sophistication involved in the objects' manufacture. So, a seemingly simple item (1920.100.49) can display complex features:

> Axe-adze with gouge-shaped blade of tridacna shell, set in a half socket and bound round. The stock which holds the blade is bound by the end of the handle and can be rotated so as to set the blade at any angle. Santa Cruz.

Codrington took a similar pleasure in describing the process of weaving, and in establishing parallels with other traditions elsewhere. One catalogue entry provides a direct link between the object and Codrington's text:

> Complete loom, with partly woven cloth (or mat) of banana fibre, showing plain weaving. Santa Cruz Islands. These looms in Melanesia are almost restricted to this group of islands but are identical with the primitive Malay form of loom [Codrington in 'Melanesians' 1891, p. 316 says 'these looms are identical with those in use in the Caroline and Philippine Islands and in Borneo']

A similar interest in manufacture is displayed in the bead-work frame that Codrington collected (**Fig. 50**) from Solomon Islands).

Codrington also speaks directly to today's visitor to the Pitt Rivers Museum. One of the displays, labelled 'Tridacna shell armlet, Solomon Islands, presented by Rev R.H.

Figure 49 Pan pipes, of seven stepped pipes with strips of reed and lashings of black thread and string, Banks Islands, h. 20.1cm, w. 8.4cm. Pitt Rivers Museum, 1920, 1920.100.92 (photo: Suzy Prior)

Codrington', has inscribed on the surface a small evaluative comment that is certainly his, 'exceptionally fine example', reminding us that Codrington held these objects in high esteem and that he had become an expert in their technology and a competent judge of their quality (**Fig. 51**).

The Pitt Rivers Codrington Collection differs from that held at the British Museum, in its richness and complexity, and also in seeming to host a series of sub-collections: fathoms of shell money from Florida in 1886 and again in 1920, and in 1920, arrows from Torres Islands, baskets from the Banks Islands and Torres Islands, and combs from Malaita. Despite Codrington's short stay in Santa Cruz in

Figure 50 Bamboo frame used for making armlets, with unfinished armlet, Solomon Islands, l. 33cm. Pitt Rivers Museum, 1912, 1920.100.64 (photo: Suzy Prior)

1881, some of the most varied items derive from this location. Indeed, it seems likely that a good proportion of them were acquired earlier and probably given to Codrington by other missionaries or acquaintances. Codrington was likely to have especially cherished acquisitions from there, as the islands had resisted missionisation and were deemed to have retained elements of traditional culture, and he recorded how Santa Cruz people continued to make objects long after people in other parts of the region had stopped. He wrote:

> The Santa Cruz people make distant voyages, far beyond Banks Islands, or New Hebrides people in this. While we were on shore, a great trading had been going on between the ship, and the canoes alongside. Curiosities can now hardly be had in other places, and the Santa Cruz people are very ingenious in making and very keen in selling the kind of things visitors like to buy, ornaments, bows and arrows, dancing clubs and mats. The latter are very fine and handsome, and what is singular, made with a kind of loom, and by the men. (Journal 1881: 30)

Descriptions of this pattern of trading by subsequent missionaries are all couched in almost identical terms of boisterous interchange tinged with danger (O'Ferrall 1908 n.p.; Ivens 1918: 241; Wench 1961: 104; see Stanley 1994b: 188–9). As late as 1911 the inhabitants of Temotu sought to kill missionary visitors (Blencowe 2007: 46). Yet these people seemed to have a particular fascination for Codrington and other members of the mission. Kolshus suggests that Polynesian men from the Santa Cruz group, in particular those from Tikopia, were accorded much respect in places like Mota. As Maori speakers they were intelligible to Patteson and others who had lived in New Zealand, and so became 'Polynesian beacons of resonance in a Melanesian sea of miscommunication' (Kolshus 2016: 9).

Codrington only indulged in one joke in his journals. He reported on 10 September 1870 on Mota that he was sitting in the *gamal* (men's sanctuary) with some local men, and the topic of Tikopians came up. Codrington summarised the conversation:

> The great points dwelt upon were: they washed every day and had no dirt on their bodies, never sat on the ground, but on a mat; in the second place they always said grace before eating and drinking, never misbehaved themselves in any way, were quite enlightened just like us. Having heard that they prayed to their canoes I enquired whether the bishop prayed to the *Southern Cross*. The old man who was the chief speaker didn't know but the others cried out against the idea. So there is some notion of difference after all. (1870 Journal, 10 September 1870)

There is in this account a nice tension between the ways in which the missionaries and Tikopians are compared, and of course, the mischievous notion that such comparisons are quite licit. There is, however, another more sober way of reading this vignette, as Helen Gardner has explained. The above quote can be read as:

> a fascinating investigation into the notion of human difference. The quote showed just how little race figured in the Motese understanding of human distinctions, instead they focused on actions. It is also a rather disconcerting comment on the Melanesian view of those in the Polynesian outliers. It feeds straight into the hierarchy of British above the Polynesians above the Melanesians! (pers. corr. Gardner)

Perhaps this contrast in missionary perceptions of the people from the Santa Cruz group made them the more significant as interlocutors and trading partners. But what is certain is that both Codrington and the traders from Santa Cruz entered into engagement over portable and durable objects with equal relish, whether, on the one side, knives, axes, tobacco or fishing gear, or, on the other, emblematic objects of dance, music or adornment.

The Cambridge Museum of Archaeology and Anthropology collection

Codrington's collection at what was formerly known as The University Museum of Archaeology and Ethnology, Cambridge (now the Museum of Archaeology and Anthropology; see Appendix 3) is the smallest of the three

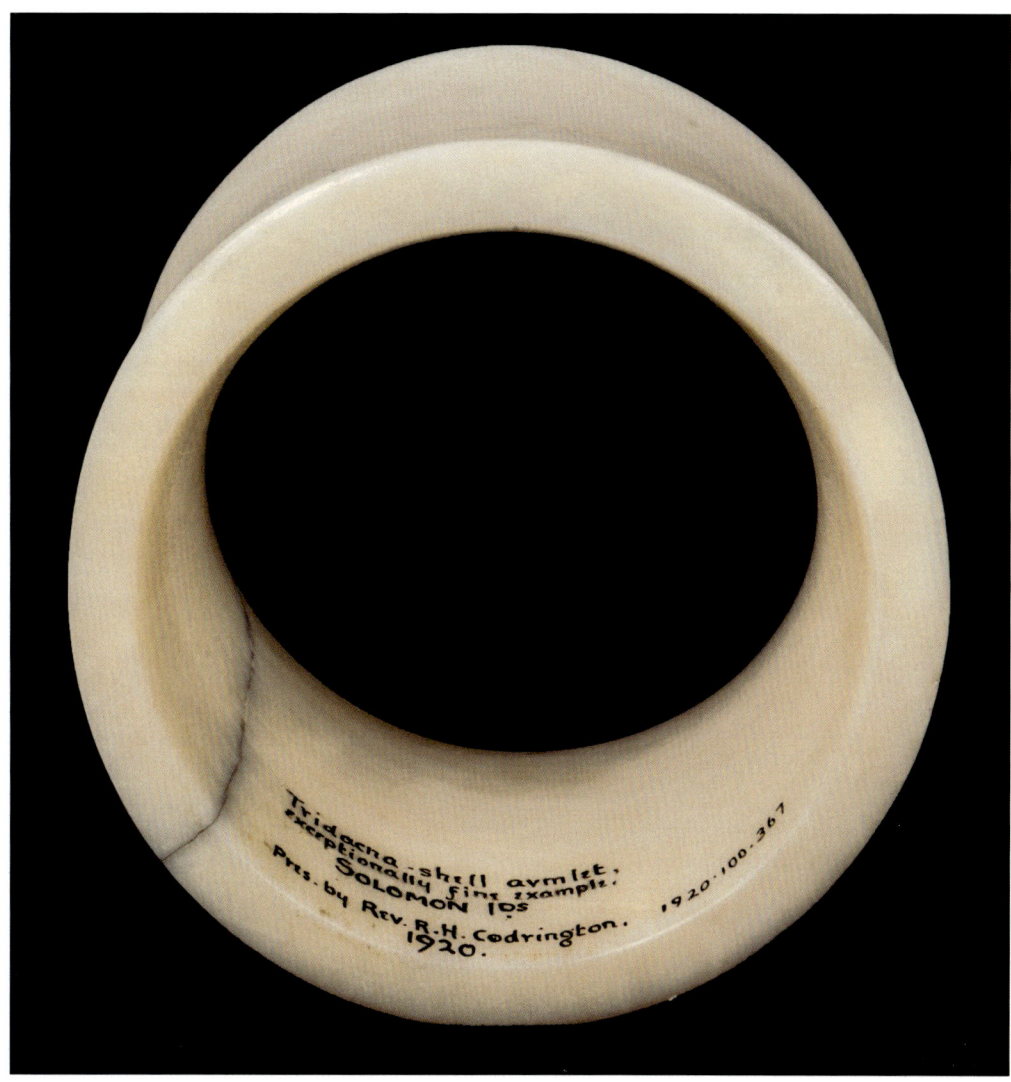

Figure 51 Tridacna shell armlet, Solomon Islands, diam. 10cm. Pitt Rivers Museum, 1888, 1920.100.367 (photo: Suzy Prior)

considered here. It consists of 21 objects, including 9 from Santa Cruz and 5 from the Banks/Torres Islands groups. Two of the objects (**Figs 52–3**) in this collection are listed as coming from the Blackmore Museum, with Codrington described as the collector and donor. Accession dates are always unreliable indicators of the age of any object, and it is unclear whether the objects were re-acquired by Codrington after the Blackmore Museum's dispersals and then donated to Cambridge or, as seems more likely, that they were acquired directly by the Museum of Archaeology and Ethnology from Blackmore.

The majority, if not all, of the other items appear to have come directly from Codrington. He was in correspondence with Anatole von Hügel from 1890, when the museum director asked about his plans for the publication of *The Melanesians* and requested a copy (MAA Outgoing Correspondence 1890: 327). A week later he wrote thanking Codrington for 'the pretty basket from the Torres Islands' that he had sent (ibid.: 331) (**Fig. 54**). In the same accession group was another very fine flat basket from the Torres Islands (**Fig. 55**) also selected by Codrington. In 1893 von Hügel asked to see a Solomon Islands tapa beater in Codrington's collection and noted with evident satisfaction, 'it is very good of you to say "I am glad when with due regard to my own university I can be of use to your museum"' (MAA Outgoing Correspondence 1893: 426).

Codrington visited Cambridge fairly frequently, staying with Mrs Annie Catherine Selwyn, the widow of Bishop John Richardson Selwyn. She was responsible for directing several former Melanesian missionaries to von Hügel. As a result, Cambridge holds probably the largest number of collections in Britain from the Melanesian Mission, including major contributions from W.C. O'Ferrall (largely Santa Cruz material) and from Walter Durrad (pers. corr. Carreau). No doubt Codrington kept an eye on the museum displays on his visits, because in 1902 he wrote to von Hügel offering a fully working Solomon Islands pump-drill to replace the defective one on display in the museum (Letters 1902, 22 September 1902). He noted elsewhere that such items were to be found in all three museums: 'pump-drills armed with flint, from the Solomon Islands, may be seen in the British Museum, and at Oxford and Cambridge' (Codrington 1903: 26). In the last letter surviving from Codrington to the director he offers to introduce to von Hügel a young man, Mr Fuller – who was to go on to collect many artefacts from members of the mission, including from Codrington, that now form the basis of the Fuller Collection at the Field Museum, Chicago. Although Codrington's contribution to Cambridge was considerably smaller than to the Pitt Rivers Museum, it did contain two dancing dresses from Santa Cruz (E 1906.312; E 1906.313) as well as two more from Ambae (E 1908.317; E 1098 318) and

Figure 52 Forehead or chest ornament of tridacna shell with plaque of turtle shell, Florida Island, formerly Blackmore Museum, collected by R.H. Codrington, 1869, diam. 13.8cm. Reproduced by permission of University of Cambridge Museum of Archaeology and Anthropology, 1937.285

Figure 53 Forehead or chest ornament of tridacna shell with plaque of turtle shell, Malaita, formerly Blackmore Museum, collected by R.H. Codrington, 1869, diam. 13cm. Reproduced by permission of University of Cambridge Museum of Archaeology and Anthropology, 1937.286

Figure 54 Deep oval basket of pandanus leaf with carrying loop, Banks Islands, h. 24cm, w. 30cm. Reproduced by permission of University of Cambridge Museum of Archaeology and Anthropology, E 1906.316

Figure 55 Deep oblong basket of coconut leaf, Torres Islands, h. 26cm, w. 57cm. Reproduced by permission of University of Cambridge Museum of Archaeology and Anthropology, E 1906.315

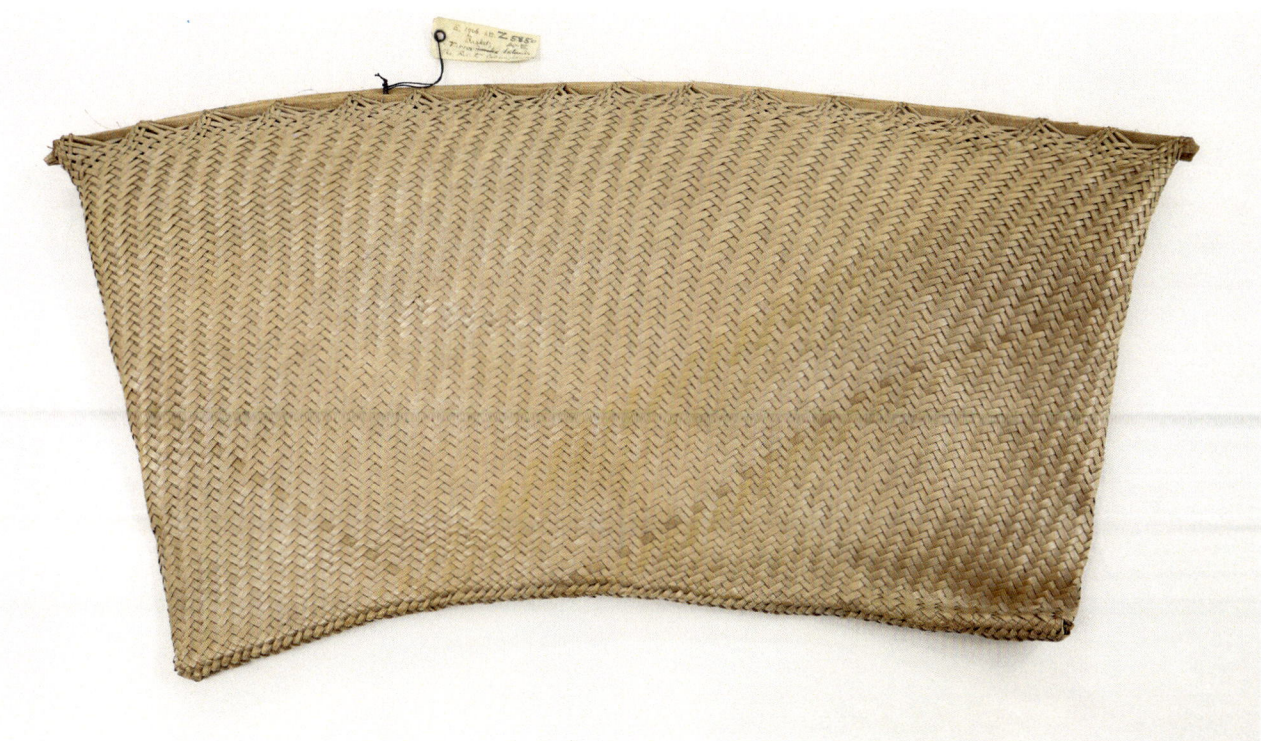

Figure 56 Charm kept with feather money, wood pigment, plant fibre, seed, glass, bead, shell, Santa Cruz, Solomon Islands, oblong piece of wood w. 10.8cm, h. 7.6cm. Reproduced by permission of University of Cambridge Museum of Archaeology and Anthropology, E 1905.183

one of that most elusive of categories, 'a feather money charm' (**Fig. 56**).

Some of the catalogue entries appear to have been composed in consultation with Codrington. As with the previous two collections, one can observe Codrington's meticulous attention to detail in ensuring that the objects are accurately described and contextualised.

Codrington's missing collection?

One curious question remains: to what extent did Codrington contribute to the Melanesian Mission Museum collection in Auckland? This museum, with 1,378 objects, was opened in 1929 and closed in 1974. It became the repository for the historic documents and objects relating to the mission, and for artefacts from Melanesia collected by missionaries, both from England and New Zealand. Potentially, the museum could have been a large and vital source of information about the dynamics of cultural change. As Ruth Ross, the historian of the Melanesian Mission in Auckland, wrote:

> The Melanesian Mission itself, by its mode of operation, must have greatly accelerated not only the adoption of European articles and techniques but also the interchange and spread from island to island and group to group of Melanesian articles and techniques which previously had been narrowly confined geographically. (Ross Papers, Box 56(2)5, Letter to John Daniels, 20 January 1978)

However, as will become evident, there were some major impediments that were to prevent such an outcome.

In its final display the Melanesian Mission Museum showed numerous large objects suspended from the ceiling (such as canoes) and attached to the walls (clubs, sticks and shields), as well as having 11 glass cases. Nine of the cases displayed ethnographic objects in groupings such as 'food and cooking' and 'musical; instruments'. Pride of place went to the first and largest case, objects associated with Bishop Patteson.

When reviewing the museum at the point of its closure Ross wrote tentatively:

> Although nothing has been found to substantiate this in the records of the Melanesian Mission or of its Trust and Finance Boards, the present writer assumes that the earlier items, which may constitute the bulk of the collection, were assembled by the Rev. R. H Codrington. (Ross Papers, Box 54(1)14, 'The Melanesian Trust')

Ross warmed to her thesis of Codrington's central significance for the Melanesian Mission collection, quoting from the preface to *The Melanesians*, 'One of the first duties of a missionary is to try to understand the people among whom he works,' and continued:

> If Codrington's precept had been followed, the primary function of the Melanesian Mission Museum would have been to foster understanding of the peoples amongst whom the mission worked. Unfortunately, the museum's controlling body

seems to have had little appreciation of the intrinsic value of the collection, as distinct from its potential as propaganda for the mission. (Ross 1983: 68)

This judgement underlines the fundamental misconception under which the museum operated: attempting to offer both a reliquary to the martyrs of Melanesia and an ethnographic display of items from the region. The Melanesian Mission Museum remains a cautionary tale, and an object-lesson in what would happen when Codrington's careful documentation procedures were ignored. As Ross noted in despair, the collection was deeply compromised by its disorganisation: 'Display cards are seldom attached to the articles they presumably identify, other articles seem to be without any identification of any kind' (Ross Papers, Box 52 (5)2, Letter to John Daniels, 26 January 1977). To complete the misery, when the collection was taken down the labels were all placed in one single drawer. Ross concluded grimly, 'If, as I suspect, attribution of unrecorded artefacts is an academic exercise loaded with trip-wires even for the experts, then I think it is something to be avoided at all costs' (Ross Papers, Box 52 (5)5, Letter to John Daniels, 20 January 1978). Although the collection was extensive, its significance in the Auckland Museum and Solomon Islands National Museum, to which the objects were deeded, has remained limited. To this day no definitive documentation has been feasible. Codrington would have been deeply offended and depressed that his artefacts should suffer such a fate. As a major collector in the field and contributor to the mission's displays, who also channelled other missionary collectors' artefacts into the museum, it is perhaps just as well that he did not live to see its failure.

Codrington's status in the museum world at the end of his life was a far cry from that of the early days of his initiation into museology. Although he had started out lamenting his lack of tuition and direction from museum curators, by the time he left the mission he had acquired a clear vision of what he wanted to collect. No doubt he was offered, and probably accepted, a variety of objects from people across the islands, including students and their parents. But what remain in the British Museum, the Pitt Rivers Museum and Cambridge collections are those artefacts that he felt worth preserving for future generations of scholars, both Melanesian and worldwide. The objects have weathered two processes of winnowing, the initial decision to acquire the items, detailed in the accessions registers, and subsequent selection to be offered for display. These decisions may have involved others in the receiving institutions selecting according to their own criteria, but they had to be agreed with Codrington, who, as the various labels show, had a clear sense of how these objects should be categorised. *The Melanesians* offers a clear window into Codrington's collecting. The illustrations and the final chapters act as an introduction to the material culture of Melanesia.

Chapter 3
'There was a spirit in my pen': Codrington's Visual Documentation

What distinguishes Codrington from other contemporary writers about Melanesia is the richness of his accounts. This is particularly apparent in his thorough documentation, which employed several visual skills in order to add to their veracity. He combined three techniques in various combinations: photography, sketching and verbal description. In this chapter these talents are explored in turn, and their contribution to his overall descriptions are discussed. His visual skills were also employed in his exploration of Melanesian graphic imagery on canoes, canoe houses and *gamal* (men's-houses in Banks Islands). His objective was to document items that were not portable, being either too large to take away or attached to buildings.

Photography

Codrington held high hopes that new photographic technology, collodion wet plate, could be used to good effect, but he quickly recognised that success would not come easily. In his diary written on Mota island in October 1869 he wrote:

> The morning as before with school. Afterwards and in the course of school exposed two pieces of paper I had little hope of. Too much wind for much. Afterwards sought and found a view over Vanua Lava (a bit) Ureparapara, Pawa Arag and Motlav and began a little sketch of it. (1869 Diary)

He later wrote to his brother:

> The collodion negatives I have sent partly that you may see them, and partly that people may have copies as they like. Scientifically, they are of value, and I should be glad if you would give to those anthropologists or whoever they may be who desire them. I don't suppose people have had any chance before of seeing what these people are really like. Compare for example the Solomon Islanders in Pritchard with any of these. I had some printed in Auckland where they damaged the negatives and I ordered some to be sent to Rolleston (Professor of Anatomy at Oxford) but I don't know whether they have reached him. I should like him to have any more that he likes. (LT, 9 October 1871)

Parenthetically, it would be interesting to know what sort of photographs he was sending to George Rolleston, the first professor of anatomy and physiology at Oxford University (for his career and commitment to evolutionary theory see Power 1885–1900). They would probably be portraits of Melanesians, but this raises a further question: as a critic of evolutionary theory, why would Codrington wish to send material to an evolutionary biologist who made a specialist study of human crania?

Codrington's photographic ambitions were regularly dashed. The problem was the medium. Wet plate collodion technology was notoriously fickle and complex. First a chemical solution had to be made, then a glass plate had to be coated with it before being placed in the camera. Exposure time was quite lengthy, and the resulting image had to be developed in a dark room using yet another chemical solution within 15 minutes. The development had then to be stopped at a precise point before the resulting image was then glazed over a flame to create a lacquered negative. In his correspondence with his brother Codrington frequently complained that his chemicals did not work in the tropical heat. Unfortunately, he left the mission field before

Figure 57 'Mota canoe', drawing by Codrington from a photograph, *The Melanesians: Studies in their Anthropology and Folklore*, 1891, fig. 13

the more reliable and easier to use gelatin dry-plate photography became widely available. It is little wonder that in *The Melanesians* there are only two photographs taken by Codrington reproduced, and that only one of these is intelligible, a Mota canoe, and this illustration looks like a drawing taken from the original photograph (**Fig. 57**).

Drawing and sketching

As his diary entry above suggests, sketching was a far simpler and a more reliable medium for recording objects, people and locations. Quite often these were pen and ink drawings, rather than pencil. Ink was a scarce commodity on Norfolk Island, as he complained to his brother. He often had to dilute the ink to eke it out when supplies were low. This, of course, resulted in fainter images. Eight of the illustrations in *The Melanesians* are drawn by Codrington, a competent and fluent draughtsman who produced good clear images. Early in the book there is an iconic image that engaged Edge-Partington sufficiently to place on a full-page plate in the 1898 edition of his catalogue (**Fig. 58**).

Codrington incorporated images into his letters and diaries. A simple example is a bowl described as 'A Mota wooden bowl for boiling on hot stones. 6 short legs' (Blue Journal, 27 August: 20) (**Fig. 59**). Sketching was useful to give a sense of place. In his 1870 journal he drew a map of Mota that he reproduced in *The Melanesians* together with another elevation from his 1872 journal (**Fig. 60**).

The frontispiece to *The Melanesians* shows Codrington's drawing skills to good effect (**Fig. 61**). Perhaps it has this prominent position because he was pleased with it. This rather gloomy scene is almost archaeological in its focus on stones and their employment in buildings. Even the pigs lying in the foreground look more like rocks than animate beings. The human figure is similarly somewhat indistinct. Depth is given to the scene by the use of cross-hatching, a common feature in all of Codrington's sketches. There are two incomplete series of drawings made by Codrington shortly after his last trip to Melanesia. The first set were to accompany his journal of the 1881 visit. This records 19 sketches, of which only 8 survive. Apart from one drawing of a canoe, all are of buildings: six of exteriors and one of an interior. Only the first drawing attempts to depict people (fig. 4, 'Wadrokal's house, Santa Cruz'), with four very indistinct figures beside a thatched house on piles (**Fig. 62**). The second set comes from Codrington's world tour of 1883. Only one of the nine sketches contains images of people ('Boats at Saigon, Cochin China, May 1883'), the rest (drawings made in China, Vietnam, Java, Ceylon and Egypt) are strictly topographical.

Figure 58 *Tamate* at Valua, Saddle Island, Banks Islands, drawing by Codrington from a photograph, R.H. Codrington, *The Melanesians: Studies in their Anthropology and Folklore*, 1891, fig. 4

'There was a spirit in my pen': Codrington's Visual Documentation | 49

I took them & undertook to get what I cared for him out of them. Two of these had their wives with them in Queensland who swam after them when they went on board Lewin's vessel to go away. All of them give the same account of their going for 3 moons, though they vary in the account of their treatment & proceedings after they were gone. It is quite enough to shew any unprejudiced person that the Queensland Regulations are a farce, that no contract whatever is entered into when "Labourers" are "recruited"; that they are got by native crimps who deceive them as a part of their business. This does not mean that all who go do not in a general way know what they are about, but that there is not the least reason to think that generally they do.

A Mota wooden bowl for boiling with hot stones, 6 short legs.

Aug. 30. Friday. C. Woolg came in from Panna to relate a circumstance which is characteristic not of this side of Mota however but of the other. A very sharp boy his brother, said to a young man who stood upon his dignity in the sq suqe (i.e. in the society in which they advance in rank by paying money, and eating in higher compartments in the gamal) "You will never be saved by your suqe", also he pointed to a sore in his leg and said "You'll soon be dead and then what will become of you?" This no doubt was very cheeky but nothing was thought of it till some time afterwards the young man Rupetar i.e. thousand butterflies who had been brooding over the insult got his bow and let fly at the school house by way of revenge. His arrow hit a tree and before he could shoot again people ran out and took hold of him and broke his arrows. They suppose it is all over but he is still sulky. On this side of Mota where people are so much advanced, an old man whose son's wife was in question the other day, couldn't sleep for thinking whether it was not his duty to do something to the offending party. So he came out in the early morning and called up Robert to consult him. Robert told

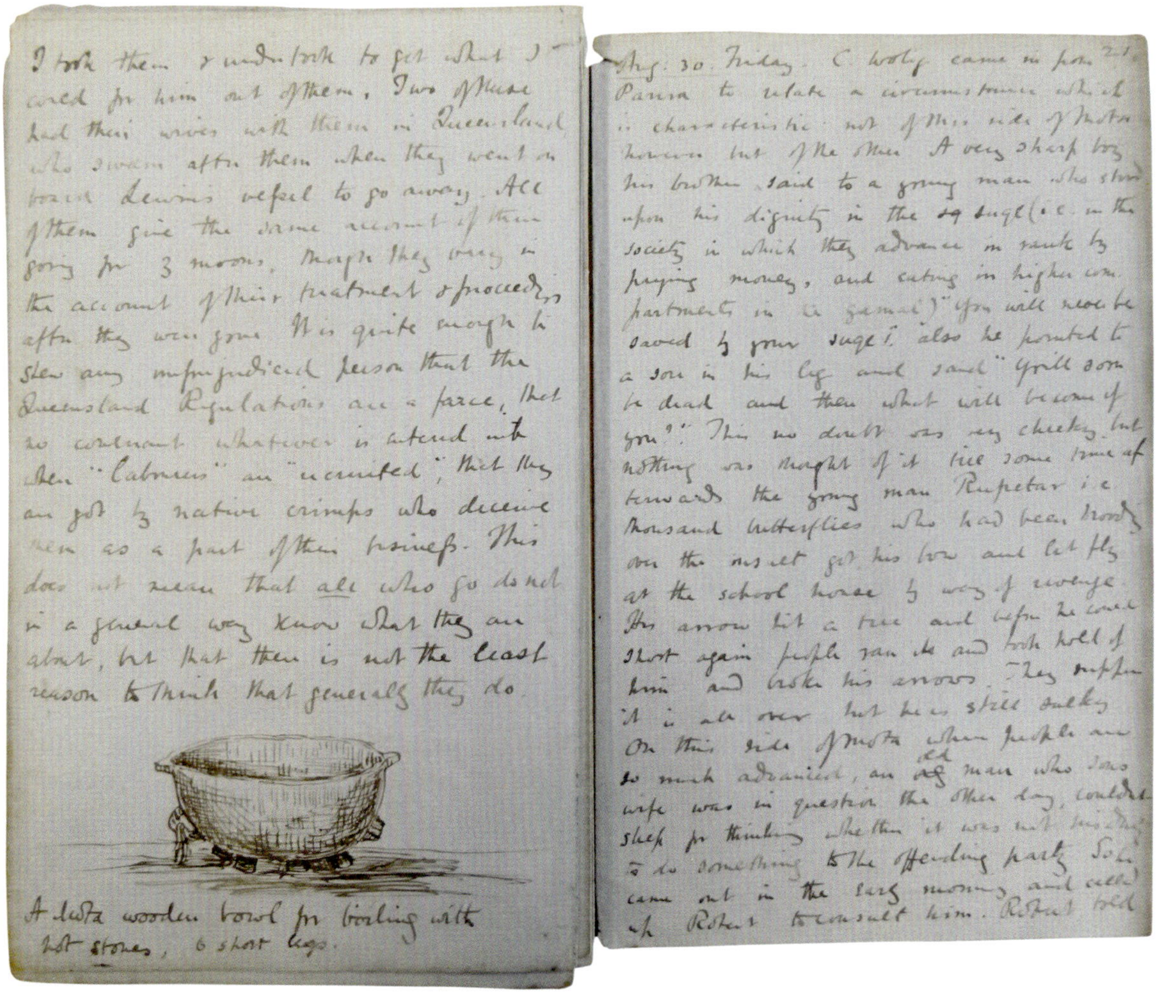

Figure 59 'Mota bowl', sketch, R.H. Codrington, 1872 Journal, 27 August. SOAS, MM 2/4

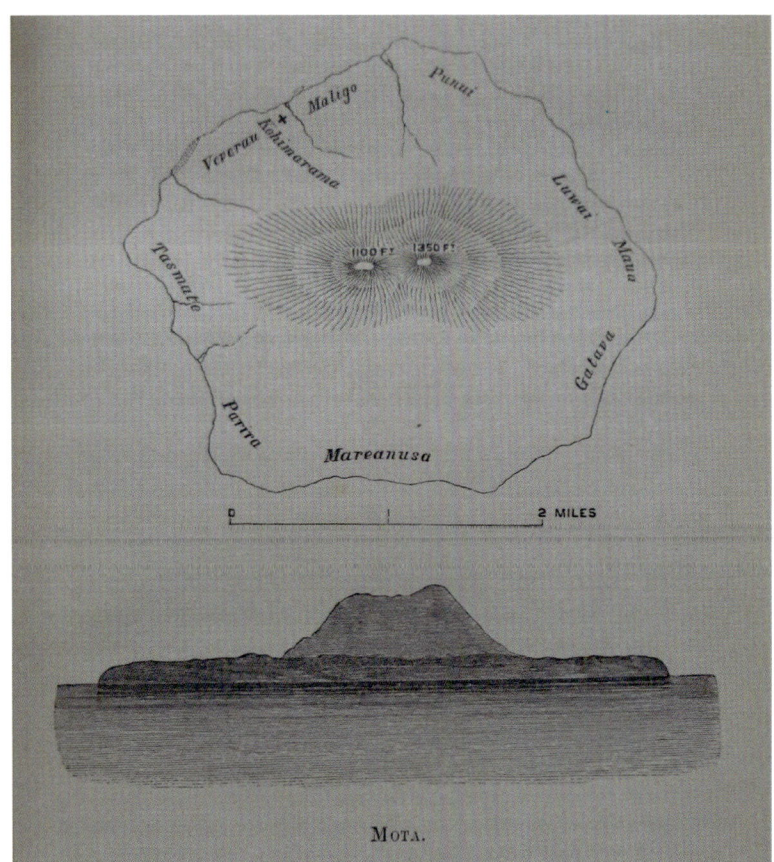

Figure 60 Map and elevation of Mota, drawing by author, R.H. Codrington, *The Melanesians: Studies in their Anthropology and Folklore*, 1891, fig. 1

Figure 61 Stone buildings at Gaua, Santa Maria, R.H. Codrington, *The Melanesians: Studies in their Anthropology and Folklore*, 1891, frontispiece

Figure 62 Wadrokal's house, Santa Cruz, drawing, R.H. Codrington, 1881 Journal. SOAS, MM 2/6

'There was a spirit in my pen': Codrington's Visual Documentation | 51

Figure 63 Drawing of man from Tewotama, Bauro, Makira (San Cristoval), R.H. Codrington. British Museum, undated, 2016.2049.1

Figure 64 Drawing of a man from New Hebrides, R.H. Codrington. British Museum, undated, 2016.2049.2

Codrington evidently had difficulty in drawing the human form. The only two extant portraits of Melanesians, 'Drawing of man from Tewotama, Bauro, San Cristoval', and 'Drawing of a man from New Hebrides' are distinctly unsuccessful, although a later touching up with colour may have coarsened the originals (**Figs 63–4**). Similarly, his 'Sketch by the author showing the dress of men and women at Bellona Island, Solomon Islands' portrays neither the costumes nor the individuals wearing them with any conviction (**Fig. 65**).

Nevertheless, Codrington's visual skills were noticed and appreciated at the time. As he noted in his journal:

After the usual early bathe and breakfast, I went to begin a sketch of the school which after prayers I finished while the daily teaching was going on. This was the first exhibition of anything in the way of drawing here, and I had an admiring circle. They said there was a spirit in my pen, the common way for accounting for wonders. (Journal 1875, 27 May)

Visualisation

The combination of drawing with verbal description could be very powerful. This I term visualisation. In his 1881 journal Codrington recorded a visit to Tega on Isabel:

We went in a boat to Cockatoo Island where we were in 1863 and up to the mouth of the stream where we landed. A most solitary and gloomy spot among mangroves. I suppose that it is under two miles to Tega, at first on the flat, then along a stream and finally after a rugged ascent and steep pitch path. The height of Tega is supposed to be about 1,000 feet, it is on the crest of the hill which is very sharp and rocky. The ridge of the hill winds along a ¼mile with 2 smaller ridges falling off from it, and on these ridges the houses are built on the projecting rocks assisted by piles, or on piles alone (sketch 7). (Journal 1881: 54)

Illustrated here is the sketch that he made as it appears in *The Melanesians*, solid and sturdy, seen over the roofs of two other thatched houses. On closer inspection, two figures can just be discerned, one standing, the other sitting on the veranda to the right of the building; but it is the building that is the subject of the composition, with attention being paid to the leaf construction and decoration (**Fig. 66**).

In his 1875 journal he described another decaying house:

Beyond this [house] there was a most picturesque view of another house on piles, and just beyond a twin pair going to ruin in graceful mourning for their master, the old rain-maker and weather prophet. When he died, his spear and shield and

Figure 65 The dress of men and women at Bellona Island, Solomon Islands, sketch by author, R.H. Codrington, *The Melanesians: Studies in their Anthropology and Folklore*, 1891, fig. 27

Figure 66 A House at Tega, Isabel, Solomon Islands, sketch by R.H. Codrington, *The Melanesians: Studies in their Anthropology and Folklore*, 1891, fig. 17

his pieces of calico and red cotton were hung up as his hatchment and a pile of food thrown up below. The yams are sprouted and are climbing up the spear and spreading over the roofs. (Journal 1875, 25 May)

He used the same skills to create an alluring landscape. Here he described a scene in 1872 on Motlav in the Banks Islands group:

> The scene as we left was very charming. The black clusters of rocks with the red brown crowd of people on them and the dark clear sea under them rippling off upon the black sand beach, light casuarina trees along the shore, behind them heavier masses of foliage with coconut palms rising into the sunshine and the white fleecy skirts of the overhanging cloud that hid the summit of the mountain. It was a very lovely and a very striking picture as we rowed away, a single canoe dancing on the nearest waves and the smoking of the parting white [surf]drifting across the shade of the trees. It is about 35 miles from Motlav to Mota and we did not get there till 5 o'clock. (Journal 1872, 29 July)

Codrington was also able to evoke mood successfully, as when he described sitting on the beach on Florida:

> It was a lovely quiet sunset evening full of soft colour, and the tide far enough out for those gleams and reflections on the wet sand and shadows which suit the repose and tenderness of evening better than a narrow sand and a line of surf. We sat till the fireflies came out, enjoying the scene. (Journal 1875, 27 May)

Architectural detail: canoes and canoe houses

Codrington had a strong interest in architecture, which came in very useful in the construction of St Barnabas Chapel on Norfolk Island between 1873 and 1880. He single-handedly refused the plans drawn up in England by George Gilbert Scott as too extravagant, and commissioned his own architect to follow his plans for a plain and decorous building (Gutch and Pinder 1980: n.p.). As head of the mission he acted as his own clerk of works, supervising the whole construction. But earlier, Codrington's architectural eye had been drawn to the most iconic and prominent of Solomon Islands buildings – ceremonial canoe houses. These were interesting for their structure, but also for their extensive decoration. In 1863, on his first visit, he depicted the interior of one, showing the roof structure as well as the sculptures and feasting pudding bowls (**Fig. 67**).

By 1872 Codrington had developed a sustained interest in these buildings. He described the 'great *kiala* boathouse' on Florida:

> This famous building is very fine indeed 180 feet long – 42ft wide, 56 ft in height; 8 great pillars support the roof and indeed the building is all roof as buildings ought to be in this part of the world. It is actually built in native fashion with bamboo tied together and thatched for the sides of the roof and whole trunks of trees for the construction. There is a little shallow carving on the great pillar and on the little studs of the side walls with conventional figures of birds … two photographs of this I sent last year. Since then the end towards the sea has been closed with bamboo work and a very strong palisade built in front of it to be ready for expected attack. (Journal 1872, 15 July)

The photographs have not survived. This canoe house contrasted with another nearby that was in a state of disrepair, but which still retained exciting carvings:

> The great curiosity of the village is now old and neglected; when I was here before it was fresh and brilliant. It is a boathouse, a building used also for public purposes, and was most elaborately decorated with carving and colour. Every post is carved with the figure of a man or a monster. Every bit of it was formerly painted black, red and white. The most curious and interesting thing was a series of scenes cut out in outline on what may be called the principal purlins of the roof. The outlines are cut in and filled in with white or they would have perished before this. They represent preparations for a feast and the feast itself, fishing for various kinds of fish and what is very curious the demons of the air most fantastic figures shooting at the people in their canoes. On the other side there is the picture of a battle in which not much is going on but it is quite Assyrian in the fight on the sea-shore and the foreground is filled in with fish to shew it. Round the middle pillars below the figures a larger picture of dancers done very fairly. There is not as may be expected any great amount of art in this decoration but there is some, and it would be very desirable to have complete copies before they perish. Old rotting canes also occupied the place, a large bundle of human skulls hung over the entrance. It was not a cheerful place at all however curious. (Journal 1872, 31 July)

In *The Melanesians*, Codrington expanded on the graphic imagery he found in the canoe house. He described one thus:

> I have seen at Fagani (Ha'ani) in San Cristoval a remarkably clever group over the apex of a gable, which represented a man climbing up to shoot an opossum, and the animal looking down upon him from the top of the pole in the most natural attitude… the canoe-houses, common halls, public-houses, called in those parts *oha*, were full of carvings in the constructive as well as decorative parts. Some of these, the posts for example which support the ridge pole and the purlins, are often figures of men. (*TM*: 173)

Later he continues the theme:

> There was many years ago at Wango a canoe-house, *oha*, full of carvings and paintings representing native life; it had along its wall-plates and lower purlins a series of pictures representing the principal affairs of life as naturally as may be seen in Egyptian tombs; a feast from the first climbing after coconuts through all the processes of preparing and cooking food; a fight upon the beach (the sea shewn to be so by the fishes depicted in it), with all its various action; voyages and accidents at sea, and among them a canoe attacked by what appeared at first sight demons horned and hoofed. These were the ghosts that haunt the sea, their forms having suffered a sea change, and composed as much as possible of fishes, their spears and arrows long-bodied garfish and flying fish. (*TM*: 258–9)

Codrington illustrates the account with two images of sea-ghosts drawn by local men (**Figs 68–9**). In contrast to these spectral forms Codrington's references to Egyptian and Assyrian graphic representation seem to be intended to insert Melanesian pictorial form into a known classical tradition that combines narrative form with decorative ingenuity in the carving.

Canoes held a similar fascination for Codrington. Like canoe houses their decoration could be read graphically. He spent a good deal of time assessing and describing them, and in his 1872 journal he wrote:

> I ought to add a word about the canoes which are so beautiful in these islands. The great *peko* [war canoe] at Boli I have already mentioned, there were some of the same kind out, the more

Figure 67 Canoe house interior, Ugi, Solomon Islands, watercolour, copy of sketch by R.H. Codrington, h. 17.1cm, w. 12.4cm. British Museum, 1863, Oc2006,Drg.734

common shape is that of a fish going head forward. They are all made of planks most carefully and skilfully fitted to the curves of the model, tied together and secured with a kind of glue from a native nut. (Journal 1872, 26 July)

In his 1881 journal Codrington included a sketch of a Santa Cruz canoe clearly showing its outrigger, sail and small cabin. He incorporated this drawing in *The Melanesians* with the accompanying gloss:

> the large sea-going canoes, *loju*, carry a large stage on either side above a very narrow hull, and have a house upon one of them for the crew. In these large canoes, with the large sail rising into curved horns, they make long voyages to Vanikoro and other islands that they know, steering by the stars. (*TM*: 293)

Codrington noted the similarity between these Santa Cruz canoes and those from Ulawa. He mentioned that an example of such canoes was held at the British Museum, which he had probably seen there. Perhaps the most successful images in *The Melanesians* are his drawings and accompanying text relating to a spear-rest in a canoe, and a figure-head (**Fig. 70**). The first captures the intricate interweaving of the animate forms within a tight circular frame. Codrington explained the imagery:

> A rest for spears forming part of a rib-piece cut out of a slab of wood and used to stiffen a canoe midships. The figures represent a crocodile and a dog above, two men and two cockatoos below. To this rib-piece the cleats on the planks are seen to be lashed. (*TM*: 296)

Another drawing is even more detailed and the explanation is similarly full:

> In the woodcut above not only are the head, which represents that taken when the canoe was first used, and the hanging board, which swings above the waves with a soothing motion, full of *mana*, but the bamboo tubes above wound round with red braid are stuffed with *tindalo* relics and leaves for protection and success. (*TM*: 296; **Fig. 71**)

MAN FISHING SHOT BY A SEA-GHOST. NATIVE DRAWING.

Figure 68 A sea-ghost shooting a man fishing, at Saa, Solomon Islands, 'from a drawing by a Native', R.H. Codrington, *The Melanesians: Studies in their Anthropology and Folklore*, 1891, fig. 10

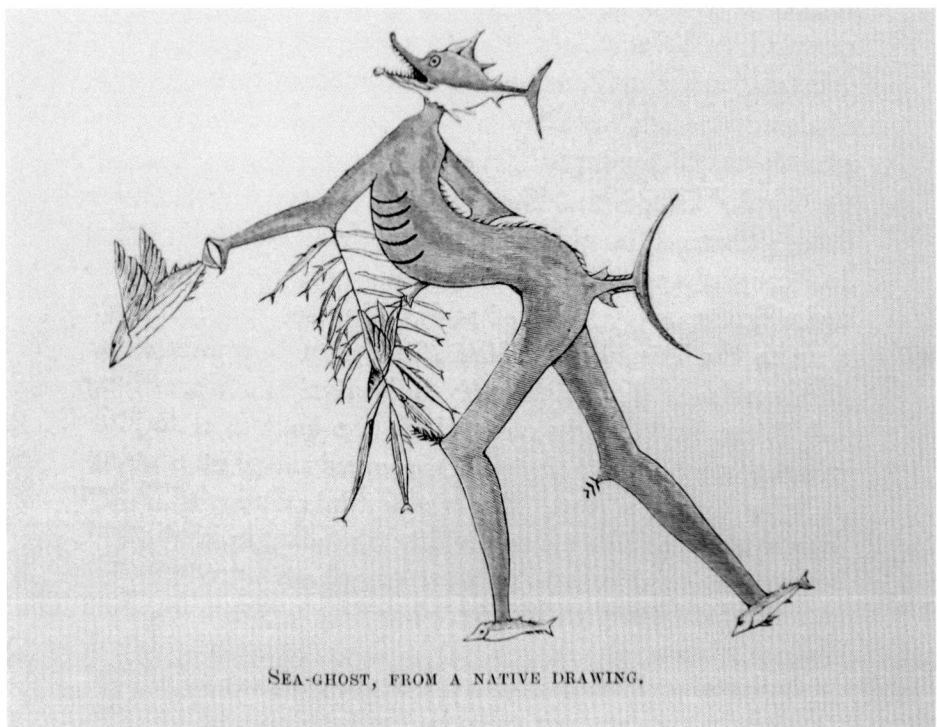

SEA-GHOST, FROM A NATIVE DRAWING.

Figure 69 A sea-ghost from Makira (San Cristoval), 'from a drawing by a Native', R.H. Codrington, *The Melanesians: Studies in their Anthropology and Folklore*, 1891, fig. 11

It becomes clear in the above quotation that at least these two sketches made by Codrington were turned into woodcuts for incorporation in his book. In all of the above combinations of imagery and description an over-arching understanding becomes available to the reader and viewer. Codrington's precise language helps explain not only the look but the symbolic work that each object performs.

Museum identification

Codrington's combination of visual form and narrative structure continued into the work he undertook on the labels accompanying the objects in the British Museum and the Pitt Rivers Museum collections. These contribute to a complex understanding of both the construction and purpose of objects. Labels attached to artefacts accorded with accession register details. There is little doubt that many of the labels were composed either by, or in consultation with, Codrington; the language and terms are consistent with those he uses in *The Melanesians*. These labels provided Codrington with the opportunity to fix the reading of an item, requiring viewers to consider the contextual information and reasoning that suggested treating the object in the way that Codrington prescribed. What is notable about the information on the labels is how they become more authoritative over time. The information in the British Museum catalogue is relatively sparse, though there is an excellent entry on the Banks Island *tamate* copied from one of Codrington's letters to his brother Tom:

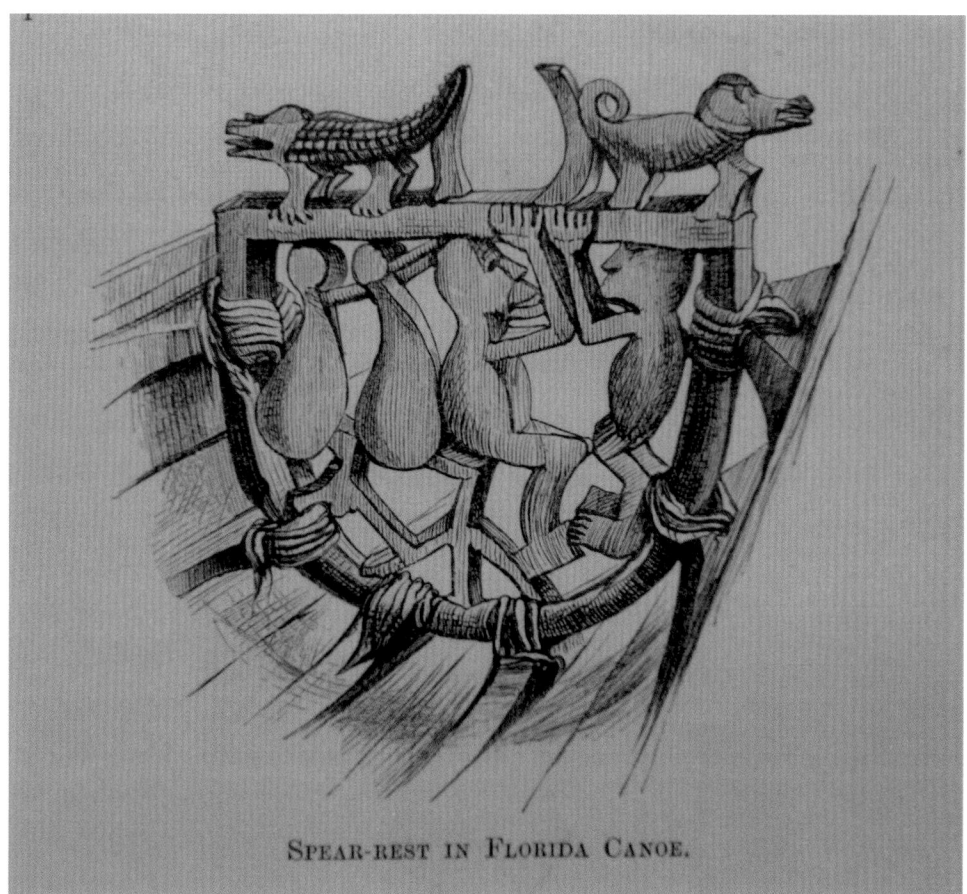

Figure 70 Spear-rest in a Florida canoe, from a sketch by the author, R.H. Codrington, *The Melanesians: Studies in their Anthropology and Folklore*, 1891, fig. 15

The Tamate – a secret society whose meeting place is in a secluded part near each village, and is called the *Salagoro*. There are many minor societies, and one or two thought more exclusive. The members have as their distinguishing marks various kinds of head dresses or masks which are called *tamates*, i.e. dead men, for the pretence was that they were ghosts, and the disguise came to have the name itself. Their secret lies in their making of these *tamates*, and in certain cries and noises. Each *tamate* has a particular leaf of a croton as a badge. (LT, 22 September 1869).

Some of the entries in the Pitt Rivers Museum's register are highly directive and full. For example, a loom from Santa Cruz (PRM 1920.30) was described thus:

> Complete loom with partly woven cloth (or mat) of banana-fibre showing plain weaving. Santa Cruz Islands. These looms are in Melanesia almost restricted to this group of islands but are identical with the primitive Malay form of loom. Codrington [1891: 316] says 'these looms are identical to those in the Caroline and Philippine Islands and Borneo'.

Another catalogue entry directs the viewer to consider the iconography of the decoration:

> Walking club [1920.100.165] Rau in Aba (the leaf, so called, of Aba, a place in Guadalcanar where they are made) very fine old specimen, blade and butt elaborately carved with combination of face and frigate birds design; butt two carved human heads back to back and above a design comprising face and frigate birds. Ysabel, Solomon Islands. (see Melanesians 1891 p 306).

The text in *The Melanesians* repeats this entry and adds as a coda, 'the spears, shields, clubs, bows and arrows of the Solomon Islands are common in museums', acknowledging

Figure 71 Figure-head of a Florida canoe, from a sketch by the author, R.H. Codrington, *The Melanesians: Studies in their Anthropology and Folklore*, 1891, fig. 16

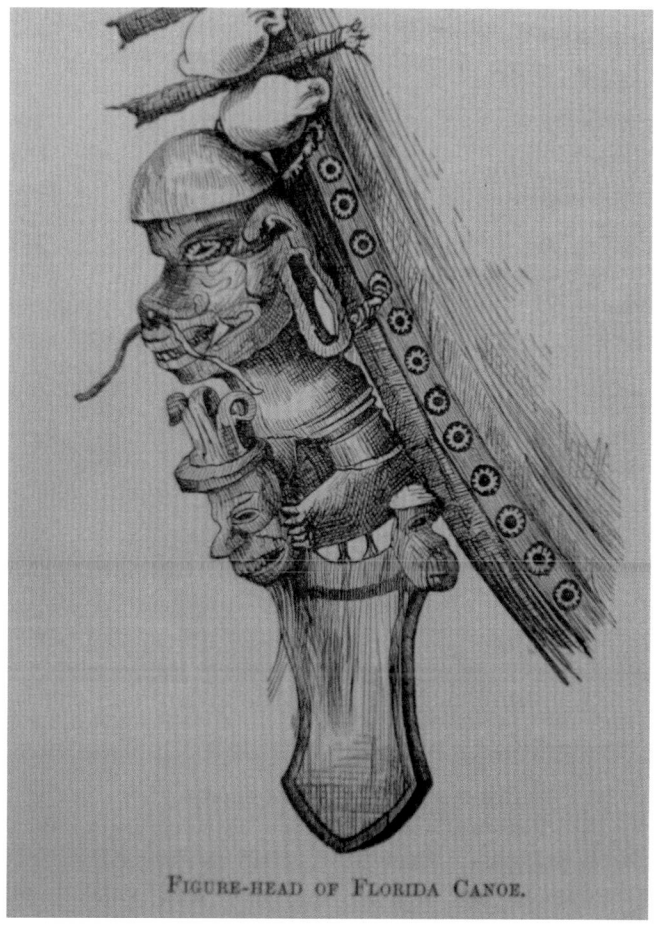

how widely disseminated Melanesian artefacts had become in the century since they were first collected by European visitors.

Finally, Codrington's visual acuity was later employed within such museums. In a late letter to von Hügel at Cambridge, he provided information about one of the major items in the Cambridge collection, as well as parenthetically adding an interesting comment about respect for cultural valuables:

> I noticed the Tamate Dress in the list of additions to your Melanesian collection para 3.21. I have no doubt that it is the same which I photographed in Norfolk Island and which figured in my book. I enclose a photograph which I happened to come across last week. It will do to put with the dress to show how it appeared when worn. I remember that it was considered rather a wonder that Bp Selwyn could find it; and was bound to find a properly initiated person to wear it for the photograph.
> (Letters 1902, 16 October 1908)

In summary, Codrington's visual intelligence was a vital component in his intellectual accomplishment. It accords with Brett's dictum that 'Seeing... is not passive reception, but the perception of complete and meaningful structures' (Brett 2005: 65). Codrington sought not only to grasp the linguistic imagination of Melanesia but also the way in which ideas took physical form. His reading of images was closely associated with the practical ability to capture them in their sensuous form, through drawing, sketching, photographing or carving. This talent in both making and thinking distinguishes Codrington's anthropology substantially from other work, both of his time and subsequently.

Chapter 4
'It has rained shell adzes today, large and small': Gifts and Exchange

This chapter considers how R.H. Codrington managed his dealings with his Melanesian students and parishioners, in terms of gifts, exchanges and purchases. Codrington's own agenda included the maintenance of harmony both in the islands and at St Barnabas College on Norfolk Island. It also involved seeking out artefacts that he could employ in deepening his study of Melanesian anthropology.

Disappearing curios

In line with his 'salvage collecting', Codrington was especially keen to obtain objects he perceived to be on the cusp of extinction. He was alive to the development of material substitution:

> One interesting thing I forgot to bring away with me but will get hereafter, a thing just like an old native adze used for chopping breadfruit. It is entirely of wood but as I said shaped like the old adze and is in constant use with no possibility of its being given up. So that in a few years when the old adzes will quite have disappeared this shape will survive in the breadfruit cutter. (LT, 30 September 1872; **Fig. 72**)

He explored the similar way in which the production of clothing was being transformed. He commissioned new work such as:

> A very fine dress from the Banks Islands called a *malo-saru* now no longer to be seen: a kind of cape, in four oblong parts, beautifully made in coloured matting, the highest product of Banks' Island art … which is worn by certain persons at festive seasons only. It is really well made with a good design. (*TM*: 107–8; **Fig. 73**)

He added: 'The value of it is that the men go stark naked, and this is the only garment worn' (LT, 25 July 1870). This latter comment needs some unpacking. As Codrington explained to his brother, what he meant was that he felt that the garment was an example of what he termed a 'survival reversed'. This type of ceremonial garment had become obsolete, Codrington argued, not because European clothes had taken precedence but as 'the men who have received the art from their ancestors have almost died out and the two that survive are too jealous to show any young men'. Why would people who currently wear little if any clothes treasure such elaborate constructions? Because, Codrington argues,

> People that go stark naked if they were rising into clothes would never begin with a very elaborate thing like that; whereas if people were losing arts (as these people <u>are</u> losing arts) they would be rather more likely to give up common tapa or anything of that kind generally than rich and great garments to give up a mark of distinction. (LT, 17 March 1873)

A pre-money economy

In order to form his collection Codrington had to construct a general network of exchange. He had a number of constituencies in the islands to satisfy, each with their own character; he also had to anticipate what goods would be acceptable to each group. Finally, he had to consider how to conduct the business of barter on a day-to-day basis. Each of these factors will be considered below.

It may be something of a surprise to learn that across the Melanesian Mission territory barter continued to the basis of normal exchange well into the 20th century. William Sinker was the captain from 1903 to 1912 of the *Southern Cross*, the

Figure 72 Adze for splitting breadfruit, carved at the head with a human face, brown wood, thick yellow patina on blade, handle end of New Caledonian type, Banks Islands, length 46cm. British Museum, 1876, Oc,RHC.12

ship that carried passengers and goods across the mission field. He wrote a racy account of his first trip, of which Codrington disapproved ('I am old fashioned and don't like the comic style.'– Letters 1891–1922, to C.H. Brooke, 12 December 1904). By the time that Sinker had arrived in Melanesia, catechists were widely established across the region. He was surprised to find on his first voyage that one of his duties was paying them: 'This paying teachers is rather a big business; much easier and simpler if they could be paid in money, but in most of the islands that would be impossible since they would be unable to use it, as there are not any traders from whom they could buy' (Sinker 1904: 8).

How then could these people be paid? The answer was through trade goods, but there was not one single system of payment. It depended upon local preferences. As Sinker (1904: 19) recorded: 'It is interesting to notice the different things the different groups of islanders go for as regards pay: some are mostly for tobacco, others cloth, or knives, lines, hats, axes, hatchets, soap, lamps, matches, jew's-harps, pipes, etc, etc.'

To further complicate things, local preferences could change quite radically at short notice, and the *Southern Cross* therefore had to stock up for all eventualities. However, trade goods had to take their place within a wider strategic plan. The ship required large quantities of coal. There were no bunker facilities once the ship had left Auckland, until its return. This meant that itineraries had to be tailored to the supply of fuel and distance between the various stations. The ship also ferried personnel, including students, catechists, priests and other missionaries, all of whom required quarters for the voyages between Auckland, Norfolk Island and the Banks and Solomon Islands. Food for the voyage and supplies for the various stations, as well as building materials for construction on the islands also had to be accommodated.

It was under these conditions that Codrington operated. He sought to free himself of the constraints of the mission's transport by urging his suppliers to send goods by other merchant ships whenever possible, but inevitably he too relied upon the *Southern Cross* for most of his supplies. These were vital ingredients for his acquisition of the objects of value he needed in order to construct his chronicle of Melanesian life.

Providing gifts

If Codrington was perplexed about what his British sponsors sought, local people in Melanesia had a very clear list of their wants – beads, fishing gear and tobacco. An early convert, George Sarawia, Codrington's protégé and the first Melanesian-ordained priest in the diocese, was quite blunt about his objectives when he first approached the Mission:

> I wanted to go myself to the real source of things, and get for myself an axe and a knife, and fish hooks and calico, and plenty of other things. I thought they were there just to be picked up, and I wanted to get plenty for myself. I did not go for any other reason but only because I had seen lots of things on the ship, and wanted to go and get plenty for myself. (Sarawia 1968: 8)

Later, Clement Marau, another local clergyman, had similar ideas: 'I thought I would get fish hooks and axes' (Marau 1906). The mission offered a new range of possibilities for Melanesians to enrich themselves and a variety of ways of doing so, whether by soliciting gifts, performing tasks in exchange for payment or, most frequently, through barter. In all cases material rewards were clearly sought. Codrington and his associates understood the material basis on which relationships were founded.

Bronwen Douglas argues that most accounts of collecting in the South Seas concentrate upon the role of European visitors, and that this approach fails to take account of the importance of reciprocity between both parties engaged in trading and collecting. Successful trading requires negotiation, consent and co-operation. Local interlocutors were important mediators between the trading parties (Douglas 2018: 41). There were also various partners in trade, such as chiefs, whose authority had to be acknowledged. They had to be thanked for permission to visit their territories and to set up stations there. Families and parents from whom students were sought for the mission school had to be compensated for the loss of the labour of their child, students to be enticed to leave home, and scholars at school to be rewarded for their progress and paid off on their return home. Each of these exchanges involved different considerations, especially when there was no

Figure 73 Dress used in dances (*malo saru*), in four scarf-like divisions united at top into a band with an opening for the neck, woven from narrow strips of buff-coloured vegetable fibre, Banks Islands, l. 148cm (with fringes), w. 156cm (with fringes). British Museum, 1873, Oc.7929

common currency of exchange. Appropriate equivalents had to be found; sometimes that involved tobacco and fishing lines as well as steel axes, at other times it meant exchanging local currency such as shell-money. What it emphatically did not include was firearms, which traders and returning labourers were bringing into the region, to Codrington's disgust and alarm. Codrington explained why trading was so important. 'Nothing could be more friendly and agreeable through the whole thing, but it [trading] is very tiring. It is well worth undergoing however because it gives them a proof of our confidence in them, and us of theirs in us' (Blue Journal, 26 September [1872?]).

In order to operate effectively, Codrington was careful to discover local preferences, which he then communicated to his brother Tom, his major provider of goods. Early on, he specified the beads that would be welcome, 'Small red, blue and white beads, opaque, for they are very particular, and small sea fishing lines will fill up corners, excellent for presents and for trade' (LT, 10 May 1869). The next year he was more specific:

> Some of the beads are also of the sorts most valued, and luckily there are some islands where anything will do. Beads represent native money very well. A few fine lines and fish hooks are always valuable. One small line is more valued as 6 large ones, and of course they fill up a box better. (LT, 29 January 1870)

Two years later he repeated his instructions:

> I hope I mentioned when I wrote some time ago that fish hooks and lines are always very acceptable as well as knives. The

smaller the lines and hooks the more valuable. Beads also of the right kind are most useful. I will send some day specimens of the right kind of beads. (LT, 4 December 1872).

Exasperated by supplies of the wrong type, he wrote to Tom:

> The beads are too large but they will do. It never occurred to me to say how big they should be. One sees beads always about the same size in circulation and imagines that such is the natural size of beads. The numbers, according to the card enclosed with the beads, which would be the right beads are 19.22.26.44.45. This is at Levin's, Bevis Marks E.C.[London]. (LT, 10 June 1874)

His complaint did not improve the quantity of fish hooks or beads supplied. Again, he wrote to his brother:

> I have just opened the box, for which many thanks. The fish hooks have amused us by their small number. I ought to be more explicit. We want them by thousands. These are very delightful in size [...] I have a lot more coming from Sydney and it is not too late to write to Auckland for 2,000 or so, though not good ones. The beads at one end show good blue ones, at the other yellow ones no good. You told me I had made a mistake about numbers. But red, blue and white are the only ones to get. (LT, 25 November 1874)

Scholars

Who received these goods? The primary recipients were the scholars. Codrington recorded in his 1870 journal, 'after school took George's report for rewards etc and gave a fishing line apiece to all' (2 September). Later his rewards were more graded, '[In the school] We distributed calico, beads, fish hooks and lines to the scholars, according to their apparent deserts, and they were abundantly satisfied' (1875 Journal, 25 May). This note of apparent contentment has an unsure echo to it. How was he sure that the persons rewarded were the most worthy, and how might one assess 'abundant satisfaction'? This remains a question one might raise throughout his ministry. Other items were also requested specifically for scholars:

> My idea of a penholder for a superior boy who writes well is about 2s 6d or 5s but I have no call for them just now since a number were given at Xmas by Selwyn. They are a nice present however. Also good strong note books, ruled of quarto or good 8 are very useful. (LT, 29 April 1876)

Most of the time supplies arrived smoothly, though not without complaint from the recipient. Boxes were a particular source of grievance. These were important both symbolically and practically. They therefore excited considerable attention. Codrington wrote rather sharply to Tom:

> I dare say there will be occasion to send a box next year. In one thing clearly I have not been very clear, as to the size of the boxes I should find useful. If the things just arrived had been sent in two boxes in one case I should have had two excellent presents of the best kind to make to superior boys, but the ones that came I should not have known what to do with if [Alfred] Penny had not taken it. Hereafter if it should so happen that things need a box larger than a deed box I should be glad if you would remember that two small boxes would be very valuable especially if of galvanised iron which won't rust. Ordinary iron or tin boxes rust through with salt water, as I know to my cost – a box in the islands which will keep things safe from rats and damp is a treasure, so long as it is of a handy size. (LT, 29 April 1876)

John Palmer, a friend and missionary associate, attempted to smooth relations between the two brothers, who were writing to each other over such a long distance and with such poor communications. From Norfolk Island, he wrote to Tom Codrington:

> I don't know what he [RHC] has told you about the box, on the whole he is satisfied but of course he had his growl. The beads satisfied him for one thing. They were enough for once but the lines, hooks, woollen comforters, all good, were too few. Wouldn't I send him enough if I had the chance again. The unfortunate box was too was a grievance. It was too large for any of the boys and should have been two smaller ones. (John Palmer, LT, 25 June 1876)

Sometimes Codrington made other requests to his uncomplaining brother. Aluminium watches were favoured at one point as 'superior' gifts:

> If you have not sent a box, or if hereafter you send one – or you might even do it by post – I should like of those aluminium watches which I am told are so good and cheap, or even two if they really are good. They would be capital things as presents to superior scholars. (LT, 23 June 1873).

Later he changed his mind, 'The watch seems very good. I don't care about it being a Russell not Waltham. I want to see whether a cheap watch of that sort is worth getting for a present for my numerous boys. People have given aluminium which is no good' (LT, 10 September 1879).

Perhaps the most singular request put to Tom Codrington was, 'Could you send a Roman coin or two with the image and superscription of Caesar? I think they are very cheap and there is nothing like the real thing' (LT, 17 January 1873). Codrington's reason for requesting this antiquarian object only becomes clearer when reading what he wrote at the end of his life about the significance of coins:

> I don't know that I told you that, when I was in Jerusalem in 1885, I got in the Temple Mount, a coin of Maximus Tiberius (582–602); the TIBER, being very legible, struck me very much in that place, recalling the tribute money... It is a pity it is not Tiberius I. (Letters 1922–6, to G.H. Haines, 11 March 1920)

In a somewhat elliptical style, he later expanded the thesis:

> Coins are like beetles in the innumerable small variations; but beetles, however otherwise interesting, have no history. A single common coin connects you with all history; you could make a long and useful lecture on a halfpenny. ——— There are I believe, 500 species of water beetles in England, but what can the little marks of variation tell us? (Letters 1922–6, to G.H. Haines, 8 February 1922)

What did a coin with Caesar's name inscribed indicate? Perhaps it might serve as an illustration for the biblical 'to Render unto Caesar' in sermons or lessons? What Codrington was probably also seeking was a teaching aid that had the aura (or mana) of antiquity, showing the interconnectedness of cultures over time. This was the appeal of antiquarianism that both brothers shared. As late as 1880 Robert was asking his brother to acquire a newly published magazine, *The Antiquarian* (LT, 3 September 1880).

Some of Codrington's entries detailing recruitment of students raise some questions for the modern reader. The distinction between gift and trade becomes particularly blurred when the question of inducement comes into play.

Gifts to parents and families of scholars both recompensed them for their loss and cemented relationships with the mission. Codrington recorded one such occasion:

> From Gaeta we sailed along to the next district, Vutuma, and came to a place where we had to put down a scholar, which we did without landing, for all the people were away for the 'gavaitona' [dance festival] and arrived at about 3 o'clock opposite the next district, Belaga. Selwyn went ashore to take one boy home. I staid [sic] on board and gave presents to the father, and brothers of our boys from this place. Yam buying and other trading was going on but with little noise and crowd thanks to the 'gavaitona'. (1875 Journal, 24 May).

Recruitment had been problematic from the earliest days. As Whiteman notes:

> There seems to have been little difficulty in attracting young people to come away for one season, but to obtain re-enlistments was far more difficult, Thus for example a report, circa 1858 of the voyage to the islands notes that mission visits to Mwaata, San Cristobal, were successful in getting only one of the previous five scholars to return with them for the second year. (Whiteman 1983: 124–5)

Codrington described a failed attempt to recruit a scholar and the reason for this particular fiasco – competition from Australian labour recruiters:

> There were two boys from the school to go, and when we were at the boat we were refused. Another boy we didn't want got into the boat, and they wouldn't let him go and made a row. The native of the place, who was a sort of teacher, seemed quite helpless and all was in a mess. Poor Clement of Motalava was left alone in a very unsatisfactory state of things. No one knew what was the cause of the people's displeasure, except they expected a great deal to be given them for letting their children go to school. They wouldn't let their boys go with us, but as soon as a labour vessel comes they will go to Queensland or Fiji. (1881 Journal: 85)

There were limits to the efficacy of trading, as Codrington sorrowfully recorded:

> Sauvi, the second great man of Boli came off as he had promised to bring me a present. It was alarmingly large, a pig and other food. I gave him what I could, but he assured me that he did not think of property or pigs, but only of one thing, that he might get back his boy who had gone for 'labour'. I never gave him credit for so much feeling, but he had tears in his eyes when he begged me to get his son back. It appeared that the boy is in Samoa and I don't know what I can do but people fancy that we all belong to the place or group of islands and that I could go and see the boy and get him away. (1881 Journal: 64)

Payment for work

Beside serving as inducements to students, trade goods were also employed as payment for work. So, for example, Codrington recorded in his journal on the island of Ugi in 1875:

> The new school house is a nice clean little place, with nicely woven bamboo sides, with a window they are proud of with a shutter to it. Thirty-three men and 12 women assisted in building it, and they expect a piece of tobacco each & five knives between them. (1875 Journal, 20 May)

As the mission expanded, so regular wages (in kind, as Sinker, the *Southern Cross* captain had noted) for employees became an ever-larger source of expenditure. Such payment probably also speeded up the reciprocal exchange of artefacts as part of general barter. Sinker recorded in Santa Cruz, 'crowds of canoes came off with yams, curios, birds, fruit, etc' (Sinker 1904: 24).

Trading

Trading was at the very heart of the mission's life. Basic staples, such as yams and fresh supplies of water, were always needed, so negotiating their supply was a constant preoccupation. The employment of trade goods by the Melanesian Mission was not always easy to distinguish from the actions of other secular traders. It also ran the same risk of getting out of control. The following account hints at potential trouble being narrowly averted:

> It was about 4 when we got back and there was trade till 6. There were a great many people on board and there was a certain amount of noise but everything perfectly friendly. The two great men Takua and Sauvui were eventually taken down below and presented by me with a hatchet, beads, tobacco and pipes. Jakua in return gave me some native money. No others were allowed below, but the doors at the top of the companion were shipped and I generally stood on guard there. It became tedious at length because there were more men on board than canoes to take them away but all was clear about 6 and we stood out for the night. (Journal 1872, 25 July, Florida Island)

Two months later Codrington recorded with some obvious satisfaction: 'My very choice shell adze arrived today, tied on to its handle, 40 years age at least and the only one known to be in existence. bought cheaply with a borrowed knife' (Blue Journal, 7 September). This sounds rather more like the cupidity of the hardened collector. Later that month Codrington described in some detail the process of trading:

> From this time until about 2 o'clock there was nothing but incessant trading. very satisfactory indeed and very fatiguing. I don't know how many there were on board altogether but 200 I suppose, not all at once though. I counted 26 in one canoe. The deck is covered with them selling all sorts of things, yams, shells, curiosities, for pipes and tobacco principally. It was a new thing to get yams here and a good thing, but it will secure them trade when curiosities are exhausted. I bought a good many stone adzes, two very good ornaments of clam and tortoiseshell and a lot of other [things] … it has rained shell adzes today, large and small. I paid so much for one or two believing them to be almost extinct that people have rummaged them up. (1872 Journal, 29 July, Florida Island)

This last sentence reveals that Codrington was very aware of the impact that his own collecting had on the objects brought forward for exchange. It is also interesting to observe how he was thinking of trading after curiosities had run out.

Trading could be risky too, as George Sarawia recorded:

> At some places they welcomed us well, traded and talked to us properly, and then we rowed back to the ship without any trouble. But at some villages or islands as we rowed back to the ship, it was as if they were chasing us off with a parting shot. Truly, we scarcely got away alive from them on those occasions. (Sarawia 1968: 20)

When things went badly wrong there was great potential for conflict and disastrous results. Codrington gives an example of just such an occasion:

> There was such a hubbub one could not hear oneself speak, but all was perfectly friendly. I did not go into the village for all the people were present, and we did not want to wait, so when I had emptied my bag I went back to the boat. I found yam buying in full swing, and the boat too high up on the beach to float. There was a good deal of confusion which I couldn't make out, in the course of which I saw Selwyn jump out of the boat into the sea, and a boy by me told us to be off for they were angry… At last by degrees, after we got away, I found that some people had been stealing trade, and that Selwyn had jumped out after a man who was carrying off his bag and that they were beginning to quarrel among themselves about the thieving. Wate and one or two others stuck with us, and I thought that at one time they were afraid on shore, but after a time it became clear that they wanted to restore some of the stolen goods, and we backed in and received two tomahawks, and rewarded the man who brought them back. Then our friends dropped into the sea and we got off, with leisure to enquire and come to some understanding [of] what it had all been about. This is the sort of thing that easily becomes serious. If we had been armed and frightened as well as ignorant of the language and the circumstances, it would be likely that a revolver would have gone off and we should have had spears at us. As it was we came to the conclusion that no threats were directed to ourselves, nevertheless when spears are quivering their long tails it is time to be off, and out of it. (1875 Journal, 22 May, Saa, Malaita)

In such circumstances the members of the Melanesian Mission looked more like ordinary traders or sailors seeking custom goods and especially rare objects, sometimes through dubious bargains. More seriously, there was a danger of being perceived in the same light as labour recruiters. In both cases, those men who left either for the furtherance of their material comforts or their intellectual development often returned bent on employing their new wealth and understanding in the cause of overturning traditional customary practice and the balance of power in local communities. Codrington was to meet scepticism and resistance from such a quarter. He mentions one such occasion with some evident rancour:

> The women and children were a formidable element in my second congregation and the 'scoffer' I am sorry to say was there; in European clothes a pipe in his mouth; who having worked on a Queensland plantation for a couple of years was much above my level. If I did no good I talked myself hoarse talking down women, children, pigs and the spitting of the smoker. I can't afford to be prolix but let the reader conceive how it is that when one is not well, tired, hoarse, striving to be intelligible in a half-known tongue, the spitting of the contemptuous smoker is in the present irritation and sticks out in the memory with obvious prominence. (Blue Journal, 22 September)

Three days later, when preaching, he met the same resistance and scepticism:

> Taking occasion rather by the gospel of the day I was deprecating worldly goods in comparison with spiritual things, when one constant and critical attendant called out gruffly that he considered a large axe a very good thing. Explanation as usual only the more convinced him that I wanted to explain away something that I held myself but didn't mean to let out. (Blue Journal, 25 September)

Codrington also drew the line at trading with persons of whom he disapproved. He was firm in his conviction that there were ethical standards that had to be maintained as the following example shows:

> As it was getting dark Padhea arrived, who was the contriver of the massacre of the Lavinia people: we would not let him come on board and I think we should have done well not to let any other concerned in it come either. For my part I refused to buy anything taken from the unfortunate people, such as money they brought, and I gave my reason that they smelt of blood. (Blue Journal, 26 September)

Material objects remained for Codrington of central importance in the interplay between European and Melanesian practices and ideas. This can be appreciated best by considering how he developed his most well-known but often controversial concept of mana.

Chapter 5
On Mana and Poisoned Arrows

Mana

Codrington's reputation as a pioneer anthropologist of Melanesia rests principally on his development of the concept of mana, first discussed briefly by earlier missionaries in the 1830s (Tomlinson and Tengan 2016: 2). He suggested that this local language concept was fundamental to Melanesian belief. For Codrington it was a key concept which provided the bridge between the physical world and the spiritual. To understand Melanesian spirituality required an appreciation of how agency was perceived, especially in the Banks Islands group, where Codrington was most at home. It will come as no surprise to learn that this somewhat abstract construct was, in Codrington's mind, based in material objects in the real world. This is why he was determined to collect sacred objects like stones and arrows.

Codrington recorded with some pride in *The Melanesians* that Max Müller, Professor of Comparative Philology at Oxford University, had cited with enthusiasm Codrington's notion of mana in the Hibbert Lecture of 1878:

> It is a power of influence, not physical, and in a way supernatural; but it shews itself in physical force, or in any kind of power or excellence which a man possesses. This Mana is not fixed in anything, and can be conveyed in almost anything; but spirits, whether disembodied souls or supernatural beings, have it and can impart it; and it essentially belongs to personal beings to originate it, though it may act through the medium of water, or a stone, or a bone. (*TM*: 119)

Codrington expanded on the way in which mana is manifested, through charms:

> If a man has been successful in fighting, it has not been his natural strength or arm, quickness of eye, or readiness of resource that has won success; he has certainly got the *mana* of a spirit or of some deceased warrior to empower him, conveyed in an amulet or a stone round his neck, or a tuft of leaves in his belt, in a tooth hung upon a finger of his bow hand, or in the form of words with which he brings supernatural assistance to his side. If a man's pigs multiply, and his gardens are productive, it is not because he is industrious and looks after his property, but because of the stones full of *mana* for pigs and yams that he possesses. (*TM*: 120)

Mana is needed, Codrington maintained, for individuals to rise through the ranks of graded secret societies (the *suqe*) in places like Mota. To rise through these levels requires money, food and pigs, and to obtain these the great man has to exhibit conspicuous mana, displayed in the charms and stones which make his pigs and yams multiply (*TM*: 56). As Whiteman notes, for Melanesians mana is judged according to its efficacy rather than as an abstract concept. So, if a man finds a stone that has some special quality he then tests it to see if it 'works' in terms of mana. He can be sure that if crops increase near the stone then it truly is a charm and has efficacy (Whiteman 1983: 73–4).

The Melanesian Mission's booklet *Religion and Customs in Melanesia* provides a useful summary:

> 'Mana'– power or influence, not physical but showing itself in enabling a man to do or get what he wants. This 'mana' may be in anything, men, wood, trees, animals, stone or any object large or small and can be invoked by charms for use. Living beings, spirits or men, liberate it and set it free for use through

Figure 74 Spherical stone believed to be possessed of mana, stone, Mota, diam. 5.3cm. Pitt Rivers Museum, 1916, 1920.100.80 (photo: Suzy Prior)

prayer and sacrifice or charms. Certain things have 'mana' for particular purposes; a stone, for instance, will have 'mana' for making yams grow big; a charm, a form of words, has 'mana', e.g. to bring rain. (Melanesian Mission 1930: 4)

Charms

Stones came in two categories: those that belonged to sacred places and others that related to a living spirit and thus acquire a mystical quality. Stones were also used to protect a house from thieves. If a thief's shadow falls across a magic stone the ghost inhabiting the stone draws out the man's life and eats it (Codrington 1915: 533). Codrington's small collection of labelled charms includes magical stones to ensure good crops (**Fig. 74**). Perceptive individuals were always on the lookout for such stones. Codrington recalled that, in the Banks Islands, if someone found a stone either on the ground or in a stream that appealed to him as resembling an animal or a fruit, then he could use it to his advantage (Codrington 1881: 18). He explained that there were special features by which such stones could be recognised:

> A stone with little disks upon it, a block of ancient coral, was good to bring in money; any fanciful interpretation of a mark on a stone or its shape was enough to give a character to the stone and to the spirit associated with it; the stone would not have that mark or shape without a reason. (*TM*: 182)

Again, in the Banks Islands, recognising these qualities could be turned to good account by the specialist recognising the stones:

> If the man desires to get the benefit of the stone, or whatever it is, known to another, with a view to increase of money, pigs or food, or success in fighting, the possessor of the stone will take him to his sacred place, where there are probably many stones, each good for its own purpose. The applicant will supply money, perhaps a hundred strings a few inches long. The introducer will shew him one stone and say, 'This is a big yam', and the worshipper puts money down. Of another he says it is a boar, of another that it is a pig with tusks, and money is put down. The notion is that the spirit, *vui*, attached to the stone likes the money, which is allowed to remain upon or by the stone. (*TM*: 141)

But dealing with stones was a serious business. They were both powerful and ubiquitous and represented a potential problem for Christian converts. How were they to be eliminated? This was left to those in authority to resolve. Clement Marau wrote in his autobiographical essay *A Story of a Melanesian Deacon* how he dealt with the requests of his parishioners on Ulawa to dispose of sacred items:

> We threw out of their houses all the things that belonged to deceiving spirits, and the stones that belonged to them they gave to me. Some of these I sank out of sight in the sea, and some we broke up, and some I kept locked up in a box… We brought out the most holy stone of all that they used to venerate, and we desecrated it, laying it down to be trampled upon by the people in the path. We destroyed the whole sanctuary and made it into a garden, as it is this day. (Marau 1906: 20)

But this was only a partial solution; there were always plenty more stones around that could tempt the waverers to use them. This was a generic problem with all charms.

Charms might be made of other materials, such as sperm-whale ivory ('heart-shaped charm *daraga* to attach to

Figure 75 Charm of shell and coral beads attached to material, l. 12.5cm, Santa Cruz. Pitt Rivers Museum, 1888, 1920.100.450 (photo: Suzy Prior)

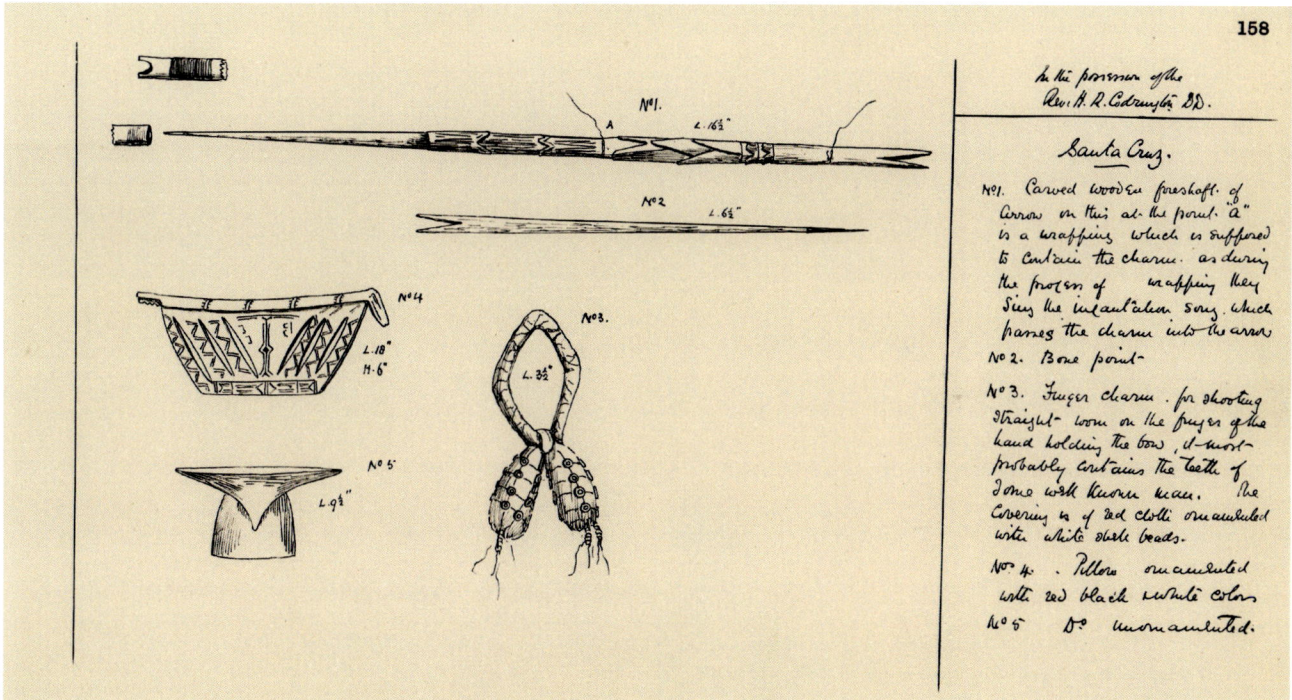

Figure 76 Charm worn on wrist, Santa Cruz, J. Edge-Partington and C. Heape, *An Album of the Weapons, Tools, Ornaments, Articles of Dress, etc, of the Natives of the Pacific Islands*, 1890, pl. 158, item 3

a shield, Isabel, Solomon Islands'), or shell and fibre ('charm worn on the finger by archer, Santa Cruz' (**Fig. 75**) – also reproduced by Edge-Partington and Heape 1890 (**Fig. 76**) with a gloss, almost certainly supplied by Codrington, describing its construction and magical properties). Charms, whether made of stones or leaves or other materials, provided the means by which men could access the unseen powers, and flatter them with sacrifices to gain their attention and help. So, what appeared to be everyday objects, in fact gave access to spirits who were omnipresent and powerful agents in the real world.

Poisoned arrows

Charms could not only be involved in obtaining goods and prestige, they could be used to do harm to, or otherwise defeat, enemies or, in extreme cases, to kill them. Such cases were commonplace across the region, as Codrington explained:

> Another charm is common to both eastern and western islands, which is called in the Banks Islands *talamatai*. A bit of human bone, a fragment of coral, a splinter of wood, or of an arrow by which a man has died, is bound up with the leaves which have *mana* for the purpose, with the *mana* song; by this means the power of the ghost is bound to the charm and the *talamatai* is secretly planted along the path which the person at whom the charm is aimed must pass, so that the virtue of it may spring out and strike him with disease. (*TM*: 204)

Bone, preferably human bone, could be incorporated in weapons to give them extra power. 'It is the human bone which gives the deadly quality to the arrow; but yet the bone must be made into an arrow with the use of certain incantations which add supernatural power, *mana*, as it is most commonly called' (Codrington 1885: 217).

Codrington collected arrows 'tipped with human leg bone' (**Fig. 77**). He explained:

> It is the human bone first of all that in the native opinion gives the arrow its efficacy; the bone of any dead man will do, because any ghost has *mana* to work on the wounded man; but the bone of a man who was powerful when alive is more valued. (*TM*: 309)

One's own relatives could be involved, as Codrington illustrated:

> In Lepers' Island (Ambae) not long ago, a young man out of affection for his dead brother, took up his bones and made them into arrows. He carried these about with him, and did not speak of himself as 'I' but as 'We two', his brother and himself, and he was much feared; all the supernatural power of the dead brother was with the living. (Codrington 1890: 216)

The structure of the arrows was everywhere similar: 'There is a shaft of reed, a foreshaft of hard wood, tree fern or palm, and a point of human bone; the point is let into the foreshaft, and that into the shaft, and the joinings are firmly bound with fine string or fibre' (*TM*: 308).

Codrington was keen to clear up any misapprehension about the real meaning of 'poison' in the term 'poisoned arrows'. He ridiculed those who took the term literally. He recounted that:

> I was once assured by a young naval officer that he had seen putrid flesh upon the natives' arrows. Asked whether he had taken one into his hand to examine it, he replied with disgust that he would not have the thing near him. He probably to this day believes that he has the witness of his own eyes to the truth of the common belief. (*TM*: 311)

His description of poisoned arrows was lengthy but very clear:

> When the word poisoned is used it is necessary to understand in what sense it is applied. The practice of administering poison in food was certainly common among the natives. I very much doubt, however, whether what was used had ever more than a very little power of doing harm; whether anything used was

Figure 77 Arrow with cane shaft and painted and carved wooden fore-shaft, with pointed bone (?) tip coated in resin, l. 120cm, Santa Cruz. Pitt Rivers Museum, 1888, 1920.100.101 (photo: Suzy Prior)

poisonous in a proper sense of the word before returning 'labourers' from Queensland brought back arsenic with them. Certainly the deadly effect of what was administered was looked for to follow upon the power of the incantations with which the poison was prepared. In the same way the deadly quality of these arrows was never thought by the natives to be due to poison in our use of the word, though what was used might be, and was meant to be injurious and active in inflaming the wound; it was the supernatural power that belonged to the human bone of which the head was made on which they chiefly relied, and with that the magical power of the incantation with which the head was fastened to the shaft. Hence the Torres Islands and Lepers' Island arrows, which have no poison, were as much valued, trusted and feared as the others; and in Lepers' Island (Ambae) both kinds are used. (*TM*: 215–16)

He concluded his discussion on poisoned arrows with a comment on the aesthetic qualities of these objects, 'In conclusion, let me call attention to the beautiful and elaborate ornamentation of the shaft from the Banks' Islands. This was executed with obsidian in Santa Maria, where certain men in former days used to make their livelihood by their art.' He added parenthetically, and with some obvious satisfaction, that Henry Balfour of the Pitt Rivers Museum had used one of the arrows collected by Codrington in a public lecture in 1888 (*TM*: 118).

But why did Codrington make such a large collection of arrows? In the Pitt Rivers Museum collection there are 57 (12 per cent of their Codrington items), with 29 from Torres Islands, and 28 from Santa Cruz. Samson follows Codrington in noting that Commodore James Goodenough died of tetanus after an attack on his party by Santa Cruz islanders in 1875, thus fanning the flames of the 'poisoned arrow' myth (Samson 2017a: 80; *TM*: 307). So perhaps the Goodenough association would be recognised by those who saw these Santa Cruz arrows. But this does not explain the number of objects collected, nor the high number from the Torres Islands. Perhaps the explanation resembles that for the stones: a desire by local people to disembarrass themselves of uncomfortable items that held negative references. But this would only explain why so many had been given, not why such a large number were preserved in the collection. Perhaps a contributory factor was Codrington's desire to explore and show the wide range of graphic designs they displayed.

Goodenough was not the only person associated with death from poisoned arrows. An earlier and more significant reference, far closer to home for members of the Melanesian Mission, was the death of Bishop Patteson's associates. Kolshus sums up the case crisply:

Even though the arrows were not poisoned per se, the tetanus threat still was the major concern when hit. After the attack on Patteson, both Stephen Taroniara and Joseph Atkin succumbed to it after a few days. Taroniara was severely injured having been hit by five arrows, but Atkins' wound was a minor one to his shoulder. It was quite common to dip arrow points for war use in faeces, and the bacterial injection would in many cases do the job. These were magical arrows with a delayed effect. (pers. corr. Kolshus 2020)

Codrington used the case of poisoned arrows as an opportunity to mock his own credulity. He introduced the scene on Mota with pathos:

I went to the Maligo Salagoro, and after a while began [to enquire] about the horrid use of poisoned arrows, and the miserable scene witnessed yesterday by me at Nuavara and still going on and to continue. They rather coolly counted the days on their fingers. This is the fourth day after his tetanus, he dies tomorrow or the fifth, being a strong young man perhaps a little later.

Codrington then introduced himself as an actor in the performance:

As far as my vocabulary went I expressed my feeling of the horrible cruelty of the thing, and they all cried out that it was indeed very bad. Yes, I said, you all say it is very bad but you have all got poisoned arrows in your possession and what for unless to shoot men, and do this horrid thing. No! they did nothing of the sort, they had given up all that was bad. But still they kept the arrows, no good to shoot birds or fish or bats to be used for nothing but man. Why don't you destroy them out the land?

The response was a piece of drama expressed in deliberately theatrical terms:

Up got the elderly man at my right, laid his arrow upon his bow and arrow and cried out 'here goes one to begin with' and shot it out of the door against a tree, breaking off the poisoned point. I praised him and another followed his example. The tall solemn man who made us such a speech on the day after the shooting got up and took fire in a cocoanut husk. 'Let him burn them.' A fire was soon blazing and they brought me one after another about a dozen of the detestable weapons from which I burnt off the spikes of human bone on which the venomous mixture with which they smeared bubbled and hissed with a foul smoke. This was a great satisfaction, and something done, something to set before the people as an example, and also creditable to these people who to some extent disarmed themselves, without waiting for a general disarmament. (1879 Journal, 11 September)

George Sarawia
Two days later on 13 September, Codrington had a chance to reflect on this incident, when he supplied his aunt with the denouement of the story, and a twist in the tail provided by George Sarawia:

> The day before yesterday as a result of a very eloquent and touching speech of mine several people brought poisoned arrows to burn. It was a sort of a scene and material for a missionary anecdote and I was rather in a glow of satisfaction when up came George without a smile and signified either that people had plenty besides at home or that they would buy fresh stock at the next opportunity. This may be true but it is a chilling remark to make. Considering, however, how little bottom there generally is in gushing dud demonstrative characters and of the danger of unreality in making such a beginning as this of a native ministry. It is a thing that at a distance to be thankful for that George is so sensible and dry. (Letters 1867–87, to aunt, 28 September 1870)

The problem for both Sarawia and Codrington was that the former did not remain a shining example of mission success. The two had known each other from early days in Auckland, and moved together to Norfolk Island in 1867. Despite Sarawia founding a successful community on Mota in 1869, which Codrington was particularly delighted to note in 1875 was so successful that the church was overflowing (Codrington 1876: 8), by late 1883 the Mota church was in rapid decline. Sarawia wrote to Codrington telling how a hurricane had devastated the island, bringing famine, dysentery and influenza with it (Gardner 2012: 157), that his wife had died, alongside 70 new converts, and that he himself was frequently ill. In the same letter, he also admitted that he had joined a secret society (*suqe*). He explained:

> It does not mean praying to the *tamate*, no we cannot pray to that *tamate*. It is true that the ceremony of making men become members of the *tamata* is still continuing. Concerning the *suqe*, they seem to be forgetting about it. It is not as before, some of its customs also we are not practicing. (Gardner 2010: 119)

For Codrington this revelation presented an immediate problem with his oldest and most favoured Melanesian colleague. For some, like Walter Durrad, Sarawia's successor on Mota, the question was how much Sarawia's membership of a *tamate* had contributed to his initial success. For others, it was rather how becoming a high-ranking member, and perhaps even chief of the *tamate*, had led to his neglecting church duties in favour of Melanesian religion (Samson 2009: 71–2). What is clear, is that these two perspectives were incompatible. Nevertheless, Codrington was left with an uneasy realisation that the objects that he had been studying were by no means just museum artefacts, they were still seen to have power in Mota and other islands in the region. Since his earliest days Codrington had engaged in local customs, such as becoming a *pulsala* (or special friend who expects reciprocal exchange of food, shelter and protection), even if, as Codrington was very aware, 'it is not disinterested benevolence that will make Mota men choose an Englishman as his *pulsala*' (Codrington 1863: 8). But Sarawia's admission put all this mutual trust into doubt. A particularly charitable solution to the issue is offered by Gardner. She emphasises the dramatic effect that the weather and imported diseases had wrought on the Christian community. This, she argues, would have diminished Sarawia's authority. How could he respond?

> If his attempts to convince the populace about the Christian God *atua* were unsuccessful as mortality rates continued to rise, it is tempting to consider that Sarawia had little choice but to influence the populace through indigenous institutions – the exclusive *tamates* or the more important and inclusive *suqe*. (Gardner 2012: 161)

Gardner consoles us with a possible response from Codrington to this problematic state of affairs:

> While his response to Sarawia's possible backsliding was not recorded, it is tempting to think he was philosophical over the swirl of deities on the islands and the shifting hold of the men's societies and the *tamates* on the minds of men and women in the first fifty years of Christianity in Melanesia. (Gardner 2012: 162)

The backlash against Sarawia
It might be tempting to finesse the problem in the way outlined above; but there is a very real possibility that Codrington would not have been sanguine or resigned to this sidestepping of the profound issues raised by any attempt to graft one religious and philosophical system onto another with a very different outlook. It would raise the huge difficulties in terms of language translation, the reconceptualisation of ideas and understanding of social mores. He would have been very aware that other European missionaries in the Melanesian Mission would have sharply different views about tolerating indigenous elements in contemporary Christianity, and that members of the mission like Walter Durrad, as well as church historians like John Garrett, would argue successfully for the suppression of *suqe* in the Anglican Church in the early 20th century (Samson 2009: 69–71). Sarawaia's reputation was further undermined by his successor on Mota, Hedley Adams, an Englishman, who maintained that Sarawaia's prestige derived not from

his priesthood but his being the head of a *suqe* (Hilliard 1978-201). This repudiation of Sarawaia's ministry was part of a wider move within the mission to loosen links with indigenous cultures. The abandonment of the Mota language in favour of English would further underline this shift. Tolerance for local practices would decline sharply, and the division, mental and physical, between European and local clergy would grow ever wider.

In Britain Codrington's reputation, as he left the mission, was extremely high. To mark his departure from Melanesia, a number of his friends raised money by subscription to pay for a portrait painted by W.E. Miller (see **Fig. 78**), which was then presented in 1886 to Wadham College, Oxford University, where he had studied. This occurred a year after the university awarded him an honorary doctorate in divinity. A final mark of Codrington's academic recognition was the award by Wadham College of an honorary fellowship in 1901.

Codrington did not, however, feel that his career had been a success. He wrote in 1919, in pain and distress, to his former fellow missionary, Charles Brooke: 'We were good missionaries – we desired to know and live with the natives. I fear that there has been in that respect a considerable deterioration in Norfolk Island and a change in the way of looking at the working of things.' He continued, 'The present conditions of the Mission makes me think that my little labours came to nothing' (Letters 1891–1922, to C.H. Brooke). Nevertheless, Codrington kept up his correspondence in the Mota language with former Melanesian colleagues, listening to their problems and worries, and giving them in turn his reflections and advice. His correspondents recorded their indebtedness to his ministry and this must have given him some comfort and satisfaction. Further support for his philosophy and work would not appear until the next century, and will be discussed in the next chapter, where a contemporary re-evaluation of R.H. Codrington's achievements and his importance for the study of Melanesian material culture are both examined to gain a proper perspective on his work.

Chapter 6
Codrington Today

This chapter attempts an evaluation of Codrington's significance in the disciplines of anthropology and museology, 130 years after the publication of *The Melanesians* (**Fig. 78**). Initially, some important critiques of his work need to be considered, before any attempt is made to form any summative judgement. Codrington's legacy is then considered under four headings. The first and paramount characteristic of all his work in collecting artefacts and folklore is his respect for local culture. It must be remembered that this flew in the face of contemporary evolutionary theory. Sometimes Codrington expressed this in a somewhat clumsy fashion, for example, 'The most wonderful thing about heathen savages is that they are so extremely like other people' (Letters 1867–87, to aunt, 28 September 1870). But this does not detract from the fundamental humanist principles he held, which he never abandoned. Second, Codrington in his study of Melanesian culture can be seen as a precursor of the modern bringing together of material and intangible culture. Third, Codrington has to be seen as a significant player in the creation of an understanding of Melanesian consciousness as expressed through language. Finally, Codrington's collection of material culture acts as a bedrock on which his accounts and theories are constructed.

Before considering each of these topics in turn, a caveat should be entered. Throughout this work I have argued that Codrington needs to be perceived and judged as an early anthropologist. I have not sought to explore his agenda for evangelisation, nor his theology or biblical translations, and, in fact, it would be very difficult to do so from the documentary evidence now available. This is not to discount the large corpus of biblical text that he translated, but this work is not considered here, apart from in its importance for the development of a Melanesian culture discussed below. I do not think that this absence is problematic for an evaluation of his anthropological work. Indeed, it perhaps helps us avoid the distractions of the anthropology/mission debate, which often risks becoming sterile. As has been argued in this work, anthropologists have largely excused Codrington from their dismissal of missionisation. Yet there have been significant authorities who have judged him a failed anthropologist, and these need to be considered.

Twentieth-century critiques of Codrington

Codrington would have been pained to learn how his reputation would suffer later in the 20th century. Perhaps it should come as no surprise that he received academic criticism from those unsympathetic to the pattern and processes of Christian missionisation. There is a long and complex history of engagement and frequent strife between anthropologists and their missionary hosts in the field, who frequently entertained them and shared with them their knowledge of local affairs. Anthropologists could be ungrateful for what they perceived as patronisation. No doubt many anthropologists could recognise Bronislaw Malinowski's experience at the start of his fieldwork on Mailu Island in 1914 in Papua, with the London Missionary Society pastor William Saville. Malinowski recoiled from the first moment against what he perceived as the missionary's narrow-minded bigotry and self-importance.

Figure 78 Portrait of R.H. Codrington painted by W.E. Millar, 1886, reproduced courtesy of The Warden and Fellows of Wadham College, Oxford University

As he recorded in *A Diary in the Strict Sense of the Term*, he considered him 'a petty greengrocer blown up by his own sense of importance into a caricature of a petty sovereign' (Malinowski 1988: 136). As Michael Young remarked, 'He [Malinowski] effectively brought the historical partnership between British anthropologists and missionaries to an end, and the gradual process of professional disengagement may be said to have begun in Mailu' (Young 2004: 333). Young immediately excused Codrington from such a judgement, 'missionary anthropologists of the stature of R.H. Codrington and Maurice Leenhardt were exceptional in Melanesia' (ibid.), but a general mistrust of missionaries and their activities grew during the 20th century and this is reflected in some of the criticism to which Codrington became subjected.

A note of discontent was recorded by Adolphus Elkin in his *Social Anthropology in Melanesia* (1953). Ernest Beaglehole in his 2001 encyclopedia entry on Codrington observed, 'in summarising Codrington's ethnography Elkin notes that although these accounts have many merits and flashes of insight, Codrington failed to depict a functioning community with discernible principles of cohesion or patterns of change'. But Beaglehole immediately added, 'In extenuation, it must be remembered that Codrington studied and wrote about Melanesia long before contemporary anthropological theory about sociocultural processes developed' (Beaglehole 2001).

Later in the 20th century, a more serious criticism of Codrington came from a respected anthropologist, Roger Keesing, a specialist on the cultures of Malaita. Keesing seems to have had an ambivalent view of Codrington's achievements. On the one hand, he gave a prominent place to *The Melanesians* in his textbook *New Perspectives in Anthropology*, which featured a two-page spread for his 'Example 30: Melanesian Secret Societies' taken directly from Codrington's text, along with a copy of Codrington's *tamate* illustration, which he captioned, 'A masked Tamate masquerader' (Keesing and Keesing 1971: 220–1). Similarly, he cited with approval Codrington's writing on ancient religions in his major work on Melanesian ideas of 'custom' (Keesing 1982: 300). Keesing also made an explicit exception of Codrington in his critique of missionisation, writing, 'In the nineteenth and twentieth centuries such figures as Junod, Codrington, Leenhardt and Schebester enormously enriched anthropological knowledge' (Keesing and Strathern 1998: 377). But, at the end of the day, Keesing had a deep suspicion and distaste for the whole missionisation project which he frequently expressed in explicit terms. Sometimes the tone was measured (Keesing and Strathern 1998: 378), but at other times he was less guarded and his real feelings were given free rein, as in this, his most candid critique of missionaries:

> The missionaries preached Jesus' message, preached of love and brotherhood. But the world they depicted was run by a White God, with a White Jesus as his agent. The white missionaries enjoined obedience to the white man's superiority, a passive acceptance by the 'natives' of their place as 'boys'– Satan's sinners rescued from his clutches, cleaned of their wild depravity, reborn as innocent children whose proper destiny was to serve Europeans obediently, peacefully and diligently. In their practice as well as in their precept, the missionaries maintained the caste superiority of the Europeans. (Keesing 1992: 89–90)

What is perhaps surprising is that the bone that Keesing chose to pick with Codrington should have been over a technical term. His accusation seems at first merely a minor issue of interpretation, the meaning of the term mana. But the consequences of the disagreement have wide-ranging ramifications. He wrote, 'I will suggest, drawing on linguistic and ethnographic evidence, that the Codringtonian interpretation of mana is deeply flawed. The linguist doubts about mana as a substantive were well taken, and the Codringtonian resolution was fundamentally erroneous' (Keesing 1984: 138). As a consequence of this perceived failure, anthropological theory in the Pacific was said by Keesing to have taken off in the wrong direction. This was, he was convinced, part of a more general disaster, 'the wholesale destruction of Oceanic religions by Christianity' (ibid.).

In a reflective review, Kolshus has disagreed with Keesing over the technical question of the usage of the term mana, arguing that it did have a substantive meaning – i.e., that it could act as a noun to describe a quality that an entity like a sacred stone can possess – and that Codrington's conception still held value. Kolshus maintained that the term was widely understood in this way on the island of Mota, and this understanding extended to the whole region, as the Mota language was used across the mission. Mana, Kolshus insisted, has as wide an applicability today as in Codrington's time (Kolshus 2013). I will return to how this plays out in contemporary Melanesia later in this chapter.

Although Codrington did not conform to the various stereotypes of the missionary, as has been discussed in the introduction to this study, he probably did attract special attention from detractors, who recognised his high profile in Pacific anthropology as well as his major role in the spread of Christianity in the western Pacific. This has resulted in probably a more important and more easily understood criticism than that raised by Keesing. The charge was that Codrington was responsible for the destruction of traditional culture: he had betrayed the secrets that provided the glue that held together societies like that on Mota, and as a result the culture had collapsed.

This charge was laid by Kirk Huffman, the first director of the Vanuatu Cultural Centre. Huffman was deeply immersed in efforts to protect and preserve *kastom* (traditional culture), and his intention was 'getting Melanesians to be interested in the … revival of their traditional cultures' (Huffman, cited in Bolton 2003: 40). His fieldwork programme, devised in conjunction with Darrell Tryon, remains to this day an institutional achievement that evokes admiration throughout the region and beyond, because of the depth and breadth of the deposits of folklore and intangible culture that it has documented and archived from villages across the nation. So, when he published in the seminal collection *The Arts of Vanuatu* in 1996, his voice was heard by a large audience. Like Keesing, Huffman held ambivalent views about Codrington. As an Anglican clergyman Codrington was not lumped together with other Christian faiths that were seen as deeply oppressive (Huffman 2013a: 1; 2013b: 32). Indeed, Codrington was commended for his work, which displayed 'an amazing amount of respect, considering the conventions of the time'. But the sting was in the tail. Huffman added, 'but the end result may have been a hastening of the decline of ritual life in the Banks Islands' (Huffman 1995: 92).

Huffman offered his reasons for this judgement in an account that he gave of a meeting he had held with customary chiefs:

> In December 1979 the writer of this commentary welcomed to the Cultural Centre a delegation of elderly chiefs from the Banks Islands, part of the 2,000 participants that had been brought to the capital to participate in the First National Arts Festival. Eventually two of the chiefs nervously asked if they could see the *Baebel blong Kastom blong Bankis* (the kastom Bible of the Banks Islands): at first a bit confused (and more used to similar 'exotic' requests from Tannese). I finally realised they were referring to R.H. Codrington's *The Melanesians* and brought out my copy. They agreed that was the book their fathers and/or grandfathers told them about. (ibid.)

Huffman then reflected how Codrington's book had become transposed into a text of sacred value akin to the Mota bible. Both held special authority. Huffman expanded on this development:

> It seems that at least one, and possibly more, copies of Codrington's (1891) work somehow ended up in Ni-Vanuatu hands in the Banks Islands at the end of the last century, and began to circulate secretly. Apparently, secretly, it may have had a devastating effect: although almost no-one could read English, some could read in Mota so were able to recognize certain language names, That, combined with the illustrations of ritual objects, and the instilled belief that a book was like the Bible 'all true and all secrets bared' seems to have convinced some Banks Islanders that the White Man now knew all their ritual secrets, that the power of the Spirits had been broken, and that ritual life had no more meaning. (ibid.)

Later, Huffman reflected on this charge and conceded that, 'Codrington's book can now, however, be a source of cultural inspiration for Ni-Vanuatu involved in cultural revival in the Banks and Torres' (Huffman 1996: 183n.2). But this concession does not answer the original question: did Codrington's book contribute to the demise of traditional culture on Mota, and perhaps elsewhere?

Lissant Bolton, closely associated with the Vanuatu Cultural Centre Women's fieldwork programme, reviewed Huffman's claim and noted the apparent contradiction implied: that Codrington's book should have had such a dire result when, ironically, the whole ethos of the mission under Patteson's direction was to refrain from unnecessary interference in popular culture (Bolton 2012: 213). She concluded that if Codrington's book had had any negative consequences, then these would have been inadvertent on Codrington's part (pers. comm. Bolton 2019).

Codrington re-evaluated

Bolton's caution has been reinforced by Kolshus's more recent robust criticism of Huffman, which also draws a contrast between Codrington's approach and that adopted by a later anthropologist, W.H.R. Rivers, who first visited Solomon Islands and other parts of Oceania in 1907–8.

> Huffman's claim sounds gratuitous. I have never come across any mention of this either in the literature or archives, nor during my close to 25 years of fieldwork engagement with the Banks Islands. A more substantial cause for scepticism is provided by two facts: since the Melanesian Mission relied on the Mota language for most communication, knowledge of English was rarely aspired to; and the only detail revealed in Codrington's *The Melanesians* that is not already *ta vareag*, 'of the open', i.e. knowable by all, is that the 'cry of the *Tamate*' is made by men. It is clear from Codrington's published work, and even clearer from his journals, that he was not interested in 'secrets'. What mattered to him was how these institutions constituted venues for power and, more importantly, for socialising. Also in this, the contrast to Rivers is striking: since the secret societies and the graded societies were centrepieces of his grand theory on the two-wave settlement of the Melanesian islands, Rivers took Codrington's lack of interest as a scientific vocation and dedicated a large part of the two volumes of *The History of Melanesian Society* to detailed descriptions of these – including a number of the most carefully guarded secrets, as I accidentally discovered when I arrived for my first fieldwork in 1996 with a copy of Rivers in my backpack. If indeed secrets were revealed through a book, Rivers is a far more likely source. (pers. comm. Kolshus, 2020)

This reasoning is, in my opinion, convincing. The rapid decline in the Christian community on Mota subsequent to Codrington's departure was part of a more general population decline on the island, with disease being the greatest threat to people's well-being. Doubts started to arise: 'Perhaps the Christian God was responsible for sending new diseases' (Hilliard 1978: 169), as the pagans had claimed all along. The rapid decline would naturally have made people dispirited, and Christianity itself was seen to have failed to deliver any material benefits, hence the renaissance of *suqe* at the end of the 19th century. This state of affairs would have grieved Codrington, not only because traditional culture was resurgent, but because the people of Mota were suffering from imported diseases.

So how does Codrington's reputation fare in the current climate? Before offering a summary of his lasting achievements, it might be worth pausing in the context of the criticisms just considered to reflect on one initially very surprising omission in Codrington's account of his life among the Melanesians – religious rhetoric. This absence is in striking contrast to much of the mission's literature, where the contrast between 'light and dark' remained a constant trope well into the 20th century (Stanley 1994b: 185). As Davidson has noted, 'There are few reflections in Codrington's letters about the underlying purpose of the mission apart from vague references to people being "Christianised". Conversion for Codrington was seen in terms of changes in peoples' way of life' (Davidson 2003: 172).

On only one occasion did Codrington offer a bridge between his anthropological and theological thinking, and, interestingly, the concept of mana was implicit in his schema. From 1895 to 1908 he delivered an annual series of 'Wittering Lectures' at Chichester cathedral, on theological topics, ranging from St Augustine to the ancient African church. His topic in 1902, quite out of character with the others, was 'The Gospel as presented to Savage Peoples'. Codrington was keen, first of all, to underline a humanist perspective that respected diversity:

> The Christian Religion may, indeed must, bear certain outward marks of difference according to the circumstances under which Christian life has to be carried on. And certainly also there have been, there are, and there will be hereafter, different methods of presenting Christian truths and laws, which arise naturally out of the differences which are sure to exist, in various times and in varying circumstances. Mankind is indeed one, but appears in many varieties; the thing taught in the gospel is one but the methods of teaching are many. (1902, 'The Gospel…': 1)

Codrington was also firm in his conviction that religious teaching had to be tailored to the world known to the potential convert:

> The gospel then is presented, whether the missionaries wish it or not, whether they know it or not, in accordance with what the hearer thinks, desires, believes. He may be very wrong, but the gospel is in fact presented to him, at least at first, as he sees it. And therefore it concerns the teacher above almost anything else to learn how it appears. What I have taken in hand is to endeavour to shew how the gospel is presented, how it comes and appears to savage people in our own time; what it meets, how it strikes, how it begins to work. And I take my own personal knowledge of such people to go upon. (ibid.: 9–10)

Codrington moved on to consider Melanesia and the people among whom he worked. Here, he wrote, the people:

> …breathe an air saturated with magical powers. Magic, to a great extent sympathetic magic, is at work in all they do and suffer. By means of this men are believed to be able to control or direct the forces of nature, to make rain or sunshine, wind or calm, to cause sickness or remove it, to know what is far off in time and space, to bring bad luck and prosperity and to blast and curse. But no man has this power of his own, all that he can do by his charms is done by the aid of the personal beings whom he influences by his spells, whether the ghosts of the dead or spirits distinct from men. (ibid.: 44)

This belief system was expressed through something akin to the power of mana:

> No heathen leaves his planted food to grow without the charm (or whatever it may be) that he depends upon, to do what is beyond his power. This is the sense of dependence on a certain power that is unseen, not human, certainly not unnatural,

because it has its place in all that is known of natural things, but supernatural, because it is beyond and above what man's nature supplies to him. On such a foundation a religion can be built up; such a foundation awaits the coming of the gospel. (ibid.: 17)

Codrington's fundamental proposition was that 'there is a moral sense in man however much it may be obscured, and there is a belief in the unseen however absurdly or grossly it conceives of the supernatural' (ibid.: 50). It was through appeal to this moral quality that conversion could become possible:

> If there be a savage who plants his food or launches his canoe without a charm of a spell or an offering he has the habit of self-sufficiency and independence. But you can say to the man who mutters his charm as he plants his food that he is quite right to seek what one may call a blessing, but that he must go to the Creator. (ibid.: 55)

What was required was a reorientation of agency for mana to be effective in a new dispensation:

> Men in the savage state in this sense of dependence are ready for prayer and for the various gifts of grace, and in their sense of right and wrong are ready to hear of forgiveness and salvation. (ibid.: 24)

Codrington's approach to his work in evangelisation was low key and seldom couched in purely theological terms. In a review of the use of anthropology in missionisation, John Hitchen has characterised Codrington as continuing to 'pursue his anthropological study primarily as a servant of his theological task' (Hitchen 2002: 467). However, from the evidence of the Wittering lectures, this does not seem to be an accurate assessment. For Codrington, anthropological understanding was a preliminary objective in its own right, evidently necessary for any interpersonal understanding, but not necessarily destined for missionary purposes. It is this reluctance to confuse the different systems of thinking that sets Codrington apart from more 'religious' missionaries. Evangelisation was one way to help Melanesians hold their own in the modern world, but it was certainly not the only or sufficient means to achieve this aim.

Codrington's lack of open religiosity should not be taken as a sign of a reluctance to embrace the mission's objectives. However, he went about his work in practical ways. So, the shock of the murder of Bishop Patteson in 1871 on the Reef Island of Nukapu, which he chronicled in great detail in both his letters home and in his 1872 journal, did not give rise to florid denunciations of those responsible for Patteson's and his companions' murders, but rather provoked Codrington to reflect, pondering on what had caused this eruption of violence. He inquired diligently into the chain of events that led to this attack, and concluded that those who had committed the crime probably mistook Bishop Patteson's party for labour recruiters. The question as to what motivated the attack remains open to this day (LT, 8 November 1871; Brooke 1872; Drummond 1930; Hilliard 1978: 66–72; Kolshus and Hovdhaugen 2010; Macdonald-Milne 2020, 208). On Patteson's death, Codrington was immediately thrust into the responsibility of running the mission. As its head, he set about memorialising his mentor not by pious accounts but by physical and aesthetic means: the construction of a memorial chapel which would become the focus of the mission life for missionaries and students alike. The design and construction of the chapel involved delicate negotiations with the Patteson family over the appointment of the architect and the furnishing of the building, as previously noted (Gutch and Pinder 1980). Here services would be conducted daily from 1880 until 1919, when the mission moved to new headquarters in Siota, Solomon Islands.

The church in Melanesia was keen to exploit memorials in the promotion of its activities. The commemoration of Patteson turned into a celebration of martyrdom. Mementos had a way of turning into sacred relics, possessed of their own particular mana. As has been noted earlier, the Melanesian Mission Museum in Kohimarama, Auckland, gave pride of place to a case devoted to Patteson's possessions. His walking stick, ink stand, pocket knife, chalice, teapot, cup, saucer and sugar bowl all served to evoke his holy presence. Similarly, a stone adze was displayed that belonged to the Reverend Joe Atkin, a fellow victim of the attack on Nukapu in 1871 (Ross Papers: box 53, folder 1, file 3). Martyrdom in the 21st century has given rise to further similar commemoration. The seven members of the Melanesian Brotherhood killed in Guadalcanal in 2003 have been inducted into the Communion of Martyrs of the Twentieth Century, created by Pope John Paul II in the church of San Bartolomeo all'Isola in Rome, where objects associated with them act as memorials or relics at the altar dedicated to them (Carter 2006: xi; Macdonald-Milne 2020).

Recent scholarship has drawn attention to the ambiguous role that historic artefacts may play in the modern Melanesian world. Sebastian Haraha has offered examples of the continuing power of charms that were kept in villages in Papua New Guinea, and which could only be made safe by being housed in the National Museum (Haraha 2007: 146). In the same collection of essays, Lawrence Foana'ota highlighted the way in which traditional objects of veneration in Solomon Islands could be captured by enemies during modern conflict, so as to do harm to their opponents (Foana'ota 2007: 41). So there is still considerable respect given in many places to the power associated with objects from the past.

In a stimulating article, Thorgeir Kolshus has argued that mana remains a significant and active concept in Mota and elsewhere in Melanesia. The power has been translated into something akin to the luck or good fortune that some individuals conspicuously enjoy. Perhaps more importantly, the Anglican Church has 'captured' mana: 'The Church's rituals and other procedures were found to have greater transformative potential than those associated with the old beliefs. It is the ordination of the bishop, who in turn ordains the priests and deacons that assures the correct transmission of ministerial powers and authority' (Kolshus 2016: 166).

Kolshus argued that clergy have been seen to acquire the power to 'distribute God's blessings and punishments at their own discretion'. Seen from such a perspective, this new mana, considered by both clergy and laity as efficacious, changes once again the notion of who has access to power from external sources. Mana has been appropriated by the church. Ritual objects can then be handled with safety by those protected by a Christian god. This is a development that Codrington could hardly have foreseen. As Davidson noted, 'what Codrington does not explore is how far Christianity was seen as offering access to a new form of mana' (Davidson 2003: 175).

Whether he would have gained any comfort from this new appropriation of mana after the previous resurgence of *suqe* is something of a moot point. Mana was indeed a slippery concept and its operations were very hard to predict, let alone control. This, Codrington was sure, was something that needed constant attention. Although he remained uneasy about Patteson's laissez-faire attitude towards traditional Melanesian culture, he still earnestly wished to respect people's attachment to old beliefs and practices. This can be seen in his comment on the *tamate*: 'It is not surprising that membership in so powerful a society should be valued and not readily resigned' (*TM*: 75). However, membership of secret societies remained a problematic issue for the mission. George Sarawia presented Codrington with a potential ethical dilemma: should he side with most of his European fellow missionaries in denouncing such membership? To his credit, Codrington never joined in the condemnation of Sarawia, neither before Sarawia's death in 1901 nor afterwards when he was accused by his successor on Mota, an English pastor, Hedley Adams, of being the head of *suqe* there (Hilliard 1978: 201).

If we set aside Keesing's and Huffman's criticisms, what is the inheritance that Codrington leaves us? How do the over 600 objects, however collected and selected for museum display and storage, represent any useful resource for the people of Melanesia?

Codrington's legacies

Respect for local culture

The answer comes in four parts. First, Codrington was a fundamental pillar in the construction of the Anglican Church of Melanesia (the present-day successor of the Melanesian Mission as a province of the Anglican Communion). He was not some antiquarian pottering around in the far reaches of the Pacific, but one of the chief architects of a post-European church, with deep respect for existing beliefs and cultures. In one of his few comments on missionisation he wrote:

> It is probably [also] not wise for any teacher of true religion to neglect or despise, even when he must abhor them, the superstitious beliefs and rites of those he would lead from darkness to light. It is far better, if it be possible, to search for and recognise what is true and good among wild and foul superstition, and find the common foundation, if such there be, which lies in human nature itself, ready for the superstructure of the gospel. (Codrington 1880: 312)

Despite the hedging qualifications in this statement, Codrington's respect for local culture shines through, and of course material objects are integral to this inheritance. His stance is in marked contrast to that of some later missionaries, who seem after his retirement to have temporarily lost the humanistic and universal principles propounded by Bishop Patteson, which he fully espoused.

Bishop Cecil Wilson (Bishop of Melanesia 1894–1917) was particularly sceptical of Sarawaia's work on Mota, writing in his autobiography:

> Every time I stayed there I felt the island was to all intents and purposes heathen and the Mission's work a ghastly failure, and I have no doubt whatsoever that the cause of the failure was *Sukwe*… This little island of Mota was, in fact, for one half of the year nominally Christian and for the other half heathen, and all because of this native freemasonry – truly described by some of our most trusted native teachers as 'partly good and partly bad'. (Wilson 1932: 76, 77)

Bishop Wilson set about creating a 'crusade of purification' in 1910, in which 'anyone participating in "heathen customs" would be excommunicated for three months' (Hilliard 1978: 201). This signified an emphatic rejection of Codrington's humanist respect for local culture. However, Codrington's legacy is still to be found in his writings and example, and these have been increasingly recognised over the past century. His collections are a further testament to this respect.

Bringing together tangible and intangible heritage

The second strand of Codrington's legacy relates to his emphasis on the intimate relationship between tangible and intangible culture. The rupture between museum-based study of material culture and anthropological theory that occurred during Codrington's lifetime meant that material-culture studies were abandoned for generations, as cultural anthropologists turned to following dynamic changes in belief systems in ever-evolving new cosmologies of the people they studied. Museum studies, it was argued, had condemned our perception of the people portrayed to a fixed, dead and unreal past that never existed outside the mind of the collector. This revolt against material culture gave rise eventually to the development of the concept of intangible cultural heritage. UNESCO enshrined this in the convention for safeguarding intangible cultural heritage that declared:

> 'Intangible Cultural Heritage' means the practices, representations, expressions, knowledge, skills – as well as the instruments, objects, artefacts and cultural spaces associated therewith – that communities, groups and, in some cases, individuals recognize as part of their cultural heritage. This intangible cultural heritage, transmitted from generation to generation, is constantly recreated by communities and groups in response to sense of identity and continuity, thus promoting respect for cultural diversity and human creativity. (UNESCO 2003)

UNESCO saw cultural diversity as being under threat from globalisation by dominant societies (Lenzerini 2011: 103). What is interesting in this complex definition is that in promoting intangible elements of culture the authors included 'instruments, objects, artefacts', thus bringing tangible and intangible elements of culture once again into synchronisation. This offers a new way of seeing Codrington, as a promoter of both tangible and intangible culture in conversation with each other.

Codrington's insistence on preserving ever-vanishing objects, beliefs and practices is underlined in the subtitle of his major work, 'Studies in their anthropology and folklore'. It was based on his understanding that both were intimately related to daily life. The historic legacy, whether it be related to fishing, marriage feasts or traditional religion, relies heavily upon the materials that were employed in their creation– fishing kites, pudding bowls and knives, as well as *tamate* masks. The *malo-saru* cape in the British Museum collection (see **Fig. 73**) provided Codrington with the opportunity to explore how cultural objects and practices were both preserved and lost. Codrington was keenly aware of this relationship between both aspects of culture, and it was for this reason that he assiduously collected and documented what he termed 'folklore' to set beside the objects. The sea-ghost figures (*TM*: illustrations 10 and 11; see **Figs 68–9**) express this double focus on narrative and image very well. The act of documentation took several forms: recording the locations from which items originated, detailing the social context in which they came, and drawing, sketching and photographing the objects – all to provide clear and unambiguous provenance. It is this wealth of circumstantial detail that sets Codrington's collections apart from more standard Pacific collections, where usually 'details of provenance and producer are not known' (Bolton 2001: 220). Furthermore, this rich documentation prevented the creep of the institutionalised redescription of artefacts in the museums, which Robert Welsh warned us against when he remarked:

> We tend to think of each accession as having a distinct identity that simultaneously reflects the collector and his social world on the one hand, and on the other the local people who made, used or sold the objects in the first place. But quite often the culture of museum administrators has also shaped the character and contents of a collection, distorting the role of both collector and villager. (Welsh 2000: 155)

Codrington's labels and his visits to museum displays served as a form of insurance against this type of creep. They also reinforced the personal connections the objects maintained with their collector, underlining the fact that they were and would remain 'social artefacts consisting of individual elements connected by a web of socially engineered meanings' (Satterthwait 2008: 51).

Does this excuse Codrington from the charge of being, like others, involved in the 'salvage collecting' of the debris of civilisations that were on the brink of disappearing? Were the objects more like archaeological evidence than emblems of living culture? As is evident in his writing, Codrington was keenly aware that he was documenting at the end of an era, before 'guns, germs and steel' (Diamond 1999) made their appearance with such devastating results. But he was not so much lamenting the disappearance of a way of life, as attempting to see, in the new situation, links back to the previous period that could be usefully employed. Objects like fishing kites and canoes remained everyday items available to be examined; the *tamate* figure could be studied in the future, as in fact has happened in the Vanuatu Cultural Centre in the 1990s (**Fig. 79**).

A Melanesian language
The third of Codrington's achievements from which Melanesians and other scholars can profit today, relates to his linguistic skills in grasping the Melanesian description of each object and how it functioned in its environment. His

Figure 79 *Tamate* ceremonial dancing cloak and mask for *suqe* festivals, Mota, Banks Islands. Vanuatu Cultural Centre, Port Vila, 1994, photograph by Nick Stanley

opportunistic employment of Melanesian individuals, first on Norfolk Island and then in mission stations, helped fill out the accounts he documented through the personal interpretation of his Melanesian associates, as well as students, their families and clan members. They gave him an excellent basis for the construction of what he considered his major achievement, the Christian gospel in a Melanesian form, which would also, he sincerely hoped, provide a framework for civil society.

Codrington was convinced that to achieve anything worthwhile, a successful translation of Christian texts was required. This necessitated a sound understanding of the Melanesian cultures from which they came. In a lecture delivered in 1894, entitled 'Various forms of paganism' he wrestled with the problem of aligning different linguistic and conceptual systems. There were two issues that needed to be addressed. First, the original terms must be clear, 'Religious terms must be found and fixed, as exact and precise as possible; definite expressions of definite doctrine. This is of immense importance, and it is very difficult. It is impossible to take too much trouble about the words in which religious teaching is to be conveyed' (Codrington 1894: 115). Second, and equally important, finding the appropriate local equivalent required a sophisticated understanding of the culture. In fact, three language systems needed to be compared:

> It will not do for one who enters into a mission already at work to take it for granted that the native words he finds in use are equivalent to those which he has been using elsewhere. They are sure not to be equivalent. The best words chosen out of an unwritten language are imperfect, inexact; they cannot express what never was in men's thoughts. He has to study the words in which religious ideas are expressed in English; he has to study them as they have come into English from older tongues; and he must study them just as much in a new tongue. (Codrington 1894: 116)

A more recent scholar from the Melanesian Mission concurs:

> My Melanesian colleague and I realized that we had quite often to go back to the Greek or consult the Bible Society's translation handbooks to discover the depth of meaning in the original Greek, remembering of course that much written in the gospels had originally been said in Aramaic. Sometimes we could bring out the fuller meaning in Pijin, as English, unlike Austronesian languages, does not, for example, have dual and trial pronouns. (pers. corr. Macdonald-Milne 2020)

In order to gain clarity in a Melanesian language, Codrington and John Palmer, together with Edward Wogale (George Sarawia's brother), spent years completing a dictionary and grammar of the Mota language (Codrington 1877; Codrington and Palmer 1896). So important did Codrington regard this work, that he made a special late trip to Norfolk Island to finish this task. However, Codrington started publishing in the Mota language before the dictionary was complete. First was *O vatavata we tuai* (Old Testament Selections in Mota) in 1873, followed by *O vatavata we tuai o tuan vavae mora prophet nan* (Selections from the Old Testament Prophets) in 1875. Codrington then moved on to translations from the New Testament, *O vatavata we garaqa. O tuan raverave mora sala* (New Testament Selections in Mota) in 1877 was followed by *O vavae vatog: Ape vasasa nan* (Lessons on the Miracles of Our Lord) in 1894. His magnum opus *O raverave nan we rono, talo vatavata we tuai wa we garaqa me sargag tuwale nol: o vava ta Mota* (The Bible in the Mota Language) also appeared in 1912. A final commentary written by Codrington appeared in 1915, *O vavae vatogo ape vavae tenegag nan amon* (Notes on the Parables in the Mota Language). Codrington was judicious in what he translated, prioritising stories, parables and injunctions that he felt would appeal particularly to people steeped in Melanesian cultures. He was opposed to translation just for the sake of it. As he noted in 1898, 'I am not altogether in favour of translating obscure passages and parts of the scripture until a fair number of natives can make something out of them' (Davidson 2003: 174). However, the sheer volume of work that he published in the Mota language meant that people throughout the mission field gained a common language, as well as a common spiritual and mental set of references, that would outlive Codrington by many years. Indeed, his *Lessons on the Parable of the Lord* was published in its third edition in Motese in 1933 and *O hymn Nan, o as nan we rono: Mota Hymn Book* appeared as late as 1957 (Pinson 1976). Although Codrington's extensive translations into Mota ceased to be used in the church in the mid-20th century, they had created a single language of study. When English was adopted, a switch from one tongue to another was fairly easily achieved. By this time a Melanesian Christianity had taken shape.

A collection of objects to inspire further reflection

Codrington's collection of artefacts provides the bedrock upon which his accounts and theories are constructed. The collection both supports and extends his contribution to Melanesian anthropology. Stones, arrows and costumes all contribute vitally to the evolving narrative that he creates. Their material presence today in the collections in Britain, as well as those returned to the Solomon Islands National Museum, helps give a sensuous appreciation of their look, manufacture and usage. This feel of the objects is something we share with Codrington. They are not just illustrations for his book; they are an autonomous and alternative way of entering into the Melanesian world that Codrington sought to comprehend. The objects also help us grasp something of the aesthetic system in which they were created. So, the plethora of arrows in the collections, rather than being merely a source of visual fatigue, become instead a repertoire of designs to entrance us afresh.

The objects Codrington collected served a range of different purposes for him. The Santa Cruz fishing kite with its spider's web lure for catching gar fish, which he so admired, represented a simple traditional artefact that had an ingenious technology, and with potential uses stretching into the future. Similarly, the wooden breadfruit splitter signified a shift in materials from earlier stone or clam shell exemplars to provide the same service under more modern conditions. Both exemplified how historic traditions could be harnessed to new circumstances. The *malo-saru* dancing dress and the *tamate* cloak and hats from the Banks Islands provided a vital link to local belief systems and rituals. The hats also provided a visual linkage between the past and the future. As Codrington reported:

> When white men were seen with hats they were supposed by the natives to wear what corresponded to their own masks. The native name for a mask worn in one of these societies is the same as that given to the society itself, *tamate*, a ghost; and *tamate* has long been established as the name for any European hat or cap. (*TM*: 79)

What Codrington was pointing to in this example, is the way modern contemporary artefacts could be incorporated into pre-existing systems, in this case, of dress. The artefacts represented the nexus for discussion between Codrington and his interlocutors: they provided for both parties the opportunity to unfold meaning and significance in concrete form. This understanding was captured in *The Melanesians* after much discussion and testing with various local figures of customary authority. However, Codrington's successful collecting career needs to be seen in the context of his other obligations.

Codrington's self-evaluation

It could be said that Codrington's success came *through* the exercise of so many different fields of work which jostled each other in his daily routine. Early on he confided to his brother:

> I hope to get my chapter 5 ready to send by the next mail to Auckland but how I am to write I don't know. I begin at 6 with a Florida translation every morning and four nights in the week I have a class or a translation till bed time. The other two evenings I now use to finish Mota translations for the press but that will very soon be over and I must make time somehow. (LT, 31 January 1877)

This was to be a vain hope. Things did not improve, and in a late letter to his brother this all came tumbling out:

> Really I can't get time to write down what I know and ought to get into print. What with school, getting lessons ready, translations, keeping the press going (with an English grammar now for Melanesians) and a good deal of the printing work also, and the cooking, I can hardly get time to do any literary work for the world at large. I have also at this time of year four gardens, besides my own on my hands and I try and photograph a bit now and then. The little I do with languages is to accumulate materials in various dialects. I am seriously contemplating the necessity of making some changes in my way of life. If I am to go on as I now do I shall never get the languages investigated and printed, and that ought to be done and no one but myself can do it. I don't know what changes can be made but I must try and get relieved of some of my school work. Of course it is hard to supply our full school with teaching, and now [Alfred] Penny is going home for a visit and [Arthur] Baker is going away for good. (LT, 3 September 1880)

Needless to say, such relief had to await his departure from the mission. Yet, many years later he was diffident about his achievements. He wrote to an enquirer:

> You ask whether I have ever written down any of my experience in mission work. I never have; but I have thought of it. There are two great objections, beside not wishing to obtrude myself on the public. One is that I should have to say so much about other people; many of them are black and couldn't read what I might say, but that is rather a reason for reserve about them. The other objection is that it would always be doubtful whether what I was writing was true. After a lapse of time events and questions take a certain form in one's mind; but often I believe they are not remembered correctly. I have too often found when looking up dates and reports that I have been quite wrong. Besides I have written too much already. I really think the translation work I have done has been decent, and I am also aware that there are not ten people in the world who know whether it is good or bad, not 100 white men who know that it has been done. This knowledge does not puff one up much. (Letters 1891–1922, to Revd Appleton, 18 July 1903)

But some points of reference were stable, and his collection remained one of these, to which he could constantly return in his own private museum. The urge to collect had carried Codrington through 20 years of what might be called fieldwork and a further 35 years of writing up. At the end of the day, he was an unapologetic collector, actively engaged in all aspects of cultural preservation and display in museums. He wrote to his young correspondent, Geoffrey Haines:

> I don't know anybody there [Fitzwilliam Museum, Cambridge] but acquaintance spreads like infection when the microbe, or whatever it is, finds the proper cultivation. There are people like you, and to a lesser degree like me, who infest museums and congregate in societies, and they naturally like to know one another. It is a most fortunate thing, I think, to be bitten by these microbes – and in address in which everyone desires to be kind to you. A curator delights in a cadet as a mosquito delights in a [rosy?] sleeper. (Letters 1922–6, 18 June 1918)

In one of the last letters that he wrote, he confessed, or perhaps even gently boasted, to Haines, 'It is a singular thing that some people are born to collect something. Very often the passion goes off early. For my part I think it is a very desirable appetite' (Letters 1922–6, 13 October 1921). Haines continued to engage with Codrington, bringing ancient coins for his inspection until a few months before his death (Letters 1922–6).

The fruits of synthesis

Despite Codrington's doubts regarding his shortcomings, these four legacies are substantial and need to be considered, though not in any formal or hierarchical order. Religious respect also involves an openness to the fluidity between the tangible and intangible worlds. Communication of the sensuous world between individuals and groups requires linguistic skills. David Brett captures this interdependence well:

> Studies of material culture, design history, cultural theory and visuality all require what I would term 'horizontal research' which spreads out and includes matters that are normally kept apart. (Brett 2005: 3)

What Codrington offers to Melanesians and followers of Melanesian cultures is a powerful 'horizontal' combination of all four features. Each requires the other three to create a satisfactory whole. Codrington's contribution to Melanesian scholarship could be said to have come about not so much despite as because of the vicissitudes under which he laboured. Teaching, cooking, providing medicine and nursing the sick, listening to people: all these enabled him to see life in its fine-grained detail, and to obtain a sense of interpersonal understanding.

The UNESCO 1982 Declaration on Cultural Policies made specific mention of Raymond Williams' concept of culture (Lenzerini 2011: 101, 104). Williams was explicit in his view that culture cannot be restricted to tangible properties, but must also embrace intangible cultural heritage. How was this to be achieved? The answer is through a slow unfolding of intellectual potential:

> The making of the mind is first, the slow learning of shapes, purposes, and meanings; second, but equal in importance, is the testing of these in experience, the making of new observations, comparisons and meanings. (Williams 1958: 4)

This prescription is one that Codrington had followed *avant la lettre* from his first days in Norfolk Island, in his numerous voyages around the islands and particularly during his sojourns on Mota. His early studies in the Banks Islands set the stage for his later work by involving judicious selection of objects to offer structure to his anthropology, and to give substance to the stories contained in his collection of folklore from this region. Folklore was of great significance for Codrington as he explained: 'The value of truly native stories is beyond all question; they exhibit native life in the particular details which come out in the narrative' (*TM*: 356). It is in the detail that the complexity and articulation of 'native life' is found. We see in Codrington's development as a collector how an initial interest in natural objects, such as stone and shell, gave way to items of manufacture such as clothing, canoes and canoe houses, and finally to the design expressions in drawings of sea-ghosts and decorated house posts, and in everyday objects such as lime boxes, water bottles and ear ornaments. Unlike many other collectors he was in the position, due to his extensive stay in Melanesia, always alert and observant, to chart changes in both the material and mental world that he encountered and registered. All collectors have an, often hidden but persistent, underlying set of objectives in their collecting behaviour; few explain their motives explicitly. Codrington is a signal exception to this rule: thanks to the variety and extent of his contextual writing about his observations and understandings, his collections remain very significant repositories even today. Perhaps Huffman's late reflection, 'Codrington's book can now, however, be a source of cultural inspiration for Ni-Vanuatu involved in cultural revival in the Banks and Torres' (1996: 183n.2) should be stated more emphatically. This is a benchmark set of collections of real importance for the history and study of Melanesian culture today.

Appendix 1
Codrington's Collection in the British Museum

Accession number	Material	Description	Location	Accession date	Other notes
Oc1944,02.1688	fibre	comb	Malaita	1869	Blackmore and Beasley collections 1931
Oc.7622	disc of clam shell	breast ornament	Santa Cruz	1870	Blackmore collections
Oc.2724	shell	large trid armring	San Cristoval	1871	
Oc.7930	shell	adze	Ambae	1872	
Oc1944,02.1057	clam shell	adze	Santa Maria	1872	Blackmore collections
Oc1944,02.1058	clam shell	adze	Santa Maria	1872	Blackmore collections
Oc1944,02.1069	clam shell	adze	Mota	1872	Blackmore and Beasley collections 1944
Oc1944,02.1070	clam shell	adze	Mota	1872	
Oc1944,02.1071	clam shell	adze	Mota	1872	
Oc1944,02.1072	clam shell	adze	Mota	1872	
Oc1944,02.1073	clam shell	adze	Mota	1872	
Oc1944,02.1074	clam shell	adze	Mota	1872	
Oc1944,02.1075	clam shell	adze	Mota	1872	
Oc1944,02.1081	clam shell	adze blade	Banks Island	1872	Blackmore collections
Oc1944,02.1042	clam shell	adze blade	Ambryn	1872	Blackmore and Beasley collections 1931
Oc.7620	loom	black patterned	Santa Cruz	1872	Blackmore collections
Oc.7621	loom	similar to 7620	Santa Cruz	1872	Blackmore collections
Oc.7623	clam shell	adze blade	Banks Island	1872	Blackmore
Oc1944,02.1058	shell	adze blade	Santa Maria	1872	Beasley
Oc.7902	shell	money	Solomon Islands	January 1873	
Oc.7903	shell	money	Solomon Islands	January 1873	
Oc.7929	veg. fibre	dress	Banks Island	January 1873	*TM*107,321
Oc.7931	basalt	adze head	Leper Island	January 1873	
Oc.7928	veg. fibre	loin cloth	Santa Cruz	January 1873	
Oc.7904	spider web	fish bait	Solomon Islands	June 1873	
Oc,RHC.44	wood and stone	adze	San Cristoval	1874	
Oc,+.2150	wood and stone	adze	San Cristoval	February 1874	
Oc,RHC.28	wood	vessel	Banks Island	February 1874	
Oc,RHC.13	shell	adze blade	Mota	February 1874	
Oc,RHC.14	shell	adze blade	Mota	February 1874	
Oc,RHC.19	shell	axe blade	Banks Island	February 1874	
Oc,RHC.21	clam shell	axe blade	Banks Island	February 1874	
Oc,RHC.22	shell	axe blade	Santa Maria	February 1874	
Oc,RHC.23	shell	gouge	Banks Island	February 1874	
Oc,RHC.27	wood & shell	food vessel	Banks Island	February 1874	
Oc,RHC.33	shell	dala	Malaita	February 1874	
Oc,RHC.34	shell	dala	Malaita	February 1874	
Oc,RHC.41	stone	axe blade	San Cristoval	February 1874	
Oc,RHC.52	stone	adze blade	Florida	February 1874	
Oc,RHC.57	stone	adze blade	Florida	February 1874	

Accession number	Material	Description	Location	Accession date	Other notes
Oc,RHC.58	stone	adze blade	Florida	February 1874	
Oc,RHC.40	shell	coconut scraper	San Cristoval	April 1874	
Oc,+.2151	wood and stone	adze	San Cristoval	1875	
Oc,RHC.29	leaf	fishing kite	Solomon Islands	1875	
Oc,RHC.35	wood	float	Malaita	April 1875	
Oc,RHC.39	shell	fish hook	San Cristoval	April 1875	
Oc,RHC.42	wood and stone	adze handle	San Cristoval	April 1875	
Oc,+.2152	wood and stone	adze	San Cristoval	April 1875	
Oc,RHC.10	shell	axe blade	Ambryn	April 1875	
Oc,RHC.15	shell	axe blade	Ureparapara	April 1875	
Oc,RHC.16	shell	axe blade	Ureparapara	April 1875	
Oc,RHC.17	shell	axe blade	Ureparapara	April 1875	
Oc,RHC.18	shell	axe blade	Ureparapara	April 1875	
Oc,RHC.24	clay	bowl	Espiritu Santo	April 1875	
Oc,RHC.26	clay	vase	Solomon Islands	April 1875	
Oc,RHC.46	wood and stone	adze	San Cristoval	April 1875	
Oc,RHC.47	wood and stone	adze	Solomon Islands	April 1875	
Oc,RHC.49	wood and stone	adze	Florida	April 1875	
Oc,RHC.50	wood and shell	adze	Florida	April 1875	
Oc,RHC.59	stone	pipe bowl	Savo	April 1875	
Oc,RHC.64	stone	tobacco pipe bowl	Savo	April 1875	
Oc,RHC.65	mother of pearl	fish hook	Savo	April 1875	
Oc,RHC.66	mother of pearl	fish hook	Savo	April 1875	
Oc,RHC.67	mother of pearl	fish hook	Savo	April 1875	
Oc,RHC.68	shell	fish hook	Savo	April 1875	
Oc,RHC.69	stone	axe blade	Savo	April 1875	
Oc,RHC.7	stone	adze blade	Ambryn	April 1875	
Oc,RHC.70	stone	axe blade	Savo	April 1875	
Oc,RHC.9	shell	axe blade	Ambryn	April 1875	
Oc,RHC.1	stone	axe blade	Ambryn	June 1875	
Oc,RHC.11	wood	breadfruit splitter	Mota	June 1875	
Oc,RHC.12	wood	breadfruit splitter	Mota	June 1875	
Oc,RHC.2	stone	axe blade	Ambryn	June 1875	
Oc,RHC.25	fibre	dress	Leper Island	June 1875	
Oc,RHC.3	stone	axe blade	Ambryn	June 1875	
Oc,RHC.30	leaf	fishing kite	Solomon Islands	June 1875	
Oc,RHC.31	wood	adze	Solomon Islands	June 1875	
Oc,RHC.32	shell	dala	Malaita	June 1875	
Oc,RHC.36	wood	fishing apparatus	Malaita	June 1875	
Oc,RHC.38	wood	fishing apparatus	Malaita	June 1875	
Oc,RHC.4	stone	axe blade	Ambryn	June 1875	
Oc,RHC.5	stone	axe blade	Ambryn	June 1875	
Oc,RHC.51	stone	adze blade	Florida	June 1875	
Oc,RHC.53	stone	adze blade	Florida	June 1875	
Oc,RHC.54	stone	adze blade	Florida	June 1875	
Oc,RHC.55	stone	adze blade	Florida	June 1875	
Oc,RHC.56	stone	adze blade	Florida	June 1875	
Oc,RHC.6	stone	axe blade	Ambryn	June 1875	
Oc,RHC.60	stone	adze blade	Florida	June 1875	
Oc,RHC.61	stone	adze blade	Florida	June 1875	
Oc,RHC.62	stone	adze blade	Florida	June 1875	

Accession number	Material	Description	Location	Accession date	Other notes
Oc,RHC.63	stone and wood	tobacco pipe bowl	Florida	June 1875	
Oc,RHC.71	stone	axe blade	Savo	June 1875	
Oc,RHC.72	stone	axe blade	Savo	June 1875	
Oc,RHC.73	stone	axe blade	Savo	June 1875	
Oc,RHC.74	stone	axe blade	Savo	June 1875	
Oc,RHC.8	stone	axe blade	Ambryn	June 1875	
Oc,RHC.45	wood and stone	adze	San Cristoval	1876	
Oc,RHC.48	wood and stone	adze	San Cristoval	1876	
Oc,RHC.20	shell	axe blade	Santa Maria	1876	
Oc,RHC.37	wood	fishing apparatus	Malaita	1876	
Oc,RHC.43	wood and stone	adze	San Cristoval	1876	
Oc1907,-.37	shell	adze	Bellona	1907	
Oc1908,-.233	wood and fibre	loom	Santa Cruz	1908	
Oc.7623	shell	adze blade	Mota	1944	Beasley collection
Oc1944,02.1042	shell	adze blade	Ambrym	1944	Beasley collection
Oc1944,02.1059	shell	adze blade	Gaua	1944	Beasley collection
Oc1944,02.1069	shell	adze blade	Mota	1944	Beasley collection
Oc1944,02.1070	shell	adze blade	Mota	1944	Beasley collection
Oc1944,02.1071	shell	adze blade	Mota	1944	Beasley collection
Oc1944,02.1072	tridacna shell	adze blade	Mota	1944	Beasley collection
Oc1944,02.1073	shell	adze blade	Mota	1944	Beasley collection
Oc1944,02.1074	shell	adze blade	Mota	1944	Beasley collection
Oc1944,02.1075	shell	adze blade	Mota	1944	Beasley collection
Oc1944,02.1081	shell	adze blade	Banks Island	1944	Beasley collection
Oc1944,02.1688	shell	comb	Malaita	1944	Beasley collection
Oc1944,02.1751	stone	adze blade	Solomon Island	1944	Beasley collection
Oc1944,02.465	shell	fish hook	Isabel	1944	Beasley collection
Oc1903,-.151	stone	axe	Vanuatu	1903	
2017,Q.169	stone	adze blade	Solomon Islands?		
2017,Q.170	stone	adze blade	Solomon Islands?		
2017,Q.171	stone	adze blade	Solomon Islands?		

Appendix 2
Codrington's Collection in the Pitt Rivers Museum, Oxford

Accession number	Material	Description	Further details	Location	Accession date	Other notes
1	shell	fathom		Florida Island	1886	*TM*: 23, 323
2	shell	fathom		Florida Island	1886	
3	shell	fathom		Florida Island	1886	
4	shell	fathom		Florida Island	1886	
5	shell	fathom		Florida Island	1886	
6	shell	fathom		Florida Island	1886	
7	shell	fathom		Florida Island	1886	*TM*: 93, 325
8	shell	fathom		Florida Island	1886	
9	shell	fathom		Florida Island	1886	
10	shell	fathom		Florida Island	1886	
11	wood	pan pipes		Torres Islands	1888	
12	wood	pan pipes		Torres Islands	1888	
13	wood	pan pipes		Florida Island	1888	*TM*: 327
14	wood	musical pipe		Pentecost	1888	
15	wood and reed	two-stringed musical instrument		Florida Island	1888	*TM*: 339; EP&H, vol. i: pl.195.7 and 43
16	stone	trimmer for flying fish		Santa Cruz	1888	*TM*: 317
17	stone and wood	trimmer for flying fish		Malaita	1888	*TM*: 317 (similar to)
18	mother-of-pearl	fish hook		Solomon Islands	1888	*TM*: 316
19	shell	fish hook		Solomon Islands	1888	
20	spider-web	fishing lure		Malaita	1888	*TM*: 318
21	palm leaf	fishing kite		Reef Islands	1888	
22	fibre	line for fishing kite		Solomon Islands	1888	
23	bamboo	knife		Torres Islands	1888	*TM*: 315
24	bamboo	knife		Torres Islands	1888	*TM*: 315
25	coco palm	boy's mask		Florida Island	1888	EP&H, vol. ii: pl. 113.2
26	fibre	complete *tamate* dress		Banks Island	1888	*TM*: 73; EP&H, vol. ii: pl. 105.1
27	wood	bow		Santa Cruz	1888	
28	wood	number of arrows		Santa Cruz	1888	exchanged
29	shell	belt of beads		Ulawa	1888	
30	wood and fibre	complete loom with partly woven cloth		Sant Cruz	1888	*TM*: 316
31	turtle shell	gorge for fishing		Banks Island	1888	
32	wood	dancing club		Santa Cruz	1888	*TM*: 333
33	bamboo	jew's harp		Solomon Islands	1888	*TM*: 339
34	bamboo	pan pipes		Banks Island	1888	
35	feathers	necklet (currency)		Santa Maria	1888	*TM*: 110, 324
36	shell	breast ornament		Santa Cruz	1888	*TM*: 111
37	nut shell	small spinning top		Florida Island	1888	*TM*: 342; EP&H, vol. i: pl. 195.8

Accession number	Material	Description	Further details	Location	Accession date	Other notes
38	string	knotted-string calendar		Isabel	1888	
39	shell	axe-adze		Santa Cruz	1888	*TM*: 71 (?)
40	stone	adze		Florida Island	1888	
41	wood	headrest		Santa Cruz	1888	
42	wood	headrest		Santa Cruz	1888	
43	palm leaf	kite	from John Palmer through R.H. Codrington	Santa Maria	1890	EP&H, vol. ii: pl. 79.4
44	palm leaf	kite	from John Palmer through R.H. Codrington	Santa Maria	1890	
45	reed	mouth flute		Pentecost	1891	*TM*: 339; EP&H, vol. i: pl. 148.6
46	bamboo	slip-joint knife		Torres Islands	1891	*TM*: 315; EP&H, vol. i: pl. 153.7
47	wood	fire-making sticks		Mota	1896	
48	stone	pump-drill	from R.B. Comins through R.H. Codrington	Alite, Solomon Islands	1897	*TM*: 325
49	shell	axe-adze		Santa Cruz	1897	
50	fibre	bark-cloth		Fiji	1897	
51	shell	fishing trimmer or float		Santa Cruz	1902	
52	wood	comb		Malaita	1902	
53	palm leaf	fishing kite		Santa Ana	1903	
54	fibre	bark-cloth		New Hebrides	1903	
55	bamboo	pan pipes		Florida Island	1912	
56	bamboo	pan pipes		New Hebrides	1912	
57	wood	pan pipes		Banks Island	1912	
58	reed	two-stringed musical instrument		Florida Island	1912	
59	bamboo	knife		Banks Island	1912	
60	bamboo	knife		Banks Island	1912	
61	shell	forceps		Banks Island	1912	
62	wood	comb		Malaita	1912	
63	shell	fish hook		Makira	1912	EP&H, vol. i: pl. 209.6
64	wood	frame for making armlets		Solomon Island	1912	
65	shell	adze blade		Banks Island	1912	
66	wood	bullroarer			1912	
67	wood	bullroarer			1912	
68	stone	greenstone celt		Florida Island	1916	
69	shell	adze blade		Torres Islands	1916	
70	shell	coconut scraper		Solomon Islands	1916	*TM*: 339–40 and fn.
71	shell	spoon		Solomon Islands	1916	
72	coconut	spoon-cup		Solomon Islands	1916	
73	coconut	kava cup		Banks Island	1916	
74	wood	kava bowl		Banks Island	1916	
75	bamboo	lime box		Isabel	1916	*TM*: 328, fig. 1
76	stone	fishing trimmer		Santa Cruz	1916	
77	shell	fish hook		Solomon Islands	1916	
78	shell	fish hook		Solomon Islands	1916	
79	shell	lure		Solomon Islands	1916	

Accession number	Material	Description	Further details	Location	Accession date	Other notes
80	stone	magical stone	to ensure good crop	Mota	1916	
81	nut shell	receptacle for small shells		Isabel	1916	*TM*: 331
82	shell	armlet		Solomon Islands	1916	
83	shell	septum stud		Solomon Islands	1916	
84	shell	string of beads		Banks Island	1916	
85	bamboo	comb		Torres Islands	1916	
86	wood	comb		Malaita	1916	
87	shell	dance ornament worn on leg		Santa Cruz	1916	
88	feathers	string of feathers worn as necklets or anklets		Santa Maria	1916	*TM*: 110, 324
89	shell	money		Banks Island	1916	
90	wood	board with string of beads		Santa Cruz	1916	
91	bamboo	pan pipes		Florida Island	1916	*TM*: 337
92	bamboo	pan pipes		Banks Islands	1916	*TM*: 337
93	palm leaf	woman's girdle		Banks Islands	1916	
94	fibre	small bag		Solomon Islands	1916	
95	palm leaf	basket		Torres Islands	1916	
96	wood and shell	ear disk		Florida Island	1916	present, T. Codrington
97	reed	arrow tipped with human leg bone		Lepers' Island	1916	
98	reed	arrow tipped with human leg bone		Santa Maria	1916	
99	reed	arrow tipped with human leg bone		Santa Maria	1916	
100	wood	bow		Santa Cruz	1916	
101	reed	arrow tipped with human leg bone		Santa Cruz	1916	EP&H, vol. ii: pl. 158
102	wood	bow		Torres Islands	1920	
103	reed	arrow		Torres Islands	1920	*TM*: 308–9
104	reed	arrow		Torres Islands	1920	
105	reed	arrow		Torres Islands	1920	
106	reed	arrow		Torres Islands	1920	
107	reed	arrow		Torres Islands	1920	
108	reed	arrow		Torres Islands	1920	
109	reed	arrow		Torres Islands	1920	
110	reed	arrow		Torres Islands	1920	
111	reed	arrow		Torres Islands	1920	
112	reed	arrow		Torres Islands	1920	
113	reed	arrow		Torres Islands	1920	
114	reed	arrow		Torres Islands	1920	
115	reed	arrow		Torres Islands	1920	
116	reed	arrow		Torres Islands	1920	
117	reed	arrow		Torres Islands	1920	
118	reed	arrow		Torres Islands	1920	
119	reed	arrow		Torres Islands	1920	
120	reed	arrow		Torres Islands	1920	
121	reed	arrow		Torres Islands	1920	
122	reed	arrow		Torres Islands	1920	

Accession number	Material	Description	Further details	Location	Accession date	Other notes
123	reed	arrow		Torres Islands	1920	
124	reed	arrow		Torres Islands	1920	
125	reed	arrow		Torres Islands	1920	
126	reed	arrow		Torres Islands	1920	*TM*: 308–9; EP&H, vol. i: pl. 153.2
127	reed	arrow		Torres Islands	1920	
128	reed	arrow		Torres Islands	1920	
129	reed	arrow		Torres Islands	1920	
130	reed	arrow		Torres Islands	1920	
131	reed	arrow		Torres Islands	1920	
132	reed	arrow dissected to show structure		Torres Islands	1920	
133	wood	bow		Santa Cruz	1920	
134	reed	arrow		Santa Cruz	1920	*TM*: 308, 312
135	reed	arrow		Santa Cruz	1920	
136	reed	arrow		Santa Cruz	1920	
137	reed	arrow		Santa Cruz	1920	
138	reed	arrow		Santa Cruz	1920	
139	reed	arrow		Santa Cruz	1920	
140	reed	arrow		Santa Cruz	1920	
141	reed	arrow		Santa Cruz	1920	
142	reed	arrow		Santa Cruz	1920	
143	reed	arrow		Santa Cruz	1920	
144	reed	arrow		Santa Cruz	1920	
145	reed	arrow		Santa Cruz	1920	
146	reed	arrow		Santa Cruz	1920	
147	reed	arrow		Santa Cruz	1920	
148	reed	arrow		Santa Cruz	1920	
149	reed	arrow		Santa Cruz	1920	
150	reed	arrow		Santa Cruz	1920	
151	reed	arrow		Santa Cruz	1920	
152	reed	arrow		Santa Cruz	1920	
153	reed	arrow		Santa Cruz	1920	
154	reed	arrow		Santa Cruz	1920	
155	reed	arrow		Santa Cruz	1920	
156	reed	arrow		Santa Cruz	1920	
157	reed	arrow		Santa Cruz	1920	
160	reed	arrow		Santa Cruz	1920	
162	reed	arrow		Santa Cruz	1920	
164	wood	fighting club		Banks Islands	1920	
165	wood	walking club		Ulawa	1920	
166	wood	walking club		Solomon Islands	1920	
167	wood	matted club		Solomon Islands	1920	
168	wood	club		Isabel	1920	
169	wood	glaive		Banks Islands	1920	
170	wood	glaive		Torres Islands	1920	*TM*: 315
171	wood	dance club		Malaita	1920	*TM*: 317
172	wood	paddle		Santa Cruz	1920	

Accession number	Material	Description	Further details	Location	Accession date	Other notes
173	wood	large staff		Solomon Islands	1920	
174	wood	walking stick		Solomon Islands	1920	
175	wood	walking stick		Solomon Islands	1920	EP&H, vol. i: pl. 209.7
176	cane	walking stick		Solomon Islands	1920	TM: 316
177	stone	adze		Solomon Islands	1920	TM: 316
178	stone	adze		Solomon Islands	1920	TM: 316
179	stone	adze		Solomon Islands	1920	TM: 316
180	wood and stone	axe		Solomon Islands	1920	EP&H, vol. i: pl. 209.5
181	wood and shell	adze		Solomon Islands	1920	EP&H, vol. i: pl. 209.12
182	shell	adze blade		Ulawa	1920	EP&H, vol. i: pl. 209.14
183	shell	adze blade		Solomon Islands	1920	EP&H, vol. i: pl. 209.13
184	shell	adze blade		Solomon Islands	1920	EP&H, vol. i: 209.10, 11
185	stone	adze blade		Solomon Islands	1920	
186	stone	adze blade		Solomon Islands	1920	
187	stone	adze blade		Solomon Islands	1920	
188	stone	adze blade		Solomon Islands	1920	
189	stone	piece of flaked obsidian		Banks Islands	1920	
190	shell	pounder and bark-cloth beater		Ulawa	1920	
191	wood and stone	pump-drills for making money		Solomon Islands	1920	
192	wood and stone	pump-drill		Solomon Islands	1920	
193	wood	bark-cloth beater		Isabel	1920	
194	shark skin	almond grater		Banks Islands	1920	
195	bamboo	slip-joint knife		Torres Islands	1920	TM: 315
196	fibre and stone	trimmer for flying fish		Malaita	1920	TM: 317
197	fibre and stone	trimmer for flying fish		Santa Cruz	1920	
198	shell	fish hook		Solomon Islands	1920	
199	shell	fish hook		Solomon Islands	1920	
200	shell	fish hook		Solomon Islands	1920	EP&H, vol. i: pl. 209.7
201	shell	fish hook		Solomon Islands	1920	TM: 316
202	shell	fish hook		Solomon Islands	1920	TM: 316
203	shell	fish hook		Solomon Islands	1920	TM: 316
204	shell	fish hook		Solomon Islands	1920	TM: 316
205	shell	fish hook		Solomon Islands	1920	EP&H, vol. i: pl. 209.5
206	shell	fish hook		Solomon Islands	1920	EP&H, vol. i: pl. 209.12
207	shell	fish hook		Ulawa	1920	EP&H, vol. i: pl. 209.14
208	shell	fish hook		Solomon Islands	1920	EP&H, vol. i: pl. 209.13
209	string	fish hook lure		Solomon Islands	1920	EP&H, vol. i: pl. 209.10, 11
210	string	fish hook lure		Solomon Islands	1920	
211	string	fish hook lure		Solomon Islands	1920	
212	string	fish hook lure		Solomon Islands	1920	
213	string	fish hook lure		Solomon Islands	1920	
214	string	fish hook lure		Solomon Islands	1920	
215	string	fish hook lure		Solomon Islands	1920	
216	string	fish hook lure		Solomon Islands	1920	
217	string	fish hook lure		Solomon Islands	1920	

Accession number	Material	Description	Further details	Location	Accession date	Other notes
218	string	fishing net		Solomon Islands	1920	
219	wood	pudding spatula		Torres Islands	1920	
220	wood	pudding spatula		Torres Islands	1920	
221	wood	pudding spatula		Banks Islands	1920	
222	wood	pudding spatula		Banks Islands	1920	
223	wood	pudding spatula		Banks Islands	1920	
224	wood	pudding knife		Banks Islands	1920	EP&H, vol. i: pl. 151.9
225	shell	coconut scraper		Santa Cruz	1920	EP&H, vol. i: pl. 162.2
226	shell	coconut scraper		Sant Cruz	1920	
227	shell	coconut scraper		Solomon Islands	1920	
228	shell	coconut scraper		Solomon Islands	1920	
229	shell	spoon		Solomon Islands	1920	
230	shell	spoon		Solomon Islands	1920	
231	shell	knife scraper		Solomon Islands	1920	
232	shell	knife scraper		Solomon Islands	1920	
233	shell	knife scraper		Solomon Islands	1920	
234	shell	knife scraper		Solomon Islands	1920	
235	shell	knife scraper		Solomon Islands	1920	
236	shell	knife scraper		Solomon Islands	1920	
237	shell	spatula		Torres Islands	1920	
238	wood	headrest		Santa Cruz	1920	EP&H, vol. i: pl. 158.4
239	wood	headrest		Santa Cruz	1920	EP&H, vol. i: pl. 158.5
240	fibre	piece of bark-cloth		Pitcairn	1920	
241	palm leaf	mat		Santa Cruz	1920	
242	palm leaf	mat		Santa Cruz	1920	
243	palm leaf	mat		Santa Cruz	1920	
244	palm leaf	mat		Santa Cruz	1920	
245	palm leaf	mat		Melanesia	1920	
246	palm leaf	mat		Melanesia	1920	
247	palm leaf	mat		Melanesia	1920	
248	wicker	basket		Banks Islands	1920	
249	wicker	basket		Banks Islands	1920	EP&H, vol. i: pl. 151.11
250	wicker	basket		Banks Islands	1920	EP&H, vol. i: pl. 151.11
251	wicker	basket		Banks Islands	1920	
252	wicker	basket		Banks Islands	1920	
253	wicker	basket		Banks Islands	1920	
254	wicker	basket		Banks Islands	1920	
255	wicker	basket		Banks Islands	1920	
256	wicker	basket		Banks Islands	1920	destroyed Dec. 1980
257	wicker	basket		Banks Islands	1920	
258	wicker	basket		Banks Islands	1920	
259	wicker	basket		Banks Islands	1920	
260	wicker	basket		Banks Islands	1920	destroyed Dec. 1980
261	wicker	basket		Banks Islands	1920	destroyed Dec. 1980
262	woven	basket		Banks Islands	1920	
263	woven	basket		Banks Islands	1920	destroyed Dec. 1980
264	woven	basket		Santa Cruz	1920	

Accession number	Material	Description	Further details	Location	Accession date	Other notes
265	woven	basket		Santa Cruz	1920	
266	woven	basket		Banks Islands	1920	
267	woven	basket		Banks Islands	1920	
268	woven	bag		Santa Cruz	1920	
269	woven	small bag		Banks Islands	1920	
270	palm leaf	bag		Torres Islands	1920	EP&H, vol. i: pl. 153.3
271	palm leaf	bag		Torres Islands	1920	
272	palm leaf	bag		Torres Islands	1920	
273	palm leaf	bag		Torres Islands	1920	
274	fibre	netted bag		Solomon Islands	1920	EP&H, vol. i: pl. 209.1
275	fibre	netted bag		Solomon Islands	1920	
276	fibre	netted bag		Solomon Islands	1920	
277	gourd	water carrier		Santa Maria	1920	EP&H, vol. i: pl. 151.10
278	coconut	cup or vessel		Solomon Islands	1920	
279	coconut	cup or vessel		Solomon Islands	1920	
280	coconut	cup or vessel		Solomon Islands	1920	
281	coconut	kava dish		Banks Islands	1920	EP&H, vol. i: pl. 151.8
282	wood	kava dipper		Banks Islands	1920	EP&H, vol. ii: pl. 86.2
283	wood	food bowl		Torres Islands	1920	
284	wood	food bowl		Torres Islands	1920	
285	shell	strings of money		Florida Island	1920	*TM*: 325
286	shell	strings of money		Florida Island	1920	
287	shell	strings of money		Florida Island	1920	
288	shell	strings of money		Florida Island	1920	
289	shell	strings of money		Florida Island	1920	
290	shell	strings of money		Florida Island	1920	
291	shell	strings of money		Florida Island	1920	
292	shell	strings of money		Florida Island	1920	
294	shell	strings of money		Florida Island	1920	
295	shell	strings of money		Florida Island	1920	
296	shell	strings of money		Florida Island	1920	
297	*Coix* seed	strings of money		Banks Islands	1920	
298	*Coix* seed	strings of money		Banks Islands	1920	
299	*Coix* seed	strings of money		Banks Islands	1920	
300	*Coix* seed	strings of money		Banks Islands	1920	
301	*Coix* seed	strings of money		Banks Islands	1920	
302	*Coix* seed	strings of money		Banks Islands	1920	
303	*Coix* seed	strings of money		Banks Islands	1920	
304	*Coix* seed	strings of money		Banks Islands	1920	
305	*Coix* seed	strings of money		Banks Islands	1920	
306	*Coix* seed	strings of money		Banks Islands	1920	
307	*Coix* seed	strings of money		Banks Islands	1920	
308	feathers	money		Banks Islands	1920	*TM*: 110, 324
309	fibre	bag to hold money		Banks Islands	1920	
310	reed	arrow used as money		Santa Maria	1920	*TM*: 327–8; EP&H, vol. i: pl. 151.4–7
311	gourd	lime gourd		Santa Cruz	1920	
312	gourd	lime gourd		Santa Cruz	1920	

Accession number	Material	Description	Further details	Location	Accession date	Other notes
313	gourd	lime gourd		Santa Cruz	1920	
314	gourd	lime gourd with spatula		Savo Island	1920	
315	bamboo	lime boxes		Isabel	1920	
316	bamboo	lime boxes		Isabel	1920	
317	bamboo	lime boxes		Isabel	1920	
318	wood	pestle and mortar		Santa Cruz	1920	
319	wood	pestle and mortar		Santa Cruz	1920	
320	wood	small mortar		Santa Cruz	1920	EP&H, vol. i: pl. 207.7
321	fibre	man's dress		Lepers' Island?	1920	
322	fibre	man's dress		Lepers' Island	1920	
323	fibre	man's dress		Lepers' Island	1920	
324	fibre	man's dress		Lepers' Island	1920	
325	fibre	man's dress		New Hebrides	1920	
326	fibre	man's dress, loom woven		Santa Cruz	1920	
327	fibre	man's dress, loom woven		Santa Cruz	1920	
328	fibre	man's dress, loom woven		Santa Cruz	1920	
329	fibre	woman's dress		Lepers' Is	1920	
330	fibre	woman's dress		New Hebrides	1920	
331	fibre	woman's dress		New Hebrides	1920	
332	fibre	woman's dress		Torres Islands	1920	EP&H, vol. i: pl. 148.3
333	fibre	woman's dress		Torres Islands	1920	
334	fibre	woman's dress		Torres Islands	1920	
335	fibre	woman's dress		Torres Islands	1920	
336	fibre	woman's dress		Torres Islands	1920	
337	bamboo	comb		Torres Islands	1920	
338	wood	comb		Malaita	1920	EP&H, vol. i: pl. 229
339	wood	comb		Malaita	1920	
340	wood	comb		Malaita	1920	
341	wood	comb		Malaita	1920	
342	wood	comb		Malaita	1920	
343	wood	comb		Malaita	1920	EP&H, vol. i: pl. 229.2
344	wood	comb		Malaita	1920	
345	wood	comb		Malaita	1920	
346	wood	comb		Malaita	1920	
347	wood	comb		Malaita	1920	EP&H, vol. i: pl. 229.3
348	wood	comb		Malaita	1920	
349	shell	armlet		Solomon Islands	1920	
350	shell	armlet		Solomon Islands	1920	
351	shell	armlet		Solomon Islands	1920	
352	shell	armlet		Solomon Islands	1920	
353	shell	armlet		Solomon Islands	1920	
354	shell	armlet		Solomon Islands	1920	
355	shell	armlet		Solomon Islands	1920	
356	shell	armlet		Solomon Islands	1920	
357	shell	armlet		Solomon Islands	1920	
358	shell	armlet		Solomon Islands	1920	

Accession number	Material	Description	Further details	Location	Accession date	Other notes
359	shell	armlet		Solomon Islands	1920	
360	shell	armlet		Solomon Islands	1920	
361	shell	armlet		Solomon Islands	1920	
362	shell	armlet		Solomon Islands	1920	
363	shell	armlet		Solomon Islands	1920	
364	shell	armlet		Solomon Islands	1920	
365	shell	armlet		Solomon Islands	1920	
366	shell	ring		Ulawa	1920	
367	shell	armlet		Solomon Islands	1920	exceptionally fine
368	bone	boar's tusk		Lepers' Island	1920	
369	shell	armlet		Solomon Islands	1920	EP&H, vol. i: pl. 195.5
370	shell	armlet		Solomon Islands	1920	
371	shell beads	armlet		Ulawa	1920	
372	shell beads	armlet		New Hebrides	1920	
373	shell and fibre	armlet		Solomon Islands	1920	
374	shell and fibre	armlet		Solomon Islands	1920	
375	grass	pair of child's armlets		Solomon Islands	1920	
376	feathers	adornment and money		Santa Maria	1920	*TM*: 110, 325; EP&H, vol. ii: pl. 86.1
377	shell and fibre	necklet		Isabel	1920	
378	shell	girdle		Santa Cruz	1920	
379	shell	girdle		Santa Cruz	1920	
380	shell	string of beads on white tape		Isabel	1920	
381	shell	string of beads		Solomon Islands	1920	
382	shell	string of beads		Solomon Islands	1920	
383	shell	necklet of seven strands		Makira	1920	unusually fine
384	dog's tooth	necklet		Solomon Islands	1920	
385	dog's tooth	necklet		Solomon Islands	1920	
386	teeth	small necklet		Solomon Islands	1920	
387	shell	brow ornament		Solomon Islands	1920	
388	shell	brow ornament		Solomon Islands	1920	
389	shell	breast ornament		Santa Cruz	1920	
390	shell	breast ornament		Santa Cruz	1920	
391	shell	breast ornament		Santa Cruz	1920	
392	shell	breast ornament		Santa Cruz	1920	
393	shell	ring pendant		Solomon Islands	1920	
394	shell	fish-shaped pendant		Solomon Islands	1920	
395	shell	shells perforated for stringing		Isabel	1920	
396	shell	shells perforated for stringing		Isabel	1920	
397	pearl	tridacna pearl		Solomon Islands	1920	*TM*: 327 n.; EP&H, vol. i: pl. 152.4
398	shell	ear ornament		Makira	1920	
399	wood	ear-plug		Ulawa	1920	
400	wood	ear-plug		Florida Island	1863	
401	shell	nose ornament		Solomon Islands	1920	
402	shell	nose ornament		Makira	1920	
403	wood and grass	nose bar		Solomon Islands	1920	

Accession number	Material	Description	Further details	Location	Accession date	Other notes
404	wood and grass	nose bar		Solomon Islands	1920	
405	bamboo	nose bar		Banks Islands	1920	EP&H, vol. i: pl. 151.2
406	bamboo	nose bar		Banks Islands	1920	
407	bamboo	nose bar		Banks Islands	1920	
408	bamboo	nose bar		Banks Islands	1920	
409	bamboo	nose bar		Banks Islands	1920	
410	bamboo	nose bar		Banks Islands	1920	
411	bamboo	nose bar		Banks Islands	1920	
412	bamboo	nose plug		Torres Islands	1920	
413	bamboo	nose plug		Torres Islands	1920	
414	shell	nose-ring		Santa Cruz	1920	
415	shell	nose-ring		Santa Cruz	1920	
416	shell	nose-ring		Santa Cruz	1920	
417	shell	nose-ring		Santa Cruz	1920	
418	shell	nose pendant		Santa Cruz	1920	EP&H, vol. i: pl. 162.5
419	pearl shell	nose pendant		Makira	1920	
420	shell	nose ornament worn on tip of nose		Solomon Islands	1920	
421	shell	nose ornament worn on tip of nose		Solomon Islands	1920	
422	shell	nose ornament worn on tip of nose		Solomon Islands	1920	EP&H, vol. i: pl. 162.6
423	coconut	vessel		Solomon Islands	1920	
424	coconut	trinket box		Isabel	1920	
425	coconut	trinket box		Isabel	1920	EP&H, vol. i: pl. 207.1
426	nut	trinket box		Isabel	1920	TM: 331
427	coconut	trinket box in shape of bonito		Makira	1920	EP&H, vol. i: pl. 207.6
428	coconut	bowl made by Waaro		Makira	1920	EP&H, vol. i: pl. 207.5
429	coconut	spoon made by Waaro		Makira	1920	
430	coconut	spoon-cup		Makira	1920	EP&H, vol. i: pl. 207.4
431	coconut	water flask		Ulawa	1920	
432	wood	large food bowl		Makira	1920	
433	wood	large food bowl		Makira	1920	
434	wood	large food bowl		Makira	1920	
435	wood	food bowl		Solomon Islands	1920	EP&H, vol. i: pl. 195.3
436	wood	food bowl in form of pig		Santa Cruz	1920	
437	wood	figure of man and dog in canoe		Makira	1920	
438	wood	small figure of man		Ulawa	1920	EP&H, vol. i: pl. 195.1
439	wood	paddle		Isabel	1920	
440	wood	paddle		Isabel	1920	
441	bamboo	flute		New Hebrides	1920	EP&H, vol. i: pl. 195.6
442	cane	transverse flute		Pentecost	1920	EP&H, vol. i: pl. 148.6
443	cane	pan pipes		Florida Island	1920	
444	cane	pan pipes		Florida Island	1920	
445	nut shell	humming top		Isabel	1920	TM: 342
446	shell beads	cat's-cradle		Isabel	1920	EP&H, vol. i: pl. 215.6
447	wood	toy canoe		Santa Cruz	1920	
448	stone	to ensure a good crop		Mota	1920	

Accession number	Material	Description	Further details	Location	Accession date	Other notes
449	sperm-whale ivory	heart-shaped charm		Isabel	1920	EP&H, vol. i: pl. 200.2
450	shell and fibre	charm worn on finger by archer		Santa Cruz	1920	EP&H, vol. i: pl. 158.3
451	wood	paddle-shaped club		Florida Island	1920	*TM*: 176
452	wood	spear-thrower		Loyalty Islands	1920	
453	bamboo	lime box		Isabel	unknown	
454	fibre	bundle of fishing nets		Solomon Islands	unknown	
455	wood	comb		Malaita	unknown	
456	shell	armlet		Solomon Islands	unknown	
457	shell	armlet		Solomon Islands	unknown	
458	bone	coconut scoop of human bone		Lepers' Island	unknown	
459	shell	fish hook		Solomon Islands	unknown	
460	reed	arrow		Santa Cruz	1920	
461	reed	arrow		Torres Islands	unknown	
462	stone	adze		Pentecost	1920	
463	wood	bowl		Makira	1920	

Appendix 3
Codrington's Collection in the Museum of Archaeology and Anthropology, Cambridge

Accession number	Description	Location	Source
E 1906.312	mat dress, woven with ornamental black bands and decorated with fringes and tassles	Santa Cruz	R.H. Codrington
E 1906.313	mat dress, woven with ornamental black bands and decorated with fringes and tassles	Santa Cruz	R.H. Codrington
E1906.315	basket, deep oblong of coconut leaf	Torres Islands (stored as Banks Islands)	R.H. Codrington
E 1906.316	deep oval basket of pandanus leaf with carrying loop	Banks Islands	R.H. Codrington
E 1906.317	mat dress woven with fringed end, bearing a pattern in red dye	Aoba	R.H. Codrington
E 1906.318	mat dress woven with fringe end of soft texture stencilled pattern in purple, openwork ends	Aoba	R.H. Codrington
Z 10844	neck ornament of clam shell	Gela	R.H. Codrington
Z 31995	loom	Santa Cruz	R.H. Codrington
Z 5271	woven dress mat	Santa Cruz	R.H. Codrington
Z 5284	feather money charm	Santa Cruz	R.H. Codrington
1890.71	small basket made of the young fronds of a coconut palm	Torres Islands	R.H. Codrington
1893.126	hand loom with grass web and shuttle	Santa Cruz	R.H. Codrington
1919.8	oblong bamboo comb with carved pattern	Santa Cruz	R.H. Codrington
1919.9	turtle shell fish hook with pearl shell representation of a fish lashed to the back	Gela	R.H. Codrington
1937.285	forehead or chest ornament formed of a large disc of tridacna shell, perforated in centre	Gela	R.H. Codrington, Blackmore collection
1937.286	forehead ornament	Malaita	R.H. Codrington, Blackmore collection
E 1905.183	charm kept with feather money	Santa Cruz	R.H. Codrington
E 1905.343	container for valuables	Solomon Islands	R.H. Codrington
E 1905.344	belt of plaited grass, narrow with fringed ends, two bands of black decoration	Torres Islands	R.H. Codrington
E 1905.345	woman's belt made of coconut bark beautifully woven with regular dark brown design	Torres Islands	R.H. Codrington
E 1906.311	loom with mat in process of weaving	Santa Cruz	R.H. Codrington

Bibliography

Abbreviations

The following abbreviations have been used to identify sources:

AIML: Auckland Institute Museum Library, New Zealand

BOD: Oxford University, Bodleian Libraries Special Collections R.H. Codrington MSS

EP&H: Edge-Partington, J. and Heape, C. 1890. *An Album of the Weapons, Tools, Ornaments, Articles of Dress, etc, of the Natives of the Pacific Islands*, 3 vols, Manchester

LT: Letters to Tom [Codrington], 1867–82 (SOAS, MM box 9, folders 2/1–2/6), 116 numbered letters, dated on sending and on receipt.

PRM: Pitt Rivers Museum, Oxford University, Collections IV: 'Chamberlain Codrington Czaplicka Dunn'

SOAS, MM: School of Oriental and African Studies Library, University of London, special collections, Melanesian Mission

TM: Codrington, R.H. 1891. *The Melanesians: Studies in their Anthropology and Folklore*, Oxford.

Codrington bibliography

R.H. Codrington publications

1863. *Lecture on the Melanesian Mission together with the Report and Accounts of the Mission*, Torquay.

1876. *The Island Voyage 1875*, Ludlow.

1877. *A Sketch of Mota Grammar*, London.

1880. 'Notes on the customs of Mota, Banks Islands with remarks by the Rev. Lorimer Fison', *Transactions and Proceedings of the Royal Society of Victoria* XVI, 119–43.

1880. *O vavae ta England* [English Grammar in the Mota Language], Norfolk Islands.

1881. 'Religious beliefs and practices in Melanesia', *Journal of the Anthropological Institute* X, 261–316.

1884. 'On the languages of Melanesia', *Journal of the Anthropological Institute* XIV, 31–43.

1885. *The Melanesian Languages*, Oxford.

1887. 'Sound-changes in Melanesian languages', *Proceedings of the Philological Society* 20(1), 271–82.

1887. *Letter in Mota to St Barnabas School, Norfolk Island, dated New York, August 17, 1887 recounting a visit to the U.S.A.*, Norfolk Island.

1889a. 'Islands of Melanesia', *The Scottish Geographical Magazine* 5(3), 113–25.

1889b. 'On social regulations in Melanesia', *Journal of the Anthropological Institute of Great Britain and Ireland* 18, 306–13.

1890. 'On poisoned arrows in Melanesia', *Journal of the Anthropological Institute of Great Britain and Ireland* 19, 215–19.

1891. *The Melanesians: Studies in their Anthropology and Folklore*, Oxford.

1892. 'Notes on the traditional connexion of Sussex and Gloucester families of Selwyns', *Sussex Archaeological Collections relating to the History and Antiquities of the County* 38, 163–5.

1894. 'Various forms of paganism', in G.A. Spottiswoode (ed.), *The Official Report of the Missionary Conference of the Anglican Communion on May 28, 29, 30 and June 1, 1894*, 112–16.

1902. *O Vatavata we Tuai: Tavaliu II* [Job to Malachi in the Mota Language], London.

1903. 'On the stability of unwritten languages', *Man* 3, 25–6.

1905. 'Ancient coats of arms in Chichester cathedral', Sussex Archaeological Collections, published at http://Anglicanhistory.org/oceania/codrington/ancient_coats1905.html 1909 (accessed 17 March 2020).

1912 (delivered in 1908). 'The councils of the church', The Wittering Lectures (*Chichester Observer*).

1912. (primary translator) *O raverave nan we rono, talo vatavata we tuai wa we garaqa me sargag tuwale nol: o vava ta Mota* [The Bible in the Mota Language], London.

1912. 'John Coleridge Patteson' and 'George Augustus Selwyn' in S.L. Ollard and G. Crosse (eds), *A Dictionary of English Church History*, London, 450–1, 550–1.

1914. *O vavaevatogo ape Vasasa nanamon* [Lessons on the Miracles], Norfolk Island.

1915. 'Melanesians', in J. Hastings (ed.), *Encyclopedia of Religion and Ethics*, vol. viii, Edinburgh, 529–38.

1915. *O vavae vatago ape vavae tenegag nan amon* [Notes on the Parables in the Mota Language], Norfolk Island.

1933. *O vavae vatogo ape vasasa nan, wa o vavae tenegag nan, mon i Lord inina* [Lessons on the parables of our Lord], 3rd edn, Maravovo.

1957. *O hymn Nan, o as nan we rono: Mota hymn book*, Taroaniara.

R.H. Codrington and J. Palmer

1873. *O vatavata we tuai* [Old Testament Selections in Mota], Norfolk Island.

1875. *O lea we wia amon s Mathew me rave* [Gospel of St Matthew], London.

1875. *O vatavata we tuai o tuam vavae mora prophet nan* [Selections from the Old Testament Prophets], Norfolk Island.

1877. *O vatavata we garaqa. O tuan raverave mora sala* [New Testament selections in Mota], Norfolk Island.

1894. *O vavae vatog. Ape vasasa nan* [Lessons on the miracles of Our Lord], Norfolk Island.

1896. *A Dictionary of the Language of Mota*, London.

R.H. Codrington, unpublished writings

1863. Voyage, 2 May – 6 August, at http://anglicanhistory.org/oceania/codrington_lecture1863.pdf.

1869 Diary. In Mota, 5–20 October (BOD Pac.s.2.1).

1870 Journal. On Mota Island (SOAS, MM box 9).

1872 Journal. Of the voyage, 6 July – 19 August (BOD Pac.s.2.2).

[1872?] Blue Journal. Undated (SOAS, MM box 9).

1873. 'Report' in 'Melanesian Mission Annual Report' SOAS, MM Box 6, folder02/02, pp. 23–4.

1875 Journal. 13 May – 11 July (BOD Pac.s.2.3).

1881 Journal. July–September (BOD Pac.s.5.2).

1883. World tour (BOD Pac.s.2.5).

1883. Eleven sketches on tour of Middle and Far East (BOD Pac.s.3).

1892–1922 Diaries (BOD Pac.s.19–27).

1895. 'History of the Wittering Lectureship', on the Wittering Lectures, a series of three weekly lectures delivered annually at Chichester cathedral (BOD Pac.s.30).

1896. 'Epistles of St John', The Wittering Lectures (BOD Pac.s.30).

1897. 'The origins of the English church', The Wittering Lectures (BOD Pac.s.30).

1898. 'Non-canonical books', The Wittering Lectures (BOD Pac.s.30).

1900. 'Church history at the time of Constantine', The Wittering Lectures (BOD Pac.s.30).

1901. 'Public worship in the early church', The Wittering Lectures (BOD Pac.s.30).

1902. 'The gospel as presented to savage people', The Wittering Lectures (BOD Pac.s.30).

1903. 'The *De Civitate*, City of God of St Augustine', The Wittering Lectures (BOD Pac.s.30).

1904. 'The *Cur Deus Homo* of St Anselm', The Wittering Lectures (BOD Pac.s.30).

1905. 'Jewel's apology', The Wittering Lectures (BOD Pac.s.30).

1906. 'St Gregory the Great', The Wittering Lectures (BOD Pac.s.30).

1907. 'The ancient African church', The Wittering Lectures (BOD Pac.s.30).

R.H. Codrington letters

1867–1923 (and undated), to R.H. Codrington (BOD Pac.s.5.29).

1867–82. Letters to Tom [Codrington], 1867–1882 (SOAS, MM box 9, folders 2/1–2/6), 116 numbered letters, dated on sending and on receipt.

1867–87, from R.H. Codrington (BOD Pac.s.4).

1891–1922, from R.H. Codrington to various correspondents, including to R.H. Codrington's aunt (unnnamed), Rev. Appleton and Rev. Charles Brooke (BOD Pac.s.28).

1902, from R.H. Codrington to Anatole von Hügel, 26 September and 10 October 1902 (Museum of Archaeology and Anthropology, Cambridge University, correspondence).

1916, from R.H. Codrington to Henry Balfour, 13 July 1916 (PRM 1920.100).

1922–26, letters and material respecting a biography of Codrington (BOD Pac.s.33).

Other manuscripts

R.M. Ross Papers relating to the Melanesian Mission Museum, Kohimarama (AIML, MS 1442).

G.W. Stocking, personal papers on Codrington, box 9, folder 2, Special Collections, University of Chicago Library.

Melanesian Mission, 1873, *Annual Report* (SOAS, GB 102MM/06/02/01).

Museum of Archaeology and Anthropology, Cambridge, Outgoing Correspondence Ledger.

Pacific Manuscripts Bureau, MS 2016, Lorimer Fison Project Handbooks, Canberra, Australian National University.

R.E. Tempest, 'Memories' manuscript, SOAS, Box 32 6/19.

References

Armstrong, E.S. 1900. *The History of the Melanesian Mission*, London.

Awdry, F. 1902. *In the Islas of the Sea: The Story of Fifty Years in Melanesia*, London.

Beaglehole, E. 2001. 'Codrington, R.H.: works by Codrington, works about Codrington', in N.J. Smelser and P.B. Bates (eds), *International Encyclopedia of the Social and Behavioral Sciences*, Amsterdam. Also published at http://www.encyclopedia.com/.../applied-and-social sciences-magazines/codrington-r-h (accessed 26 November 2019).

Blain, M. 2019. 'Bibliography of sources of information for the *Blain Biographical Directory*', published at http://anglicanhistory.org/nz/blain_directory/ (accessed 16 September 2019).

Blencowe, P. and Blencowe, S. (eds) 2007. *Letters Home: Jack Blencowe*, Chichester.

Bolton, L. 2001. 'The object in view: Aboriginese, Melanesians and museums', in A. Rumsey and J.F. Weiner (eds), *Emplaced Myths: Space, Narrative, and Knowledge in Aboriginal Australia and Papua New Guinea*, Honolulu, 215–32.

— 2003. *Unfolding the Moon: Enacting Women's Kastom in Vanuatu*, Honolulu.

— 2012. 'Incursions: loss, continuity and adaptation 1840–1900', in P. Brunt, N. Thomas, S. Mallon, L. Bolton, D. Brown, D. Skinner and S. Kuchler (eds), *Art in Oceania: A New History*, London, 186–217.

Bolton, L., Thomas, N., Bonshek, E., Adams, J. and Burt, B. (eds) 2013. *Melanesia: Art and Encounter*, London.

Brenchley, J. 1873. *Jottings during the Cruise of HMS Curacao among the Pacific Islands in 1865*, London.

Brett, D. 2005. *Rethinking Decoration: Pleasure and Ideology in the Visual Arts*, Cambridge.

British Association for the Advancement of Science. 1874. *Notes and Queries on Anthropology for the Use of Travellers and Residents of Uncivilized Lands*, London.

Brooke, C.H. 1872. 'The death of Bishop Patteson', in J.J. Halcombe (ed.), *Mission Life: An Illustrated Magazine of Home and Foreign Church Work*, vol. iii, part i (NS), London, 1–23.

Brown, G. 1910. *Melanesians and Polynesians: Their Life-histories Described and Compared*, London.

Campbell, F.A. 1873. *A Year in the New Hebrides, Loyalty Islands, and New Caledonia*, Geelong.

Carreau, L. 2009. 'Collecting the collector: being an exploration of Henry Geoffrey Beasley's collection of Pacific artefacts 1859–1939', PhD thesis, University of East Anglia.

— 2018. 'A glimmering presence: the unheard Melanesian voices of St Barnabas Memorial Chapel, Norfolk Island', in L. Carreau, A. Clark, A. Jelenik, E. Lilje and N. Thomas (eds), *Pacific Presences Volume Two: Oceanic Art and European Museums*, Leiden, 235–48.

Carter, R. 2006. *In Search of the Lost: The Death and Life of Seven Peacemakers of the Melanesian Brotherhood*, Norwich.

Codrington, O. 1904. *A Manual of Musalman Numismatics*, London.

Codrington, T. 1918. *Roman Roads in Britain*, London.

Davidson, A.K. 2003. 'The legacy of Robert Henry Codrington', *International Bulletin of Missionary Research* 27(4), 171–6.

Diamond, J. 1999. *Guns, Germs, and Steel: The Fates of Human Societies*, New York.

Douglas, B. 2018. 'Ethnohistory – collecting and representing', in B. Douglas, F.W. Veys and B. Lythberg (eds), *Collecting in the South Sea: The Voyage of Bruni d'Entrecasteaux 1791–1794*, Leiden, 41–62.

Dresser, C. 1873. *Principles of Decorative Design*, London.

Drummond, H.N. 1930. *John Coleridge Patteson, Pioneer and Martyr: With an Account of the Memorial Chapel*, Parkstone. Also published at http://anglicanhistory.org/oceania/patteson/drummond1930 (accessed 6 February 2020).

Durrad, W.J. 1920. *The Attitude of the Church to Suqe*, Norfolk Island.

Edge-Partington, J. 1883. *Random Rot: A Journal of Three Years Wandering Around the World*, Altrincham.

Edge-Partington, J. and Heape, C. 1890. *An Album of the Weapons, Tools, Ornaments, Articles of Dress, etc, of the Natives of the Pacific Islands*, 3 vols, Manchester.

— 1898. *An Album of the Weapons, Tools, Ornaments, Articles of Dress of the Natives of the Pacific Islands Drawn and Described from Examples in Public and Private Collections in England*, third series, Manchester.

— 1996. *Ethnographical Album of the Pacific Islands originally published as Album of Weapons, Tools, Ornaments, Articles of Dress of Natives of the Pacific Islands* (second expanded edn, ed. B.L. Miller), Bangkok.

Elkin, A.P. 1953. *Social Anthropology in Melanesia*, Oxford.

Eves, R. 2000. 'Dr Brown's study: Methodist missionaries and the collection of material culture in the Pacific', *Museum Anthropology* 24(1), 26–41.

Fison, L. 1904. *Tales from Old Fiji*, London.

Foana'ota, L. 2007. 'The future of indigenous museums: the Solomon Islands case', in N. Stanley (ed.), *The Future of Indigenous Museums: Perspectives from the South Pacific*, Oxford, 38–46.

Fox, C.E. 1958. *Lord of the Southern Isles: Being a Story of the Anglican Mission in Melanesia 1849–1949*, London.

Gaillard, G. 2004. 'Codrington, Robert Henry, Reverend', in *The Routledge Dictionary of Anthropologists*, London, 30.

Gamble, C. 2021. *Making Deep History: Zeal, Perseverance and the Time Revolution of 1859*, Oxford.

Gardner, H. 2006. 'Missionaries, evolutionism and Pacific anthropology: the correspondence of Lorimer Fison and Robert Codrington', in *The New Pacific Review: Proceedings of the 16th Pacific History Association Conference*, Canberra, 122–33.

— 2010. 'Practicing Christianity, writing anthropology: missionary anthropologists and their informants', in P. Grimshaw and A. May (eds), *Missionaries, Indigenous Peoples and Cultural Exchange*, Brighton, 110–22.

— 2012. 'Defending friends: Robert Codrington, George Sarawia and Edward Wogale', in K. Fullager (ed.), *The Atlantic World in the Antipodes: Effect and Transformation Since the Eighteenth Century*, Newcastle upon Tyne, 146–65.

Gill, W.W. 1876. *Myths and Songs from the South Pacific*, London.

— 1880. *Historical Sketches of Savage Life in Polynesia*, Wellington.

Gosden, C. 1999. *Anthropology and Archaeology: A Changing Relationship*, London.

Gunson, N. 1969. 'Brown, George 1835–1917', in *Australian Dictionary of Biography*, Canberra, published at http://adb.anu.edu.au/biography/brown-george-3075/text4541 (accessed 18 March 2020).

Gutch, J. 1971. *Martyr of the Islands: The Life and Death of John Coleridge Patteson*, London.

Gutch, J. and Pinder, J. 1980. *Patteson Memorial Chapel, Norfolk Island*, Watford.

Haddow, E. 2020. 'Excavating Eden: missionaries, material culture and migration theories in the history of Pacific archaeology: 1797–1940', PhD thesis, Australian National University.

Haraha, S. 2007. 'The Papua New Guinea National Museum and Art Gallery as a modern *Haus Tambuna*', in N. Stanley (ed.), *The Future of Indigenous Museums: Perspectives from the South Pacific*, Oxford, 137–50.

Hilliard, D. 1978. *God's Gentlemen: A History of the Melanesian Mission 1849–1942*, St Lucia.

Hitchen, J.M. 2002. 'Relations between missiology and anthropology then and now – insights from the contribution of ethnography and anthropology by nineteenth-century missionaries in the South Pacific', *Missiology: An International Review* XXX(4), 455–76.

Huffman, K. 1995. 'Travails and travels with Speiser: a personal commentary', *Pacific Arts* 11 & 12, 90–101.

— 1996. 'Trading, cultural exchange and copyright: important aspects of Vanuatu arts', in J. Bonnemaison, C. Kaufmann, K. Huffman and D. Tryon (eds), *Arts of Vanuatu*, Bathurst, 182–94.

— 2013a. 'Holemtaet graon, lanwis, kastom mo kalja: protect your land, languages and cultures', *Vanuatu Daily Digest*, 18 October.

— 2013b. 'Noho'n'dou yene nieve nungute'i numowo'h yene – respect is the foundation of life: rituals, respect, ancestors, spirits, "art" and kastom in Vanuatu', in C. Howarth, *Kastom: Art of Vanuatu*, Canberra, 30–5.

Ivens, W. 1918. *Dictionary and Grammar of the Languages of Sa'a and Ulawa, Solomon Islands, with Appendices*, Washington D.C.

Jones, O. 1868. 'The ornament of savage tribes', in *The Grammar of Ornament* (Folio edn), London, 13–17.

Keesing, R. 1982. 'Kastom in Melanesia: an overview', *Mankind* 13(4), 297–301.

— 1984. 'Rethinking mana', *Journal of Anthropological Research* 40, 136–56.

— 1992. *Custom and Confrontation: the Kwaio Struggle for Cultural Autonomy*, Chicago.

Keesing, R. and Keesing, F. 1971. *New Perspectives in Cultural Anthropology*, New York.

Keesing, R. and Strathern, A. 1998. *Cultural Anthropology: A Contemporary Perspective* (3rd edn), Fort Worth.

Kolshus, T. 1999. 'Purism, syncretism, symbiosis: cohabiting traditions on Mota, Banks Islands, Vanuatu', Cand.Polit.-degree, University of Oslo.

—— 2011a. 'Letters from homes: maintaining global relationships in the Victorian Age' in I. Hoëm and R. Solsvik (eds), *Identity Matters*, Oslo, 1–21.

—— 2011b. 'The technology of ethnography: an empirical argument against the repatriation of historical accounts', *Journal de la Société des Océanistes* 133(2), 299–308.

—— 2013. 'Codrington, Keesing and Central Melanesian *mana*: two historic trajectories of Polynesian cultural dissemination', *Oceania* 83(3), 316–27.

—— 2016. 'Mana on the move: why empirical anchorage trumps philosophical drift', in M. Tomlinson and T.P. KāwikaTengan (eds), *New Mana: Transformations of a Classic Concept in Pacific Languages and Cultures*, Acton, 155–201.

Kolshus, T. and Hovdhaugen, E. 2010. 'Reassessing the death of Bishop John Coleridge Patteson', *Journal of Pacific History* 45(3), 331–55.

Lenzerini, F. 2011. 'Intangible cultural heritage: the living culture of peoples', *The European Journal of International Law* 22(1), 101–20.

Lonergan, D. 1991. 'Codrington, Robert Henry', in C. Winters (ed.), *International Dictionary of Anthropologists*, New York, 116–17.

Macdonald-Milne, B. 2020. *Seeking Peace in the Pacific: The Story of Conflict and Christianity in the central Solomon Islands*, Leicester.

Malinowski, B. 1988. *A Diary in the Strict Sense of the Term*, Palo Alto.

Marau, C. 1906. *A Story of a Melanesian Deacon Clement Marau Written by Himself* (trans. R.H. Codrington, D.D.), London. Also published at anglicanhistory.org/aus/melanesia/marau.html (accessed 22 September 2019).

Mazzarella, W. 2017. *The Mana of Mass Society*, Chicago.

Melanesian Mission 1930. *Religion and Customs in Melanesia*, Southern Cross Booklet No. 2, Oxford.

Nash, J. 2012. 'Melanesian Mission place names on Norfolk Island', *Journal of Pacific History* 47(4), 475–89.

O'Ferrall, W.C. 1908. *Santa Cruz and the Reef Islands*, Westminster.

Pinson, W.J. 1976. *How Can You Sing the Lord's Song Without a Book? A Checklist of Books Printed 1855–1975 by the Anglican Church in Melanesia on the Mission Press*, Honiara.

Pomo, P. [C.H. Brooke] 1884. *The Autobiography of a South Sea Islander: A Fiction*, London.

Power, D. 1885–1900. 'Rolleston, George', in *Dictionary of National Biography*, vol. 49, 167–8.

Quanchi, M. and Cochrane, S. 2007. 'Introduction', in S. Cochrane and M. Quanchi (eds), *Hunting the Collectors: Pacific Collections in Australian Museums, Art Galleries and Archives*, Newcastle, 1–15.

Read, C.H. 1898. 'Introduction', in Edge-Partington, J. and Heape, C., *An Album of the Weapons, Tools, Ornaments, Articles of Dress of the Natives of the Pacific Islands Drawn and Described from Examples in Public and Private Collections in Australasia*, third series, Manchester.

Ross, R.M. 1983. *Melanesians At Mission Bay: A History of the Melanesian Mission in Auckland*, Wellington.

Samson, J. 2009. 'Christianity, masculinity and authority in the life of George Sarawia', *Review of the Canadian Historical Association* 20(2), 60–84.

—— 2010, 'Translation teams: missionaries, islanders and the reduction of language in the Pacific', in P. Grimshaw and A. May (eds), *Missionaries, Indigenous Peoples and Cultural Exchange*, Brighton, 96–109.

—— 2017a. *Race and Redemption: British Missionaries Encounter Pacific Peoples 1797–1920*, Grand Rapids, Michigan.

—— 2017b. 'The 'sleepiness' of George Sarawia: the impact of disease on the Melanesian Mission at Mota 1870–1900', *Journal of Pacific History* 52(2), 156–71.

Sarawia, G. 1968. *They Came to My Island: The Beginning of the Mission in the Banks Islands* (trans. Rawcliffe, D.A.), Siota.

Satterthwait, L. 2008. 'Collections as artefacts: the making and thinking of anthropological museum objects', in N. Peterson, L. Allen and L. Hamby (eds), *The Makers and Making of Indigenous Australian Museum Collections*, Melbourne, 29–60.

Shankland, D. 2012. 'Introduction: archaeology and anthropology: divorce and partial reconciliation', in D. Shankland (ed.), *Archaeology and Anthropology: Past, Present and Future*, London, 1–18.

Shineberg, D. 1999. *The People Trade: Pacific Island Labourers and New Caledonia 1865–1930*, Honolulu.

Sinker, W. 1904. *By Reef and Shoal: Being an Account of a Voyage Amongst the Islands in the South Western Pacific*, London.

Sohmer, S. 1988. 'A selection of fundamentals: an intellectual history of the Melanesian Mission of the Church of England 1850–1940', PhD thesis, University of Hawai'i.

Stanley, N. 1994a. 'Recording Island Melanesia: the significance of the Melanesian Mission in museum records', *Pacific Arts* 9 & 10, 25–41.

—— 1994b. 'Melanesian artifacts as cultural markers: a microanthropological study', in S. Riggins (ed.), *The Socialness of Things: Essays on the Socio-Semiotics of Objects*, Berlin, 173–99.

Stevens, E.T. 1870. *Flint Chips: A Guide to Pre-Historic Archaeology as Illustrated in the Blackmore Museum, Salisbury*, London.

Stocking, George W. 1987. *Victorian Anthropology*, New York.

—— 1995. *After Tylor: British Social Anthropology: 1888–1951*, Madison.

Thomas, N. 2018. 'Reflections' in B. Douglas, F.W. Veys and B. Lythberg (eds), *Collecting in the South Pacific: The Voyage of Bruni d'Entrecasteaux 1791–1794*, Leiden, 295–7.

Tomlinson, M. and KāwikaTengan, T.P. 2016. 'Introduction: Mana Anew', in M. Tomlinson and T.P. KāwikaTengan (eds), *New Mana: Transformations of a Classic Concept in Pacific Languages and Cultures*, Acton, 1–36.

United Nations Educational, Scientific and Cultural Organization. 2003. *Convention for the Safeguarding of the Intangible Cultural Heritage*. Published at https://ich.unesco.org/en/convention (accessed 8 December 2019).

Waterfield, H. and King, J. 2005. *Provenance: 12 Collectors of Ethnographic Art in England 1760–1940*, Paris.

Weir, C. 2008. '"White man's burden', 'white man's privilege': Christian humanism and racial determinism in Oceania, 1890–1930', in B. Douglas and C. Ballard (eds), *Foreign Bodies: Oceania and the Science of Race 1750–1940*, Canberra, 283–306.

Welsh, R.L. 2000. 'One time, one place, three collections: colonial processes and the shaping of some museum collections from German New Guinea', in M. O'Hanlon and R.L. Welsh (eds), *Hunting the Gatherers: Ethnographic Collectors, Agents and Agency in Melanesia 1870s–1930s*, New York, 155–79.

Wench, I. 1961. *Mission to Melanesia*, London.

Whiteman, D.L. 1983. *Melanesians and Missionaries: An Ethnohistorical Study of Social and Religious Change in the Southwest Pacific*, Pasadena.

Williams, R. 1958. 'Culture is ordinary', in his *Resources of Hope: Culture, Democracy, Socialism*, London, 3–14.

Wilson, C. 1932. *The Wake of the Southern Cross: Work and Adventures in the South Seas*, London.

Wiltshire Archaeological and Natural History Society 1864. *Some Account of the Blackmore Museum, Salisbury*, London.

Woodford, C.M. 1890. *A Naturalist Among the Head-Hunters: Being an Account of Three Visits to the Solomon Islands in the Years 1886, 1887 and 1888*, Melbourne.

Yonge, C.M. 1875. *Life of John Coleridge Patteson, Missionary Bishop of the Melanesian Islands*, 2 vols, London.

Young, M.W. 2004. *Malinowski: Odyssey of an Anthropologist 1884–1920*, New Haven.

Index

Page numbers in *italic* refer to images and their captions only

Adams, Hedley 69
anthropologists and missionaries 71–4
anthropology and theology 4, 74
antiquarianism 5, 14, 62, 76
archaeology and anthropology 21
artefact types
    adzes and axes *19, 21, 22,* 29, 56, 60, 63, 75
    armlets 27, 39, *42, 43*
    arrows 27, 29, *36, 68–9*
        poisoned arrows 67–8
    bags and baskets 27, 29, 36, *37,* 43, *45*
    beads 60–2
    bowls *27, 49, 50,* 54, 77
    boxes 62
    breast ornament *39*
    canoes *27,* 48, *49,* 54
    canoe houses 48, 54, 55
    charms 29, 39, *46*
    club *37*
    combs 27, 39, 41
    currency
        feather 41, 46
        shell *23,* 36, *38,* 41, 46
    dala 19, *20*
    drills 36, 43
    ear discs *36*
    fish hooks 21, *22, 23, 25,* 35, 60, 61, 62
    fishing equipment 21, *24,* 27, 60
    flints 14, 17, 21
    food vessel *22, 38*
    headrest *37*
    human figure *40*
    kites 36, 77, 78
    knives 29, 77
    looms 22, *41*
    mats 22, 36, 42
    musical instruments 39, 46
        flute 29, 35, *35,* 36
        pan pipes 27, 41
    ornaments 10, 14, 19, 39, 42, *44,* 63, 80
    paddles 27
    pottery 22, 26, *27*
    sea-ghosts 54, *56*
    shields 46, 57
    spears 27, 54, 55, 57, *64*
    string calendar 41
    tapa beater 43
    textiles 22, 35
        clothing 26, *39,* 48
        dresses 43, *53*
            malo-saru 59, *61,* 77, 78
            tamate 49, 58, 69, 72, 74, 77, 78
    tools 36
    toys 39
    water bottles 27
    weapons 36
Atkin, Joe 15, 68, 75
Awdry, Frances 8

Beaglehole, Ernest 72
Beasley, Harry 18, 27, 29
Blackmore Museum 4, 14–16, 18, 19, 21, 29, 43
    Blackmore, William Henry 14, 16, 18, 29
    Codrington collection 15–16
    Hill, Shirley 15, 16, 21
    Stevens, Edward Thomas 14, 15, 19
Bolton, Lissant 73–4, 77
Brenchey, Julius 16, 18
Brett, David 58, 79
British Museum 4, 18
    and Augustus Wollaston Franks 16
    and Charles Read 27, 29
    Codrington collection 18–27
Brooke, Charles (Percy Pomo) 6, 7, 8, 13, 17, 60, 70, 75
Brown, George 6

Cambridge Museum of Archaeology and Anthropology 4
    Codrington collection 42–8
    Melanesian Mission collections 43
    von Hügel, Anatole 17, 27, 43, 58
Carreau, Lucie 10, 29, 43
Carroll, Lewis (Charles Dodgson) *vi*, 5
charms 15, 39, *46*, 66–7
    magic stones 66, 73
    modern significance of 75
Charterhouse School 5, 17
Codrington, Oliver 5, 14
Codrington, R.H. *vi*, 72
    achievements
        bringing together tangible and intangible heritage 71, 73
        respect for and non-interference in local culture 76, 77
        translating through working in a Melanesian language 77, 78
        using objects as a way of entering the Melanesian world 78
    aesthetic preferences 4, 68, 75, 78
    artistic accomplishments 9–10
        architecture 54–6
        carving 10
        drawing and sketching 4, 49–52, 55, *57*
        photography 48–9
        printing 9, 78
        visual documentation (visualisation) 4, 48–58
    biography 1, 4–5
    collecting and material culture
        artefact labelling 41, 56–7, 77
        cataloguing Melanesian material culture 41
        coins 62, 79
        collecting strategies and practices 14–15, 42, 47, 59–62, 79
        conceptual ordering and sub-collections 41
        construction and purpose of objects 29
        personal collection 16, 17–25
        'salvage collecting' 59, 77
            and material substitution 19
            and 'survival reversed' 59
    critique of colonial culture 7, 11
    critique of evolutionism 4, 7, 14, 48, 71

humanist perspective 4, 71, 76
    on the moral sense in man 75
impact of Codrington's writings on Melanesian communities 73–4
informants, role of 7
jokes 42
on language 8–9, 78
    Mota language 4, 9, 13, 70, 73, 74, 78
    translation 13, 77, 78
local knowledge, importance of 5, 7
on magic 4, 7, 74
observation and listening, importance of 4, 6, 7, 18, 39, 79, 80
philosophy
    absence of religious rhetoric 74
    Codrington's empiricism 4, 7, 13
    paganism and Christianity 74
    promotion of self-reliance 10–11
    response to local scepticism 64
    self-evaluation and self-doubts 78–9
    views on missionaries 6–8
publications
    'The Gospel as preached to savage people' (The Wittering Lectures) 5, 74
    The Melanesian Languages 4, 39
    The Melanesians: Studies in their Anthropology and Folklore 4, 6, 7, 10, 17, 18, 35, 39, 41, 43, 46, 47, 49, *50*, 51–7, *57*, 65, 71–4, 78
Codrington, Tom 5, 9, 11, *12*, 14–18, 21, 26–7, *36*, 36, 54, 62
    collection *15*, 18, 27, *28*, 36, 62
Comins, Richard 27, *29*
critiques of R.H. Codrington
    destruction of traditional culture 73
    lack of discussion of social change 72
    misunderstanding of meaning of mana 73
    thesis repudiated by Kolshus 73
curios 1, 5, 15–18, 42, 59, 63

Davidson, Allan K. 9, 74, 76, 78
design and ornamentation 35, 80
Douglas, Bronwen 60
Dresser, Christopher 35
Drummond, Nelson 10, 75
Durrad, Walter 43, 69

Edge-Partington, James 17, 27, 36, 49
    album of weapons *30–4*, 67
    documenting changes in local culture 27
    on pattern and decoration 75
Elkin, Adolphus 72
exchange, trading and purchase; *see also* gifts
    conflicts arising from 64
    patterns of trading 63
    reciprocity in 60
    trade goods 60

Field Museum, Chicago 43
Fison, Lorimer 6, 7, 35
Foana'ota, Lawrence 75

folklore 5, 6, 71, 73, 77, 79,
Fuller, Captain A.W.F. 18, 29, 43

Gardner, Helen 7, 42, 69
geography of Melanesia and place names
    Solomon Islands *23, 25*
        Bellona 55
        Florida 18, 22, 26 ,36, *36, 38, 44,* 54, *57,* 63
        Guadalcanal *57,* 75
        Isabel (Ysabel) *37, 53,* 67
        Malaita 18, *24,* 26, 27, 41, *44, 56,* 64, 72
        Makira (San Cristoval) 5, 18, *40, 52,* 54, *56,* 63, *69*
        Nukapu 75
        Santa Ana 36
        Santa Cruz group *26,* 29, 36, 42, 43, 55, *66, 67, 68*
            Temotu 5, 42
            Tikopia 42
        Savo 18, *21,* 23
        Ugi 26, *55,* 63
        Ulawa 55, 66
    Vanuatu (New Hebrides) 52
        Ambae (Lepers' Island) 29, 43, 67, 68
        Ambrym 22, 29
        Banks Islands 1, 18,29, *37,* 38, 41, *45, 49,* 60, *61,* 65, 66, 73, 80
            Gaua (Santa Maria) 19, 26, 30, 41, *51,*
            Mota 1, 22, 26, 37, 49, *49, 50,* 66, 68, 69, 73, 74, 75
            Mota Lava 48, 54
            Ureparapara *19*
            Vanua Lava 13, 26, 48
        Pentecost 26, 36
        Torres Islands 1, 29, 36, 41, *45,* 68, 73, 80
Gill, William 5
gifts 60–3
Gosden, Chris 21
Gutch, John 8, 10, 54
Gutch, John and Pinder, John 10, 75

Haines, Geoffrey 17, 79
Haraha, Sebastian 75
heritage, tangible and intangible 29, 71, 73, 76
Hilliard, David 74, 76
Hitchen, John 75
horizontal research 79

Jones, Owen 35

kastom 73
Keesing, Roger 72
Kolshus, Thorgeir 9, 11, 42, 68, 73, 74, 75

labour recruitment in the Pacific 11, 16, 27, 63, 64, 75
Lubbock, John 6

Macdonald-Milne, Brian 75, 78
Malinowski, Bronislaw 71
Marau, Clement 60, 63, 66
Melanesia(ns) *passim*
Melanesian Brotherhood 75
Melanesian Mission 1, 26, 27, 43, 46, 59, 63, 64, 68, 69, 74, 76, 78
    collections in Britain 43
    museum in Auckland 46–7, 75
    policy on indigenous beliefs 69
mana 4, 55, 62, 64, 65–7, 73, 74, 75, 76
    in contemporary Melanesia 75
Miller, W.E. 70, *72*
Müller, Max 5–6, 65

Norfolk Island
    chapel 4, 54
    St Barnabas College 4, 13, 59

O'Ferrall, William Chamberlain 43

Palmer, John 62, 78
Patteson, Bishop John Coleridge 1, 8, *9,* 10, 14, 42, 46, 74, 76
    Codrington on the death of Patteson 6, 68, 75
Pitt Rivers Museum, Oxford
    Balfour, Henry 17, 37, 68
    Codrington collection 18, 35–42
Polynesians 5, 6, 9, 39, 42
private collections, vulnerability of 17, 29
pulsala (special friend) 69

Rivers, W.H.R. 74
Rolleston, George 48
Ross, Ruth 46–7, 75

Samson, Jane 68
Sarawaia, George 7, *8, 9,* 60, 68–9
    Bishop Wilson's criticism of 76
    involvement in *suqe* 69
Satterthwait, Leonn 72
Selwyn, Annie C. 43
Selwyn, John R. 1, 8, 10, 43
Sinker, William 59–60, 63
Sohmer, Sarah 6
Solomon Islands National Museum 78
Southern Cross ship 15, 42, 59, 60, 63
Stocking, George 4, 6, 7
students and scholars 8, *10,* 13, 60, 62, 63
suqe (graded societies) 10, 74, 76

teachers 8, 9, 60, 76
Tempest, Roger 8
Thomas, Nicholas 18

UNESCO 76, 79

Vanuatu Cultural Centre 73–4

Wadham College, Oxford 5, 70
Welsh, Robert 77
Whiteman, David 8, 65
Williams, Raymond 79
Wilson, Cecil 76
Wogale, Edward 77
Woodford, Charles 7

Young, Michael 72